China, Africa and Responsible International Engagement

China's increasing involvement in Africa is a controversial and hotly debated issue. On the one hand, China has brought significant economic and political opportunities to the continent with large amounts of investment and infrastructure. On the other hand, however, China's interests in Africa – including international strategy for multipolarity, a boom in China–Africa trade, and a strategic focus on energy – have been challenged as a form of neo-colonialism with claims that support for authoritarian governments has come at the expense of human rights, the environment and good governance.

This book analyses China's responsibility in Africa through the lens of good governance, China's African policy, policy implementation, feedback from host countries, and feedback from international society. Arguing for a new framework for evaluating China–Africa engagement, it looks at four countries – Sudan (South Sudan), Nigeria, South Africa and Ethiopia, all of which represent typical features of China-Africa relations – to test China's impact on the country and to analyse the factors in Africa that affect China's ability to shoulder responsibility. It proves that China's responsibility in Africa is affected by both the Chinese and African environments and that China's positive or negative impacts on the host African countries are largely constrained by the political and economic situation within the host state.

Containing information from first-hand interviews with African officials, officials from China's Ministry of Foreign Affairs, employees from Chinese State-owned enterprises who have been assigned to Africa, and Chinese self-employers in Africa, and using fieldwork from three African countries, this book will be of significant interest to students and scholars of African and Chinese Politics, International Relations and Development.

Yanzhuo Xu is an Assistant Professor at the Institute of World Economics and Politics, Chinese Academy of Social Sciences, China. She received her PhD from the School of Government and International Affairs at Durham University, UK. This research is supported by China's National Social Science Fund, Project No. 16CGJ025.

Routledge Contemporary Africa Series

The Development of African Capital Markets
A Legal and Institutional Approach
Boniface Chimpango

China, Africa and Responsible International Engagement
Yanzhuo Xu

China, Africa and Responsible International Engagement

Yanzhuo Xu

LONDON AND NEW YORK

First published 2018
by Routledge

2 Park Square, Milton Park, Abingdon, Oxfordshire OX14 4RN
52 Vanderbilt Avenue, New York, NY 10017

*Routledge is an imprint of the Taylor & Francis Group, an informa
business*

First issued in paperback 2020

British Library Cataloguing-in-Publication Data
A catalogue record for this book is available from the British
Library

Library of Congress Cataloging-in-Publication Data
Names: Xu, Yanzhuo, 1983– author.
Title: China, Africa and responsible international
engagement / Yanzhuo Xu.
Other titles: Routledge contemporary Africa series.
Description: New York, NY: Routledge, 2018. |
Series: Routledge contemporary Africa series |
Includes bibliographical references and index.
Identifiers: LCCN 2017027535
Subjects: LCSH: China—Foreign relations—Africa. |
China—Foreign economic relations—Africa. | Africa—Foreign
relations—China. | Africa—Foreign economic relations—China.
Classification: LCC DS740.5.A34 X8 2018 | DDC 327.5106—dc23
LC record available at https://lccn.loc.gov/2017027535

ISBN: 978-1-138-03761-8 (hbk)
ISBN: 978-0-367-59433-6 (pbk)

Typeset in Times New Roman
by codeMantra

This book is dedicated to my beloved son Wang Wei.

Contents

List of maps, figures, and tables

Maps

Figures

Tables

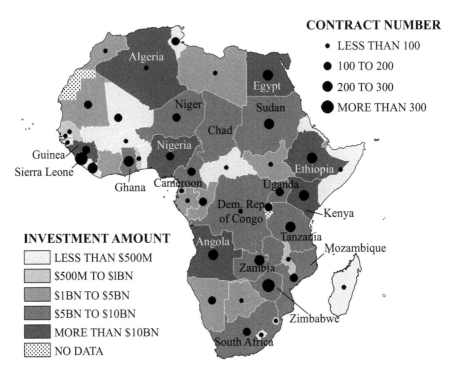

CONTRACT NUMBER

- • LESS THAN 100
- • 100 TO 200
- ● 200 TO 300
- ● MORE THAN 300

INVESTMENT AMOUNT

- LESS THAN $500M
- $500M TO $1BN
- $1BN TO $5BN
- $5BN TO $10BN
- MORE THAN $10BN
- NO DATA

Algeria
Egypt
Niger
Sudan
Chad
Nigeria
Ethiopia
Guinea
Sierra Leone
Ghana   Cameroon   Uganda
Dem. Rep.   Kenya
of Congo
Angola   Tanzania
Mozambique
Zambia
Zimbabwe
South Africa

Map 1: Chinese investment 2005–2015 (US$ billion) and contracts until 2013 (num-
ber) in Africa

Source: Author.

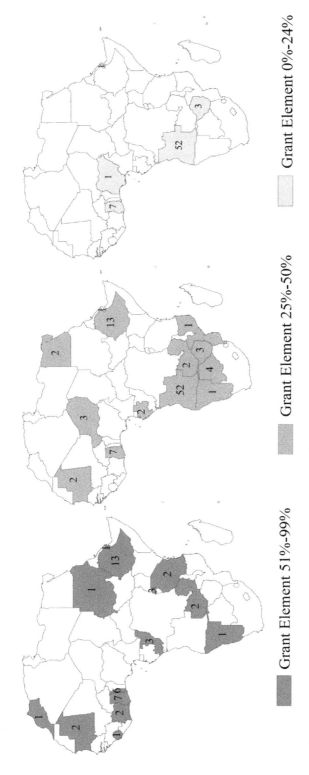

Grant Element 51%-99%   Grant Element 25%-50%   Grant Element 0%-24%

Map 2: China assistance to Africa: grant element and number of project
Source: Author.

Acknowledgments

I would like to thank Dr David Kerr, Durham University, who gave me many inspiring ideas and support in finishing this book. He is a wise and humorous person who has a deep understanding and empathy toward Chinese politics, society, culture and history, as well as the developing countries in Africa. On many occasions, his comments and suggestions saved me days and nights of searching.

I would also like to Thank Dr Gillian Boughton, Honorary Fellow of Durham University, for her kind assistance during my stay at St. Mary's College. This kind and elegant lady has long been dedicated to helping women's education in developing countries, such as Afghanistan. Her efforts and her work have changed many underprivileged but aspirant girls' lives. Her experiences in helping people from underdeveloped areas largely influence my research on understanding from Africa's perspectives.

Then I would like to give my gratitude to Dr Xue Li, Institute of World Economics and Politics, Chinese Academy of Social Sciences. It is always a pleasure to work and talk with Dr Xue. Not only does he have an objective attitude toward China's foreign strategy, but he is also very generous and provides opportunities and support to all young scholars in their early career.

I owe great gratitude to my family, my husband Dr Wang Xinting, my son, parents and grandparents. Without their emotional and financial support, I would have been unable to finish the research.

I would also like to thank my friends Dr Hsin-che Wu and Dr Florence Chen for their sincere friendship and their integrity.

Finally, I would like to express my gratitude to the anonymous interviewees in Beijing and London for their patience in sharing valuable ideas; to the faculty at SGIA for their academic and technical support; and to the editors at Routledge for their hard work in getting this book published.

List of abbreviations

AFP	Agence France-Presse
AGOA	African Growth and Opportunity Act
ANC	African National Congress
AMU	Arab Maghreb Union
APC	All Progressives Congress
AU	African Union
BBS	Bulletin Board Systems
BBC	British Broadcast Company
CADFund	China-Africa Development Fund
CCS	Center for Chinese Studies
CCECC	China Civil Engineering Construction
CDB	China Development Bank
CDD	Center for Democracy and Development
CITIC	China International Trust Investment Corporation
CMEC	China Machinery Engineering Corporation
CNCRC	China National Cotton Reserves Corporation
CNOOC	China National Offshore Oil Corporate
CNPC	China National Petroleum Corporate
CPC	Communist Party of China
CSR	corporate social responsibility
CREC	China Railway Engineering Corporation
CUD	Ethiopian Coalition for Unity and Democracy
DDA	Doha Development Round
DPA	The Darfur Peace Agreement
ECCAS	Economic Community of Central African States
ECOWAS	Economic Community of West African States
EEPCo	Ethiopian Electric Power Corporation
EPRDF	The Ethiopian People's Revolutionary Democratic Front
EU	European Union
EXIM	Export–Import Bank
FAOUN	Food and Agriculture Organization of the United Nations
FAO	Provincial Foreign Affairs Office
FDI	Foreign Direct Investment

FOCAC	Forum of China-Africa Cooperation
FT	Finacial Times
FTECC	Foreign Trade and Economic Cooperation Commission
GDP	Gross Domestic Product
GNI	Gross National Income
GNPOC	Greater Nile Petroleum Operating Company
IAEA	International Atomic Energy Association
ICC	International Criminal Court
IGAD	Intergovernmental Authority on Development
IMF	International Monetary Fund
IR	International Relations
JEM	Justice and Equality Movement
LDCs	Least developed countries
MEND	Movement for the Emancipation of the Niger Delta
MOF	Ministry of Finance of the PRC
MOFA	Ministry of Foreign Affairs of the PRC
MOFCOM	Ministry of Commerce of the PRC
MNCs	Multinationals
NCP	National Congress Party
NEPAD	New Partnership for Africa's Development
NG MOFCOM	Nigerian Ministry of Commerce
NGO	non-governmental organization
NIPC	Nigerian Investment Promotion Commission
NNPC	Nigeria National Petroleum Corporation
NYU	New York University
ODA	Official Development Assistance
OECD	Organization for Economic Cooperation and Development
OFDI	Outward Foreign Direct Investment
OML	Oil Mining Lease (petroleum rights)
OOF	Official Flows
OPL	Oil Prospecting License
PASDEP	plan for accelerated and sustained development to end poverty
PDOC	PetroDar Operating Company Ltd.
PDP	People's Democratic Party
PERE	Program for Environmental and Regional Equity
PIB	Nigeria's Petroleum Industry Bill
PLA	People's Liberation Army of the PRC
PPP	Purchasing Power Parity
PRC	People's Republic of China
QQ	quantile quantile
RMB	Renminbi
ROC	Republic of China
ROI	Return on Investment

SADC	Southern African Development Community
SAPETRO	South Atlantic Petroleum Limited
SASAC	State-Owned Asset Supervision and Administration Commission
SINOPEC	China Petroleum and Chemical Corporate
SPF	Sudan Police Force
SPLM/A	Sudan Peoples' Liberation Movement/Army
SOEs	State-owned enterprises
SRF	Sudan Revolutionary Front
UK	United Kingdom
UN	United Nations
UNCTAD	United Nations Conference on Trade and Development
UNDP	United Nations Development Program
UNIDO	United Nations Industrial Development Organization
US	United States
USAID	United States Agency for International Development
WTO	World Trade Organization

Foreword

Why China?

The new millennium has witnessed a significant transformation in the field of international relations theory and world political patterns. China, as an emerging political and economic power, has experienced remarkable changes as a result of its high-speed development and expansion in international affairs. However, as it maintains a different political system and pursues a different developmental path in the name of "crossing the river by feeling the stones", its rise and unpredictable future have evoked wide debate. Consequently, the rise of China has become a subject of global interest. The consensus could be reached on China as a major global economy, but its political, developmental and humanitarian influences, along with its growing strength, remain controversial. On the one hand, China has been unable to fully "project itself onto [the] international scene" (Taylor, 2006b, p. 1), which is dominated by Western political discourse. It portrays itself as different from the West and a leader of the developing world by emphasising "sovereignty and non-interference" and "international democracy" (multi-polarity 国际关系民主化). These claims place it in opposition to traditional powers and as a challenge to the international system they created. On the other hand, the Chinese government has paved the way for its economic growth through "going out" policy, which requires it to actively involve itself in the international community and abide by global norms and institutions. At the same time, its ambition to be a great power on the world stage also called for it to play a constructive role within the current system. These paradoxical motivations gave China a complex and uncertain reaction to the existing international system. Even now, when China has undergone a transformation on the international stage, "moving from a hostile, aggressive 'rogue' state outside the international system" to "an active participant in global institutions and a sometimes constructive player" (Nina Hachigian & Beddor, November 2009, p. 3), it remains reluctant to fully accept the shared rules and norms advocated by international institutions. The answers to China's new role and its impact on the global order are far less straightforward. China's record of solving hot world crises differs from time to time, and from case to case. For instance, China has incon-sistent responses to the "Responsibility to Protect" norm, employed during the "Arab Spring": it abstained from voting on Security Council Resolution 1973, on 17 March 2011, which helped to "establish a no-fly zone" (Garwood-Gowers, 2012, p. 11) and authorized "member states to take all necessary measures to protect civilians and civilian populated areas under threat of attack" (UNSC, 17 March 2011). However, shortly after Libya's vote, when all the Western countries expected China to agree to condemn or sanction Syria, China, followed Russia, opposed collective measures directed against the Assad regime (Qu, March/April 2012). Secondly, it has a double-faced attitude towards international institutions, organisations and initiatives. China has actively joined international institutions launched and estab-lished by traditional players, such as the International Monetary Fund (IMF), World Bank, International Atomic Energy Association (IAEA), and World Trade Organization (WTO) since the 1980s. It became a member of 52 intergovernmental institutions in 2009 (UIA, 2009) and signed more than 270 international treaties (Kent, 2007), many of which were the ones it once rejected. At the same time, it enthusiastically supported regional organisa-tions and initiatives, despite its weakness, in order to dilute US influence in Asia, Africa and other developing areas. After the East Asian financial crisis, China helped with the creation of the ASEAN+3 forum and the East Asia Summit in 2005 that is considered with "a possible alternative to the US-led Asia-Pacific Economic Cooperation" (Hawke & NZIER, Nov. 19, 2011). Similarly, China launched the Forum on China-Africa Cooperation (FOCAC) that provided the continent with an alternative funding re-source to the traditional OECD donors. These kinds of examples can also be found in China's support for the Chiang Mai Initiative, Shanghai Co-operation Organization, and so forth. Thirdly, in terms of international cooperation on hot topics, it has also shown inconstancy. Regarding the non-proliferation of nuclear weapons, it has played a constructive role in dealing with the North Korea nuclear crisis by facilitating Six-Party Talks and passed the Security Council's Resolution 1718 and 1874 which placed financial and commercial sanctions on DPRK (MOFA, July 7, 2009). On the other hand, it hesitated to impose sanctions on Iran, and instead, Chinese companies continue to be involved with the regime in Tehran. The BBC reported in 2012 that, as "Tehran's largest trading partner and customer for its crude export (about 20% of Iranian oil goes to China), it roughly im-ported 500, 000 barrels a day", (Pei, January 20, 2012) which is criticized as "undermin[ing] US-led efforts to shut off the supply of fuel on which Iran's economy depends" (Blas & Hoyos, September 23, 2009).

In short, China's response to international issues and institutions have evolved, as China expert Kenneth Lieberthal described, "taking steps but without a clear agenda of where to go" (Nina Hachigian & Beddor, November 2009, p. 9). China's unclear, sometimes contradictory agenda has received lots of criticism and experienced difficulties in cooperation in solving global issues. However, considering its size and growing power and influence, nearly all solutions for global topics could hardly be achieved without China's active involvement. Indeed, it is unrealistic to expect China to change overnight; understanding its logic and motivating the country to be more cooperative is a compromised but better way. As a result, this book's research on China aims to provide a realistic suggestion for understanding China's diplomatic agenda, further to exploring the possibility of promoting its contribution to international issues from the perspective of China-Africa engagement.

Why international responsibility?

In order to ascertain China's diplomatic agenda, one should first attempt to clarify its motivations. Like all other countries in the international arena, China's foreign policy and diplomatic strategy are shaped through the balance of the domestic and international environments. Evaluating the term "international responsibility" provides a perspective to view both China's national interests at home and international requirements, and the interaction between them. This norm could reflect the contradiction and compromise between China's domestic agenda and international expectations and demands. Furthermore, it is a new concept to look beyond narrow traditional state sovereignty and yet to emphasize the interdependency of modern countries. By exploring China's attitude towards "international responsibility", it could help to understand the state's motivation to become more cooperative. Thirdly, "international responsibility" is a dual term which could be interpreted as both negative consequences and positive commitment, it offers a neutral stand from which to comment on China's activities. Fourthly, it is a comprehensive term which combines foreign strategy with economic consideration and international ethics, with a combination of central policy and real implementation. In short, to analyse this concept is a useful tool for understanding the interrelated domestic interests and international environment that features in and informs Chinese foreign policy discourse.

Why Africa?

China, as a rising but lonely power on the international scene, inevitably requires political, diplomatic and economic support. Sharing similar backgrounds and grievances, the majority of the developing world forms the foundation of China's diplomatic clout. Africa, a continent with the largest number of developing countries, is a traditional arena in which China can address [and exercise] its influence and attention. Recently, the long-marginalized continent is hotly discussed and has drawn the world's attention due to China's high-profile involvement. Nevertheless, China has attached a particular attention to its African brothers, from the time when

"Chairman Mao said that we were carried into the UN by African friends" (Y. Liu, March 11, 2011), to new President Xi Jinping's statement that "China will be a reliable friend and genuine partner of African countries forever" (J. Yang, March 29, 2013).

The China-African relationship can be traced from the 1950s, but the growing close relations have drawn the world's attention since the Forum of China-Africa Cooperation- (FOCAC) Ministerial Conference in Beijing, in 2000. Despite the fact that China's outward foreign direct investment (OFDI) in Africa only accounted for 2.2% of its total OFDI, (US$ 1.7 billion out of US$ 74.65 billion) in 2011 Ministry of Commerce of the PRC (MOFCOM, 2011), and China's foreign direct investment (FDI) in Africa accounted for only 4% of the world's into the continent, (US$ 1.7 billion out of US$ 42.65 billion) (United Nations Conference on Trade and Development [UNCTAD], 2012, p. 38), the world is still concerned with the impact and influence of China's sharply increasing engagement, which is reflected in China's FDI figures for Africa, which have dramatically increased from US$ 56 million in 1996, to US$ 1.5 billion in 2005, and US$ 15 billion in 2011 (MOFCOM, 2011). China's growing engagement in the continent has received plenty of criticism and given rise to much doubt and concern, notably for "New Colonialism" and "come in, take out natural resources, pay off leaders and leave", as express by then-Secretary of State Hillary Clinton (Krause-Jackson, June 12 2011), and violations of humanitarianism, environment and human rights, and notably Beijing's close relation with certain pariah regimes, including Sudan and Zimbabwe. There is also criticism that the influx of cheap Chinese manufacturers and labour has destroyed the development of Africa's local industry.

Apart from Africa's significance to China and the world's concern for China's involvement in the continent, China's asymmetrical strength in Africa also provides an opportunity to evaluate China's dilemma agenda, that is, hesitating between national interests and international expectations, between economic benefits and international ethics. As an independent actor, Africa's attitude towards China-Africa relations could serve as a mediator to avoid neither too "West" nor too "Chinese".

Why China's international responsibility in Africa?

China's political discourse has developed from "why China should take the responsibility of Africa's development" (T. Cheng, August 27, 2012; Yuchuan Zheng, June 8, 2013) into, "What kinds of responsibility should China take for the development of Africa" (D. Li, 2011). The international community, Chinese government and African countries all have expectations for China to be more responsible for African's current situation, so it is worth exploring how to make full use of China's engagement and avoid negative consequences.

First, there is no consensus definition of the term "international responsibility". The most commonly accepted definition cannot fully explain China's role in Africa because it does not take into consideration the various factors behind it. The research on China's international responsibility can help with an empirical assessment of the norm within China-Africa context. The assessment of China's impact on Africa can complement the current definition of "international responsibility" by viewing the term from developing countries' perspectives and attempt to create a more balanced standard with which to judge a state's behaviour.

Second, it attempts to formulate a compromised way that can take into account the full scope of China's assistance to Africa. Since Chinese presence in the continent is inevitable, it is practical to push China to become more cooperative rather than undermine existing efforts/policies. Currently, the literature focuses on the either negative or positive impact China has brought to the continent, but the research on China's international responsibility does address China's different way of approaching Africa with both its positive and negative influence. In addition, it goes further by exploring the possible ways to motivate Beijing and how to take advantage of Beijing's funds and policy by understanding China's presence and policies in Africa.

Introduction

China's increasing involvement in Africa during this past decade is one of the most controversial and hotly debated issues in the region, maybe even worldwide. It appears to contradict not only the idea of an internationally marginalised Africa but also the traditional North-South engagement pattern; specifically, humanitarian intervention and foreign aid mechanism. On the one hand, China has brought significant economic and political opportunities to the continent with large amounts of investment and infrastructure. While on the other hand, China's interests in Africa-including international strategy for multipolarity, a boom in China-Africa trade, and a strategic focus on energy – have been challenged as a form of neo-colonialism and support for authoritarian governments at the expense of human rights, the environment and good governance. Comparing these two arguments, it shows that there is a lack of appropriate criteria with which to evaluate China's impact on African countries.

The existing literature has presented two faces of China in Africa: it has provided an alternative source and approach to conditional Western aid, but a generally asymmetrical relationship has made China-Africa links little different from previous Western-African relations. This book argues that the Western way is not the best criteria for evaluating China-Africa engagement when considering the emerging power's new role as a donor. Instead, it attempts to establish a reasonable standard for a state being responsible in international society and employs five standards on China-Africa involvement to analyse China's responsibility in Africa, in terms of good governance, China's African policy, policy implementation, feedback from host countries, and comments from international society. Since the good governance is considered to be an inner responsibility, the rest four criteria will be mainly discussed.

To assess whether China is responsible for Africa is a difficult question. In order to clarify China's role in Africa, this book has divided China-Africa involvement into two parts, the factors that shape China's responsibility in Africa at the policy level and the factors that impact China in Africa (policy implementation).

In general, three factors have shaped China's responsibility in Africa at the policy level: China's Africa policy motivation, Africa's demands and international expectation. It has been concluded that China holds a different approach and political philosophy for helping Africa's development, but it shows a willingness to cooperate with the traditional players on the continent, and its own African policy is not always incompatible with Africa's demands.

Moreover, the factors at policy implementation level are diverse, including Chinese governmental branches, Chinese enterprises, and the host African countries' environment. At this level, Chinese companies shoulder Beijing's 'going out' strategy, using aid and infrastructure to expand overseas markets and acquire assets, especially energy assets, in Africa. Theoretically, this approach does not necessarily undermine development in Africa. However, in order to reach the central government's goals, and constrained by the competition in the overseas market, Chinese companies have to invest in highly risky areas or provide generous loans and credit to outbid competitors, including overpayment for equity positions or underbidding contracts. Due to the profit-driven nature of enterprises, Chinese companies sometimes try to reduce costs during the implementation of projects by reducing quality, cutting labour costs, or sacrificing worker safety and lowering environmental protection. Their irresponsible behaviour deviates from the central government's policy, but also badly damages the reputation of both Chinese companies and China as a whole.

Although the host African countries and their markets were considered to be untapped and less competitive, compared to developed countries and well-established markets, Chinese companies still have difficulty in operating there. This book selected four case countries – Sudan (South Sudan), Nigeria, South Africa and Ethiopia, which represented typical features of China-Africa relations – to test China's impact on the country and analyse the factors in Africa affecting China's ability to shoulder responsibility. It proves the hypothesis that China's responsibility in Africa is affected by both the Chinese and African environments. China's positive or negative impacts on the host African countries were largely constrained by the political and economic situation within the host state.

1 Overview of the book

1.1 Literature review

Few researchers have analysed China's international responsibility in Africa. The most relevant paper is by political scientist Dr. Sven Grimm, "China as Africa's Ambiguous Ally – Why China has a Responsibility for Africa's development" (Grimm, June 2011). In this paper, Grimm emphasises China's importance to the world and provides a broad overview of the impact of China's engagement in Africa. It inspired me to look at the differentiation between actors that take responsibility for Africa's development. However, the paper does not clarify what responsibility means in China-Africa discourse, nor does it clarify China's motivation behind responsibility. A body of research focuses on the enterprise-level, that is, China's Corporate Social Responsibility (CSR) in Africa, (S. Cheng & Liang, May 10, 2012; C. Yang, August 2008; Zadek et al., November 2009), but little addresses state level engagement, and much neglects the interaction between the state and enterprise levels. Therefore, in order to figure out the background of this research, two fields of literature need to be discussed. One is China's engagement in Africa, and the other is China's international responsibility.

1.1.1 The implication of China's engagement in Africa

As for the hotly debated topic in international relations, there is a large body of research focused on China's engagement in Africa. Generally, three strands of thought and two scopes inform the on-going discussion about the impact of China in Africa: these are "Sino-optimism, Sino-pragmatism and Sino-pessimism" (Adem, 2012), and the macro and microscope.

I Three strands of China in Africa

From the perspective of Sino-optimism, China's involvement in Africa is a blessing. Africa gains much from its close relationship with Beijing because China's economic involvement in Africa has provided great opportunities for Africa's growth and development. Wang, Foster and others point out that

China provides substantial funds for infrastructure, for example in power (mainly hydropower), transport (mainly railroads), and information and communications technology (mainly equipment supply), where traditional donors allocate relatively little assistance (Corkin, December 2007; Foster, Butterfield, Chen, & Pushak, 2009). Some have suggested that Chinese investments in Africa have provided opportunities for African countries. For example, Alden has found examples of African entrepreneurs in small and medium businesses who have benefited from Chinese investments, particularly through "the growth of informal and formal linkage with Chinese ... business networks outside of government sponsorship". He has further argued that Chinese investments in Africa are much needed, especially in the face of declining investment from Western countries, and should, therefore, be welcomed (Alden, August 1, 2005, March 1, 2005). Some researchers have paid attention to China's technical transfers – for example, Muekalia has argued that Chinese agricultural technology will undoubtedly "increase productivity in Africa, reduce hunger and create jobs" (FAO, 2012; Moyo, 2010; Muekalia, 2004, p. 10; R. Rotberg, 2008).

From the perspective of Sino-pragmatism, China's involvement in Africa has its strengths as well as weaknesses; whether it benefits the continent or China depends on how the host African governments take advantage of China's activities. Brautigam compared the impact of Chinese investment in manufacturing industries among several African countries, and concluded that some countries with supportive investment environments have successfully formed a "flying geese" model with Chinese enterprises, while other countries that failed to "establish an environment that would allow either domestic industry or export-oriented firms to thrive and grow" may perceive China as a threat to local industry (Brautigam, March 2007, pp. 13–15). As for Chinese exports to Africa, Taylor argues that the cheap products made in China should not be condemned as a scapegoat for the decline of Africa's own manufacturing sector. It is, rather, Africa's internal problems that have caused this decline. In spite of these contentious issues, Chinese products have provided African consumers with more choices (Taylor, 2009, pp. 82–86). Adem summarised that "since the logic of capital is the same whether those in the driving seat are Europeans, Americans or Chinese" (Adem, 2012, p. 144).

A Sino-pessimist perspective prevails in media, journals and research. In this view, China's engagement is a curse for Africa and threats the development of the continent. Sino-pessimists analyse trade between China and African countries as highly imbalanced (with the exceptions of oil and other resources exports to China) in favour of Chinese exporters, which has the effect of debilitating and even shutting down local manufacturers and traders (Alden, March 1, 2005, p. 7; Draper, March 9, 2006; Wilson III, July 28, 2005). Thus, not only do Chinese imports threaten local manufacturers, but also the labour market, since the closure of local retailers and manufacturers results in thousands of job losses as well (Alden, March 1, 2005; Draper,

March 9, 2006, p. 7; Zafar, 2007, p. 122). Mills and Shelton predict that, despite South African President Thabo Mbeki's hopes, China is unlikely to promote development in Africa through more direct involvement in the New Partnership for Africa's Development (NEPAD), because of China's own domestic need to alleviate poverty in rural areas. Furthermore, they forecast that, in South Africa's case, future investments would be discouraging; increasing trade will become more challenging due to the competitive nature of the Chinese economy (Mills & Shelton, 2004, p. 37).

Furthermore, this strand holds that China's involvement in Africa is self-serving for oil and other raw materials and that the political rhetoric of a "win-win" situation only favours China. Hellström argued that the "centrepiece of China's African policy became 'mutual benefit' and 'win-win cooperation', roughly translating into a relationship where Chinese investments, mainly in infrastructure, were offered in exchange for African natural resources" (Hellström, May 2009, p. 8). The thirst for resources leads China to aggressively pursue shady methods in ways that can violate the democratic development and human rights of these African nations. A number of scholars have criticised China's foreign policy towards Africa of "non-interference" in the affairs of another state, and the emphasis on state sovereignty ahead of humanitarian protection. Due to this principle, China does not attach any political conditionality to its engagement with Africa (Taylor, 2006a, pp. 956–950). According to Wilson III (Wilson III, July 28, 2005, p. 11) and others (e.g., Giry, November 5, 2004), principles such as democracy, transparency and human rights do not feature in China's Africa policy. As Taylor has pointed out, this policy stance allows China to engage with the more despotic and undemocratic regimes in Africa (Taylor, 2004, p. 94; 2005). This lack of political requirements for China's engagement with Africa appeals to African elites, who are often the primary beneficiaies, while there is little to gain for the ordinary populations and democratic societies in Africa (Alden, March 1, 2005, p. 7; Taylor, 2004). Alden argues that these African governments are happy to do business with China since it provides them with a new source of regime security (Alden, 2005, p. 145) when most Western companies are unwilling or unable to do business with them (Giry, November 5, 2004). Taylor summarised that Beijing has contributed towards creating a discourse in Africa that "effectively legitimises human rights abuses and undemocratic practices" in pursuit of profits and resources (Taylor, 2004, p. 99).

II The impact of China in Africa: macro and micro

Some analysts view China's involvement in Africa from the governmental level. Van der Wath describes relations between China and Africa as "constructive, stable, friendly and co-operative" (Van der Wath, 2004, p. 73). Several authors pay attention to the flow of developmental aid from Beijing to Africa and make a comparison between the Chinese methods and amount with those aid flows from OECD members (Brautigam, 2008a; Kragelund, 2008; X. Wang & Ozanne, September 2010). Foster and others, using a database based on information released by the press, estimate that Chinese infrastructure finance commitments to sub-Saharan Africa accounted for US$16 billion between 2001 and 2007. While some of this financing appears to be concessional, most of it does not meet the OECD definition for aid (Foster et al., 2009). It was given to Africa as subsidies provided by government support programmes with low cost loans (Asche & Schüller, 2008).

Broadman's research is one of the few studies based on microeconomic data, using a survey of both Chinese and non-Chinese firms in South Africa, Ghana, Senegal and Tanzania. He finds that China's trade and investment in Africa tend to reinforce each other, and notes significant investments have been made in non-primary industries such as clothing, food industry, transport, building, tourism, power plants, and telecommunications (Broadman, 2007). Chen and others surveyed Chinese firms involved in the African construction sector, and found that the success of Chinese firms was due both to cost competitiveness – deriving from access to cheap capital, low-cost labour, and cheap building materials – and to political support from the Chinese government. However, the political support enjoyed by Chinese construction firms does not exempt them from the challenges faced by other construction firms in terms of economic and political instability, poor quality of local inputs and weak infrastructure in Africa (C. Chen, Chiu, Orr, & Goldstein, 2007). Kernen emphasises the importance of multiple private sector networks and the increasingly significant role of Chinese privatised companies (Berthelemy, 2011, p. 8). Gu looks at Chinese private companies in Africa through "evaluating characteristics and motivations of Chinese private firms in Africa and assesses their development impacts" and concludes, "China's Africa Policy and its implementation in terms of private sector engagement is lacking" (Gu, 2009).

In summary, the assessment of China in Africa varies from case to case, country to country, and perspective to perspective. To be good, neutral or bad depends on various factors, notably, from what perspective (the traditional OECD donors; Chinese central government; Chinese enterprises; African government or African people) and what the criteria used to evaluate China's presence and actions in Africa (comparing it with the West, China in the past, or with other emerging economies). The three strands of thought "Sino-optimism, Sino-pragmatism and Sino-pessimism" provide a panorama through which to look at both China's contributions to and negative impacts on Africa. However, no matter if the praise or criticism is drawn from the perspectives of either the West or Africa, little concern is given to China's strengths and limitations within this continent. Since China's policies in Africa are driven by multiple factors, one could hardly get the whole story and a relatively balanced judgment without broader considerations. Secondly, the research on Macro and Minor engagement are separated from one another, with either central policy or enterprise activities discussed.

It lacks, therefore, a dynamic connection between the two layers. Many Chinese scholars have pointed out the fact that China is not as a monolithic entity as outsiders may expect (Taylor, 2009) (see also reslin, 2007, p. 61). This argument fits into the China-Africa discourse as well. A fragmented China has become involved in Africa, and vice versa: different layers (central government, enterprises and individuals) shape the image of "China" in Africa. In this case, it is worth discussing the dynamic interaction between different Chinese actors in Africa. Thirdly, Taylor emphasised,

> When talking of 'Africa', we are required to generalise even as we recognise that each state in Africa is different and, as a consequence, that the way in which Chinese engagement with any particular African country will always be contingent on the latter's political economy.
>
> (Taylor, 2009, p. 9)

However, most of the research on China in Africa is either assessing 'Africa' as a whole or discussing specific bilateral relations, such as China-Angola, China-Nigeria or China-Zimbabwe, and so forth. Few have paid attention to comparisons between African countries.

1.1.2 The concept of international responsibility

As mentioned in the previous paragraph, the assessment of China's engagement in Africa requires balanced criteria, the recognition of a fragmented "China", and a diversified "Africa". Locating China-Africa into "international responsibility", a new norm in international relations, could help to complement the existing research and provide a multi-layer and multi-perspective evaluation.

"International responsibility" is a new concept in the international relations field. Most of the research, which uses the term, is from the field of international law. Obviously, China's "international responsibility" in this book will not focus on the juridical aspect. Instead, it is more like "international ethics", which concerns the obligations between states in an era of globalisation. At the same time, it acknowledges the national interests within the boundaries and avoids the empty rhetoric of morality among countries. Since there is no existing systematic theory on "international responsibility", Chapter 3 will explore the term.

Based on the existing literature, this book aims to fill these gaps and to create relatively objective criteria that could better evaluate China's involvement in Africa. Considering the limitation of the literature, the assessment of China's impact on Africa in the context of "international responsibility" is divided into two parts: the first is "international responsibility", and the second is "China-Africa" on the basis of "international responsibility". At the same time, it attempts to understand China-Africa relations in a more complex context, including both policy and economic activities, both a fragmental China and a diverse Africa.

1.2 Research questions and hypotheses

This book considers China's international responsibility in Africa. The assessment of China's impact on Africa in the context of "international responsibility" should be divided into three parts: The first requires criteria of China's "international responsibility". The second is, "What are the influential factors in China-Africa" on the basis of international responsibility? (Policy) The third is, "How does the context of China-Africa relations shape the conduct of international responsibility?" (Implementation) This requires three hypotheses and their related research questions.

I International responsibility

Hypothesis I: The term 'international responsibility' is flawed because it does not take into account the developing countries' perspectives, such as a state's capability in shouldering responsibility and the varied character of states' interaction on economic development. (Chapter 3 will answer the research questions of hypothesis I.)

Question 1. What is international responsibility? Question 2. What are the criteria of international responsibility?

II China-Africa

Hypothesis II: According to some of the literature, China's behaviour in Africa is not responsible since China places its own economic and political interests ahead of the African societies' interest in development. Based on the discussion of influential factors, China's motivations and African requirements (and international expectation) are not always compatible (Chapter 4 and the second part of each case chapter will answer the research questions of hypothesis II).

Question 1. What are the influential factors that shape China's motivations and responsibilities in Africa? Question 2. Are China's motivations and African requirements (and international expectation) incompatible?

III The context of China-Africa relations

Hypothesis III: Most ideas of international responsibility place emphasis on state agencies and major institutions. Part of the character of China's involvement is the many kinds of an actor in varied circumstances. China has a complex role in international responsibility because of these varied contexts (Chapter 5 will answer the question 1 of hypothesis III, and the case studies part – 6, 7, 8, and 9 – will answer the question 2 of hypothesis III).

Question 1. Which actors from China are involved in its responsibility in Africa? Question 2: How does the situation of many actors in many different environments effect China's ability to be a responsible actor in African development?

BOOK CONCLUSION: On the basis of the hypotheses and research questions, is China a responsible actor in Africa? (To what extent is China responsible in Africa?) (Chapter 10 will answer this final question.)

1.3 Research structure and research outline

1.3.1 Research structure

In order to answer the research questions and test the hypotheses, the book will be divided into two parts: the first part is complementary to the literature review, while the second part is a case study analysis to test the above hypotheses. The first part will be used to construct a framework for analysis and to answer research questions of hypothesis I ("international responsibility") and hypobook II ("China-Africa"), and then to confirm the hypotheses I and II; the case studies will be used to evaluate and further test hypothesis II and answer the research questions of hypothesis III ("the context of China-Africa relations").

I Framework part

The framework part will be divided into three chapters: international responsibility, China's Africa policy, and a fragmental China.

The international responsibility chapter will lay a foundation for the whole analysis. It will discuss hypothesis I of the flawed term "international responsibility". This chapter will also attempt to complement the current research on this norm in international relations, and it will set original criteria for the assessment of China in Africa on the basis of three perspectives: international society (dominated by the OECD countries), China and Africa, with the consideration of both political strategy and economic interests. The analysis and evaluation of the whole book will be conducted according to the findings of this chapter.

The chapter on China's Africa policy is designed to make a comparison between Chinese political discourse and the current literature on China in Africa. The current literature on China-Africa focuses on "What China did" rather than "What China said". In order to test hypothesis II of whether China's political and economic interests' could be compatible with African's demands, it is important to first identify China's Africa policy and the interests and strategy between the lines. Policy analysis will help to identify the Chinese government's priorities and latest development trends, to further explore hypothesis II, to what extent China could cooperate with the traditional OECD donors in Africa's development at a policy level.

The chapter addressing China's domestic environment will present a fragmented China in Africa. It will combine with the China's Africa policy chapter to explore which branches or institutions may be involved in China-Africa interactions. It will argue not only is China fragmented, but also that it is a fragmented implementer with respect to its strategy in Africa. Instead of working as a national 'team', every Chinese actor involved in Africa has its own motivations, priorities, aims and agendas; they often operate in a compromised way that combines both central policy and their own interests. Sometimes, they may undermine each other in order to pursue their own agendas. After the analysis, this chapter will show how China's responsible and irresponsible behaviour comes out and which actors encourage China to be fully responsible in Africa.

II Case studies part

The case studies will analyse hypotheses II and III of this book, and answer their respective research questions. In response to the literature of a diversified Africa, the case studies address four specific African countries: Sudan (South Sudan), Nigeria, South Africa and Ethiopia. Sudan is considered to have a pariah regime with large oil reserves the two features that China has long been accused of courting. Nigeria has a partly democratic government with large oil reserves, and is also the largest African country. South Africa is a democratic country without much in the way of oil reserves, but it has the largest and most developed economy on the continent. Ethiopia is a one-party state with regular elections; it is one of the least developing countries in Africa, is landlocked and does not much in the way of natural resources. The four cases are representative because they have different types of government, different levels of development, different attitudes towards Beijing, and different amounts of energy reserves (see Table 1.1).

Table 1.1 The comparison of four cases

	Sudan	*Nigeria*	*South Africa*	*Ethiopia*
Government type (according to freedom house)	Pariah regime	Semi-democratic	Democratic	One party rules
Economy	Least developed	Lower-middle income country	Largest and most developed in Africa	Least developed
Energy reserve	Oil	Oil	Mining	None
Regional strength	Used to be largest, now third largest African country	Largest African country; regional leader	Regional leader	Landlocked
Security	Conflicts	Armed groups	Stability with violent protests	Stability with some anti-government protest

Source: Author.

The case studies will be divided into four chapters, the four chapters will focus on each individual African country and to answer the following questions: (the questions of hypothesis II and III)

1 What are the influential factors that shape China's responsibility in Sudan, Nigeria, South Africa and Ethiopia, respectively? This question is designed to respond to the three influential factors of state responsibility, as discussed in Chapter 3 – that is, since each case has its own features, China has different motivations and pressures to shoulder the responsibility there; which factors play a bigger role against the background of the host country's situation, and how can they be compatible with each other?

2 Since China's involvement in Africa involves multiple kinds of actor in varied circumstances, what elements have affected China to be fully responsible for African countries, based on different situations in the four host countries? And how do they affect the implementation of China's Africa policy?

3 Since the four case countries have represented different features as showed in Table 1.1, the discussion section of case studies part will conduct a horizontal comparison among four states, to explore China's attitude and approach towards the different kinds of African countries and further to respond to the final questions of "is China a responsible player in Africa?"

4 The two hypotheses tested in the case studies complement the concept of "international responsibility" by adding developing countries' ideas – that is, Chinese researcher's arguments of considering capability into state's responsibility and African countries and their real demands and environment. The conclusion will, therefore, employ the five standards to evaluate whether China is a responsible country (with its unique features) in Africa.

III Conclusion

The final chapter will answer the question using the findings in the framework and case studies sections,, "Is China a responsible player in Africa? (Or what extent is China responsible in Africa?)"

Through the comparison of the four case countries, the conclusion will evaluate China's responsibility according to the established criteria in Chapter 3. The evaluation will be arranged into five parts, each addressing one criterion. In the analysis the criterion, the conclusion will respond to the common criticism of China-Africa engagement, "non-intervention" in the case of Sudan; "oil for infrastructure" in the case of Nigeria; "influx Chinese manufacture products" in the case of South Africa; "China as a model" in the case of Ethiopia. In addition, it will address the gap between China's African policy and its implementation as a general trend or a specific case in different types of African countries.

1.3.2 Research outline

The book will be presented in the following chapters:

Chapter 1 is an introduction. This chapter introduces the topic of the book and the significance and relevance of the research. Then it describes the research questions and hypotheses. In order to answer the research questions and test the hypotheses, it also introduces the research design, which will be organised into two parts: the framework and the case studies. Meanwhile, it presents the whole structure of this book.

Chapter 2 is a methodology chapter that will talk about how to conduct the research. Considering feasibility and accessibility, documentation, elite interviewing, focus group observation, and comparative qualitative approaches will be most appropriate to achieve the research goals. The main instruments adopted for the book framework will be documentation and discourse analysis, while the data collected from interviews and observations will be used in the case study chapters. Fieldwork will be conducted through elite interviews of officials from China's Ministry of Foreign Affairs (MOFA), employees from Chinese State-owned enterprises (SOEs) who have been assigned to Africa, Chinese self-employers in Africa, and China's African scholars. Additionally, in order to get first-hand information on each case country, rather than Africa as a whole, data from observation of the chatting groups and BBS among Chinese people in the host country will be analysed.

In Chapter 3, by reviewing the definition of "international responsibility", the book will establish criteria of the norm; that is, what is a responsible country? How does one make a judgment of whether a country is responsible or not? The chapter will then employ China's current strengths, identity and capabilities together with external expectations into these criteria in order to analyse China's international responsibility. That is, for a country like China, what are the requirements to become responsible?

Chapter 4 is the policy analysis chapter. This chapter is designed to assess China's responsibility in Africa at the policy level and to test hypothesis II of the relations between China's national interests and its responsibilities in Africa. At the beginning, it will review China's African Policy and its trends by explaining China's understanding of and logic for engagement in the continent, notably Beijing's increasingly flexible interpretation of its "non-intervention" principle in dealing with the crisis in Africa. After that, it will analyse Beijing's policy and approach from the perspective of responsibility. Indeed, China has held different positions and conducted different approaches to Africa from the traditional OECD donors, but its "oil for infrastructure" measures and the controversial China Model share similar expectations for the continent's stability and development with that of the Western countries. Hence, at the policy level, even if China's interpretation of being responsible is different to that of traditional players, it does not necessarily mean those differences are necessarily irresponsible.

Chapter 5 will present a fragmental China, with diverse interests and considerations that might influence its African policy implementation. It will introduce the first layer that shows China's Africa policy has deviated in implementation. Since China's involvement in Africa is mainly conducted in terms of foreign assistance, trade and investment, this chapter will ascertain which Chinese governmental departments or branches have been involved in China-Africa projects, what are their motivations and interests, and to what extent and how they can impact the achievement of the central government's pledge. Generally, after the policy has been announced by the central government, the state council, and three major players – MOFCOM, MOFA and Export-Import Bank (Exim), are responsible for the policy's management, supervision and implementation. Chinese companies will undertake the projects in the host country. Not only the official branches may have different strategies for Africa's development, but Chinese companies' in the host country may also undermine Beijing's policy as a result of their profit-driven agendas.

> After the discussion in the framework part, this book will use four case studies to answer and test the research questions of hypotheses II and III. Since Africa is heterogeneous, to evaluate the influence of China's engagement in the respective host country should be tailored to the particular situation of each subject. Four featured African countries are selected, Sudan (South Sudan), Nigeria, South Africa and Ethiopia (a pariah regime friendly to the Chinese government with oil reserves, an oil-rich country under partly democratic government, and a regional leader, and the least developed state with no resources) will be discussed in Chapter 6, 7, 8 and 9.

China's responsibilities in Sudan mainly focus on its effectiveness in facilitating the resolution to the humanitarian crisis there. Chapter 6 will start with a brief introduction to the conflicts in Sudan and China's evolving policy towards Darfur and South Sudan in terms of its "non-intervention" principle. This chapter will also highlight international criticism, and the serious situation in Sudan, which put important pressure on China's evolving policy towards more cooperative and international joint efforts. However, the international society and the opposing sides in Darfur and South Sudan failed or were slow to recognise China's changing policy, and still consider Beijing a close ally of the Bashir regime. It faced China with a dilemma and limited its capability to be responsible for solving the crisis.

Chapter 7 will mainly discuss the typical Chinese involvement in resource-rich African countries; that is, the "oil for infrastructure" approach as evidenced in the case of Nigeria. It will first introduce the China-Nigeria relationship against a background of Chinese companies' sharply increasing presence in Nigeria's oil industry, along with the infrastructure projects supported by the central government. Then, the chapter argues that on a policy level, there is no evidence to suggest China is irresponsible in Nigeria since its "oil for infrastructure" strategy was put forward to diversify China's overseas energy supply on the one hand, and to fuel Nigeria's economic growth on the other. But, in reality, multiple factors affect China's level of responsibility in the country. The electoral politics between north and south Nigeria and mismanagement and corruption in local government have made the "oil for infrastructure" approach highly unstable. Oil-related violence and incompetent governance have prevented the Nigerian people from enjoying the benefits of national oil income. Chinese companies also lose profits due to these same problems. In addition, the Nigerian government and its people have great ambitions for its national strength and economic performance, but because of the insufficient local infrastructure, it is difficult for local Nigerian businesses to compete with Chinese counterparts. The impact of Chinese products on local business has raised the satisfaction for Chinese involvement as well, which is a common phenomenon in China-Africa relations.

Chapter 8 will talk about South Africa. Currently, China has a close relationship with South Africa and a similar stance on international affairs. Economically, China's involvement in this country is different from other African countries due to South Africa's national strength and leading role in the region. The bilateral relationship between these two countries is more akin to that of competitors, rather than donor and recipient. As the most developed country on the continent, South Africa is expected to become a political and economic gateway between international society, and the region. Beijing considers its responsibility clear in this aspect. However, in reality, its representation and influence in other African countries are limited. Hence China's engagement in South Africa is much more out of bilateral consideration. The domestic situation in South Africa shows two features to Chinese investors. On the one hand, it has a democratic government with a sound legal system and advanced awareness of international standards. However, on the other hand, it has serious corruption, instability and a huge wealth gap between white and black South Africans. Chinese businesses that lack experience in overseas operations have met with difficulties and negative feedback in the South African market.

Chapter 9 looks at Ethiopia, a landlocked country with neither valuable reserves of natural resources nor sufficient, quality infrastructure. China's responsibility in this country is mainly economic development and financial assistance because the China-Ethiopia relationship is asymmetric. Beijing's active involvement in the least-developed country is much more out of political and diplomatic consideration than economic profits. Generally, the Ethiopian government and its people hold a positive attitude towards Beijing and Chinese enterprises. The only problem arises at the implementation level because some Chinese companies lack the awareness of international standards on environmental, labour force and community protections.

Chapter 10 is the conclusion. This chapter will review China's engagement in the four case studies and apply the five criteria established in Chapter 3. It will give a summary of the extent to which China is responsible in Africa. And, finally, it will answer the research question of whether China is responsible or irresponsible in Africa. It will make a comparison between each type of African country in order to respond to the common criticism of China's involvement in Africa, and further answer the question of "Whether China is responsible in Africa".

2 Methodology

Having formulated the research questions and hypotheses, and specified the research scope, this chapter on methodology is designed to explore how best to conduct the research and to obtain the required information and data. The chapter begins with a discussion of research methods and a practical research design. It will then specify the main methods of interviewing; observation, documentation and discourse analysis, while also detailing the research procedures and explain any issues arising from the data collection and analysis.

2.1 Research methods

In order to evaluate the facets of China's presence in Africa, the book begins by setting up a standard for the term "international responsibility". Although it is unlikely to provide access to pure facts that might enable us to declare that particular interpretations and narratives are either true or false, it still could maintain an element of objectivity through criteria of comparison (Bevir & Rhodes, 2010). In this case, Chapter 3 will attempt to establish reasonable criteria for "international responsibility" for China that will not be considered as a given truth, but rather a pragmatic demand, which will be achieved through a process of gradual comparison of internal capabilities and external expectations. Then it will go further through the ideas, doctrines and Chinese policy and explore the real interests and impacts between them, in order to reveal whether there is the potential for cooperation between China and the West in Africa. The fourth chapter's policy analysis will favour a form of interpretation that lies between hermeneutics and post-structuralism and will attempt to interpret the reality of China's African policy as neither nihilistic nor irrational. It will try to investigate from neither the pure interpretation of Chinese documents, nor the pure characteristics of CPC's subjective interests, but rather to offer a combination of China's national interest with the policies and measures to Africa's development announced by the central government. The following chapter will focus on China-Africa connections in practice, and attempt to explain the relationship between the central government and the key actors in Africa, such as Chinese enterprises, African's regulations and environments, through interpretation of evidence acquired during interviews and the materials available on discourse, from news media and various other documents. In comparison to Chapter 4, Chapter 5 will discuss Chinese governmental branches and enterprises in Africa, and analyse the gap between policy and implementation based on the data from interviews with Chinese officials and also documentary evidence.

After that, in order to further explore China's activities in different kinds of African countries, it will use four national cases of China's involvement in Africa – Sudan (South Sudan), Nigeria, South Africa and Ethiopia – to confirm hypothesis II and test hypothesis III. Chapters 6–9 will discuss the influential factors that shape China's Africa policy and the reason for China being or not being responsible to the respective host country in its policy implementation, according to the findings from interview materials and documentary analysis. It will point out the gap between Beijing's African policy and its implementation and how it comes about in different countries. In discussing the gap, the tone must also discuss the fragmented nature of China and a diversified Africa. One emphasises the Chinese situation – that is, Chinese enterprises' activities – due to the contrast and contradiction between their patriarchal relationship with the Chinese government and also their self-interested nature. The other focuses on China's limitations and capabilities in the host country.

The conclusion to the case studies part will adopt a comparative method between each country that refers to the need to employ an analysis from a sense of perspective to a familiar environment and discourages parochial responses to political issues (Hopkin, 2002). The case studies will enable the research to explore China's motivations for shouldering responsibility in different kinds of African countries. Furthermore, it can reveal China's featured approaches to different types of African countries, as different countries have different strategic meanings to China, politically, economically or diplomatically. Each case represents a unique Chinese feature in Africa. ("Non-intervention" in Sudan; "Oil for infrastructure" in Nigeria; overwhelming Chinese products in South Africa and China as a model in Ethiopia.) In Part 2 conclusion, it will use a comparative approach to explore since the four case countries are different, whether China has particularly favoured some countries, such as oil-rich countries or pariah regimes, as the common criticism said.

It is worth noting that it is unrealistic to create an ideal model that excludes the variance for comparison in political science. Peters described the problem as "extraneous variance", caused by factors outside the theoretical proposition being examined, which is a serious obstacle to comparative research (Peters, 1998, pp. 30–36). In order to narrow the scope and find the most similar system research design, as suggested by Przeworski and Tenure, it should aim to minimise the variance problems (Burnham, Lutz, Grant, & Layton-Henry, 2004, pp. 63–68; Hopkin, 2002, pp. 255–256). For this reason, the case studies will horizontally make a comparison across different types of African regime and vertically focus on China's different levels of engagement.

Having decided on the interpretative research approach and comparative method, the next step is to define the appropriate way to collect original data for the case studies. Burnham has pointed out the "purpose of the research design is to propose an operational plan, and to ensure that the strategies and procedures adopted within the plan are adequate to provide valid and accurate solutions to the research questions" (Burnham et al., 2004, pp. 29–33). It is necessary to clarify the general aims for carrying out the research, which are stated as follows: first, to analyse the proper scope of China's African responsibility. Second, using the "international responsibility" criteria discussed in the framing part to evaluate China's African engagement during the last decade. Third, to find out the factors obstructing China from fulfilling its responsibility. Generally, there are three perspectives that count in the debate about China-African responsibility: the Chinese central government, Western governments and international agencies; and the perspectives of different African states. However, in practice, the key actors on the front lines are the assistance groups, the Chinese enterprises (including managerial personnel, Chinese workers, and self-employed), Chinese migrants, Western companies, and local African people. In this case, the data collection process will be divided into two groups: official documents, discourse, news and opinions from the enterprise and people levels.

The key issue is which research method (or methods) will be most appropriate to achieve these stated research goals? Considering the capability and energy of a PhD student, I decided to collect the first-hand information through Small Ns (a small number of cases), as suggested by qualitative comparative methods. Qualitative comparative research tends to explain political phenomena in terms of the combined effect of several factors (Hopkin, 2002). Comparing to the greater reliability of findings from large Ns (a large number of cases), in other words, quantitative comparative methods, Ragin argued that there is no a priori reason to regard case-oriented, qualitative comparative research as methodologically "soft" and indeed this approach can provide a far more rigorous and sophisticated response to some types of research questions (Ragin, 1987). Considering the China-Africa connections, sophisticated response qualitative studies enable the researcher to look at the enterprise-level within Chinese political contexts, at the cases individually and as a whole, while revealing the influence of domestic interests on outside behaviours. At the same time, it would "explore people's subjective experiences and the meanings they attach to those experiences which are good at capturing meaning, process and context" (Bryman, 1988, p. 62). As a result, the main instruments adopted for data collection are interviews, observations, documentation and discourse analysis, which will be detailed respectively in the sections below. The use of such a combination of methods will check the accuracy of data and provide complementary information to strengthen the findings.

2.2 Research design

2.2.1 In-depth interview

A qualitative method is intended to "explore people's subjective experiences and the meanings they attach to those experiences" (Cassidy, Reynolds, Naylor, & De Souza, 2011). Intensive interviewing allows people to talk freely and offer their interpretation of events. Qualitative methods are good at capturing meaning, process, and context and eliciting people's subjective experiences, opinions, beliefs, values, and so forth (Bryman, 1988). An intensive interview is a popular approach used by political science to collect first-hand information and increase the interaction between the interviewer and the respondent. The research design of the in-depth interview is flexible and open to new ideas and interpretations (Burnham et al., 2004, p. 219). Open-ended questions are also valuable for discovering what the respondent really feels. Moreover, the perspectives provided by experienced people will be useful for further discourse analysis. At the start of interview design, it is important to identify who will be interviewed, since what questions will be asked is inevitably shaped by who is going to answer them. The size and categories of interviewees – from International Relations scholars, officials, SOEs employees and self-employers – are deliberately defined, and interview questions are accordingly designed. Then one should draw up an interviewing schedule. This section will involve the real procedures and problems encountered during the interviews, followed by the process of transcription and analysis.

By categorising the key actors involved in China's operations in Africa, research was conducted on the following four sample groups: (1) officials from central government (former Chinese ambassadors to African countries, staff from Chinese embassies in Africa); (2) Chinese-African scholars from universities and research institutions affiliated to ministries; (3) employees assigned to Africa by central state-owned enterprises; and (4) staff from private firms and self-employers. With the limitations of time and funding, fieldwork was carried out in Beijing, China, which is not only the political, economic and cultural centre of China with global significance but also the location of all Chinese ministries, top universities and leading institutions. For those subjects currently working in Africa, I used emails, telephones or voice-over-internet software applications to gain the information and conduct interviews.

The sample size was about 20 people in total, depending on their availability. Though the number is small, it is enough for intensive and in-depth interviews. In addition, according to the casual conversations with relevant respondents, people from similar backgrounds seemed to provide similar perspectives. More information could be supplemented from other sources, such as observation, discourse, documents, news, and so forth, but not from more interviewing. Since the research not only seeks to evaluate China's activities in Africa but also to see which level (central-enterprises' or African countries' capability) impact China's African policy, what the people who have experience in Africa have to say is more important than simply discussing theory. Because of the number and specified groups of samples, I employed snowball sampling, by which I mean asking them to nominate potential informants during the interview. The request is usually made at each subsequent interview until the required number is reached, which is a valuable strategy to generate a sample of people or groups, and it is more suited to in-depth interview research (Burnham et al., 2004, pp. 92–93). In each of the four groups of people, according to the availability and accessibility of a certain level or category, the interview survey may choose to interview some people from the entry and medium levels, instead of high position; this is because middle-level staffers are more likely to provide true stories rather than stalling with official jargon.

Since all the interviewees, regardless of the level or groups they belong to, are experienced in China-Africa issues, the intensive interviews would be more appropriate for this research. In contrast to the structured interview, intensive interviews are open and flexible, allowing the informants to elaborate on their values and attitudes and account for their actions (Brenner, 1985). When it comes to the perspective of China, all the stories from Chinese officials, scholars, employees, and private owners in Africa are paramount for this research. The intensive interviews are conducted in Chinese, which allows the key informants to tell their stories in the language they are familiar with and helps them to express their logic and positions better. The intensive interviewing techniques are based on a general interview guide. Therefore, questions in the case studies are prepared as topic headings and general questions targeted at each group to facilitate a discussion of issues in a semi-structured or unstructured manner (Devine, 2002). It is worth noting that, although the interview guide is just served as a checklist of topics to be covered, the order in which they are discussed is not preordained (Bryman, 1988, p. 66). The design of the interview questions of each group is detailed below for each targeted group – its general aims, specific research areas, and interview topics.

I Interview questions

According to the general aims of the research, the data collection process focused on a comparison between different groups, officials and civil citizens. Furthermore, in order to ascertain the relationship between the Chinese government and state or province-owned enterprises, the information should be collected from both sides. For the civil citizens group itself, opinions included both SOEs and private companies. Opinions were collected from the following angles: (1) the awareness of China's international responsibility; (2) the impression of Chinese ways in Africa; (3) their own experiences of what has happened as part of China-Africa links. To be more specific, the respondents were divided into four groups based on their occupations, and interviewing questions were prepared to meet the requirements of each of the four groups.

Question schedule 1 was designed for officials from the central government, such as former Chinese ambassadors to certain African countries, and officials from China's African embassies. The people confirmed for interviews are the former ambassador to Morocco, the former second secretary to Ghana, and the former Chinese Ambassador to Nigeria and Namibia. Because of the accessibility of diplomats, "snowball" or referral sampling were used during the interview. I started with a few key informants who were identified as relevant and then asked them in turn to name other key individuals who would be relevant to this research. In this way, more accurate and specific first-hand information could be acquired. For those officials who held a higher position and better understanding of China's African policy, elite interviewing was most appropriate, as this treated each respondent as an expert in the topic (Leech, 2002, p. 663). During the interviews with these diplomats, the balance was usually in favour of the respondents' high level of position, and bureaucratic tones could hinder the successful completion of the research. Therefore, I chose the respondents who were not currently holding office, in the hope of fewer constraints and apprehensions of what they say. At the same time, I sent a topic guideline in advance and chose to interview those who showed the most interest in the topic.

The aims of interviewing this group were: (1) to compare their understanding of international responsibilities with the Western expectations and Africa's demands, and to test hypothesis II to see the possibility of cooperation between China and Western countries on African issues; (2) to become acquainted with the central government's motivations towards and strategies for Africa; (3) to get first hand information on China's governmental assistant projects in Africa; (4) to assess the connections between Chinese enterprises in Africa and central government. Based on these goals, the following eight questions were discussed during the interviews:

1   What's your opinion towards the idea of China's international responsibility, for example, as proposed by the then-U.S. Deputy Secretary of State Robert Zoellick?
2   What kinds of responsibilities should China take in Africa's development?
3   Do you think China is a responsible stakeholder in Africa? Why?
4   What do you think are the biggest problems that blocked African development? Please take the country you worked in as an example.
5   To what extent and in what ways do the Chinese enterprises operating in Africa liaise with, and get help from the local embassy? What are

the issues between the Chinese diplomats and the representatives of the Chinese enterprises?

6   How do China and African states achieve a win-win situation when the two countries have an unbalanced development status?

7   Please name the most successful assistance project conducted by China, and why it turned out to be successful.

8   What do you think are the biggest problems that affect China's image in Africa?

Questions Schedule 2 was targeted at the employees of SOEs. People from these groups have worked or are currently working in Africa for certain Chinese projects, which has enabled them to have a greater chance of communicating with local communities and is more prone to discover the problems that exist between central policies and practical feasibility. Two sectors, the energy and construction industries, have the most Chinese SOEs operating in Africa. The respondents who confirmed were all from these two industries: an African projects manager from China Gezhouba Group Company Ltd., a project manager in Ghana from Sino Hydro Corporation Limited, and an engineer in Nigeria from CNPC. Meanwhile, an employee from provincial or municipal level companies was included as well: a project manager of Guinea-Mali, China Geo Engineering Corporate. This research focuses on the people who have work experience in Africa, even if they are from lower positions because they were more likely to provide the truth about the front line. In order to unearth true stories, I avoided interviewing employees from public or communication departments, who were more likely to regurgitate their press releases. However, people from this group are often not familiar with research interviews, sometimes they may ask the interviewer to offer their own opinions on the topics under discussion (Finch, 1984), so the guidelines needed to be more specific.

By interviewing this group, one would expect to get the following information: (1) their awareness and understanding of China's African policy; (2) the gap between foreign policy rhetoric and actual economic activities; (3) Chinese enterprises' problems in Africa. Finally, the interview questions were prepared as follows:

1   How does your company decide who will be assigned to Africa?

2   Please describe the aims of the projects you've worked on, or are currently involved, in Africa.

3   What percentage of funding in this project is from a government, central or provincial, respectively? Compared to projects elsewhere, is there obvious governmental support?

4   Comparing to other projects domestically, or in other developing countries, how profitable are the projects in Africa?

5   How many African colleagues do you have, and what positions do they hold? How do they get along with Chinese counterparts?

6 How does your company accomplish the industry chain? In the example of transportation, how do they get the necessary components for the projects? Do you favour Chinese or African partners when accessing supply chains?
7 Please describe the advantages and disadvantages of Chinese enterprises in Africa compared to Western competitors.
8 What difficulties do Chinese companies have during their cooperation in Africa?

Question Schedule 3 was conducted with the hope of getting information from private companies in Africa. Chapter 5 specifically discusses the ambiguous lines between China's SOEs and private firms. Considering the fact that most of the large Chinese private companies have close connections to the government, the samples for these groups were from small or medium-sized private firms. The private firms randomly involved in Africa, it is difficult to find them for an interview. Only one translator for a small trading company in Nigeria confirmed interest in being interviewed, via Internet communication software. Other first-hand information of private companies was acquired from observation, which will be addressed in the next section.

The aims of interviewing employees of private firms were: (1) the impact of Chinese engagement in Africa at a grassroots level; (2) to evaluate the gap between China's Africa policy and its implementation in terms of the private sector. The prepared topics are as follows:

1 When did you come to Africa for the first time?
2 Why do you invest in Africa?
3 What's your opinion towards the going global strategy and China's Africa responsibilities; do they have any influence in your daily operations in Africa?
4 What constraints have you experienced during your operations in the African market?
5 Will you introduce your friends or relatives to Africa? Why?
6 How many employees do you have? Will you employ African staff? Why?
7 Did you receive any help from the local embassy?
8 Who is your biggest competitor?

Question Schedule 4 was for China's African scholars. Although the opinions of Chinese academia can be accessed through their books and articles, considering the prudence of Chinese scholars, the interviews for this group aim to achieve the following goals: (1) to address the notion of "international responsibility" from China's African scholars' point of view; (2) to access the latest information about China in Africa; (3) to serve as a supplementary source for the previous data collection. Due to the high level of knowledge and expressive abilities, the interview favoured the respondent in this group.

Therefore, the questions prepared for each scholar were based on their existing publications. The confirmed respondents were a professor from Beijing University who specialises in African studies and energy studies; a research professor of African studies from the China Institutes of Contemporary International Relations; and researchers from the Chinese Academy of Social Sciences. Their opinions were collected in order to deepen the other research findings and to modify the data from the three non-academic groups. The questions and topics for these people were (modified questions and more specific queries were added following the completion of the other three groups' interviews):

INTERNATIONAL RESPONSIBILITY

1   What's your opinion of China's international responsibility, as proposed by the then-U.S Deputy Secretary of State Robert Zoellick?
2   What kinds of responsibilities should China take in Africa's development?
3   Do you think China is a responsible stakeholder in Africa? Why?
4   What kinds of positions does Africa have in China's foreign strategy?
5   In your book, Great Powers' Responsibility, you've emphasised the possibility of cooperation between China and the West; do you think this perspective suits the situation in Africa?
6   Both your articles and books on China's responsibility are from national policy level perspective. What do you think is the role of lower levels in the responsibility process?

AFRICAN STUDIES

1   Why does the Chinese government enthusiastically promote the FOCAC, while also being the focus of much criticism, such as Chinese neo-colonialism, and kidnapping targeted at Chinese labours by local African people?
2   What do you think are the problems affecting China's image in Africa?
3   Has China's African policy experienced big changes during last 10 years?
4   What do you think of the Chinese model (Beijing Consensus)? Do you think China has provided an alternative development road for Africa, and why?
5   According to statistics, African elites favour China's presence, while non-governmental people express resentment. How do you think the different attitudes came about, and how could the problem/disparity be solved?

II Interview procedures

A pilot study was conducted, based on the literature review, in order to test the interview structure, respondents and questions, to assess the quality of elite interviewing, to reveal the meaningless or embarrassing questions, and to discover the new issues raised during the pilot study. The rehearsal of the actual survey provided an opportunity to discover how the respondents might react to the survey, and thus to estimate the level of non-responses (Burnham et al., 2004, p. 39) and the quality of the data. The pilot research was conducted as follows: (1) to choose one or two representatives from each group and initiate a flexible and open conversation to test their openness to this kind of interview, and their attitudes towards the questions; (2) the interviews were conducted via email and telephone because all the potential interviewees were not in the UK; (3) the pilot study was conducted between 10 and 30 May 2012.

During the pilot study, the interview questions and process were modified, new questions and potential informants were added. At the same time, the unforeseen difficulties were revealed. The lack of interaction has blocked the successful completion of an elite interview, especially using emails where the respondents may provide lots of anecdotes, such as complaints of the harsh conditions in Africa, which are not relevant to this research. Limited by the length of the interview, more attention should be paid to interaction. Furthermore, more detailed stories, not only personal experiences but also accurate investment figures were expected to be obtained through interviews. At the same time, nearly all the respondents expressed willingness to recommend other informants – as noted in the previous section, snowball sampling designs will be used to select interviewees from the existing four groups for the further subcategory. It was expected to achieve a total number of 20 people; that is, approximately six officials, six SOEs employees, three employees from private firms, and five scholars.

The formal interview research will be titled "Assessment of China's African Policy and its Implementation", with an introductory letter issued by the School of Government and International Affairs at Durham University. The fieldwork was carried out between July 15, 2012, and September 15, 2012, in Beijing, China. The interview order for the four groups was fixed. Officials from the central government were the first group interviewed, their interviews and information focused on the policy level. The second group to be interviewed was the employees from SOEs, focusing on their awareness of central African policy, and to what extent they might receive support from the central government, and the implementation in practice could offer a useful comparison with the policy advocated by the officials. Then it came to the private firms, investigating their motivations for investing in Africa, and their ways of operation could offer a comparison with both official policies and those of SOEs. Finally, the evidence generated by these three groups was assessed in order to inspire new questions, which would be asked during the interviews of the fourth group. This discussion focused on the interpretation of their reactions to the former interview transcripts.

Case studies are an extremely popular part of research design and are widely used throughout the social sciences. The qualitative research method embraces it, as it generates a wealth of data relating to one specific case that can be used to generate hypotheses and theories (Burnham et al., 2004). It enables a researcher to focus on one area and study it in depth. After the first round of elite interviews, I conducted a second round of interviews focusing on the case study countries and interviewed Chinese-African studies scholars who are specialised in, and have work experience or have done fieldwork, in the four case countries. The second round of interviews will be carried out while writing the case studies, conducted through emails or interviews in Beijing. (The information from interviewees is included in an appendix I.)

It is worth noting that the interviews were conducted in difficult situations. First, due to accessibility, some of the key informants were not from the case study countries. As a result, there was a lack of a subcategory based on host countries. Second, the number of interviewees from Group 3 (self-employers) was too small. Not only were they difficult to reach, but they also showed limited interest in academic interviews. Third, as Witness 7, an African researcher who has six years' work experience in Africa, suggested, it was hard to get information from Chinese enterprises... because they tend to talk about their contributions to African countries but to neglect their weaknesses, as they believe "Don't wash your dirty linen in public". In this case, I employed the following methods to adjust for these deficiencies.

2.2.2 *Participant observation*

Participant Observation is a research strategy used by researchers who participate in a social environment to understand people's behaviour. The researcher needs to establish a tight connection or themselves become group members for this method (Wax, 1968). The participation can be deep or slight, public or secret, but this participation would need a specific period of time, during which the researcher would observe and record people's behaviour, in formal or informal interviews, or collect documents that describe these people's activities in this environment (Lofland & Lofland, 1984, p. 12). The key to implementing a successful Participant Observation is a long-term observation (Burnham et al., 2004, p. 256).

Gold is one of the pioneers who offer a clear category for this method and identified four kinds of a participant for this method: complete participant, participant-as-observer, observer-as-participant, and complete observer (Gold, 1958, pp. 30–39). The first one is a full participant in the group, and other members of the group do not know the researcher's real identity. The difference between the first type and the second is that the researcher in the second variant needs to clarify the researcher's purpose to the other group members. In the third category, the group members understand the research's purpose, and the researcher can freely interact with group members without excuses. In the final category, the researcher just observes the group without any interaction (Burnham et al., 2004, pp. 227–235; Frankfort-Nachmias & Nachmias, 1996) (Frankfort-Nachmias and Nachmias Chapter 12, but in their book, there are only two types: complete participant and participant-as-observer). In order to reach the informants from the four host countries – Sudan, Nigeria, South Africa and Ethiopia, as well as Chinese self-employers in Africa and some African veterans, the book took the third and the fourth of Gold's categories and conducted an observation in QQ and BBS to obtain essential data from the informants.

Tencent QQ is the one of the common instant message software for Chinese to communicate with each other via mobile phone, laptop, or computers. One function of it is group chat, which enables its members to create a discussion group (Qun) under certain subjects. Thus, I applied to some Chinese in Africa QQ chatting groups based on the four African countries. After being rejected by some exclusive chat groups, and considering the relevance of those who accepted, as well as their numbers and levels of activity, the following chat groups were selected for observation:

1 Sudan

    i Walking Across Sudan (Xingzou zai sudan 行走在苏丹) with 999 group members (the maximum number of members for a QQ group).

2 Nigeria

    i Home of Chinese Enterprises in Nigeria (Niriliya zhongzi qiye zhijia 尼日利亚 中资企业之家) with 332 members;

    ii Nigerian Association of Trade and Commercial Enterprises (Niriliya shangmao qiye xiehui 尼日利亚商贸企业协会) with 213 members.

3 South Africa

    i South Africa-China Chamber of Commerce (Nanfei zhongguo shanghui 南非中 国商会) with 306 members;

    ii South Africa chrome ore (Nanfei gekuang 南非铬 矿) with 338 members.

4 Ethiopia

    i Ethiopia Autonym Business Group (Aisaiebiya shiming shangwu qun 埃塞俄 比亚实名商务群) with 465 members;

    ii Ethiopia Boss Group (Aisaiebiya laoban qun 埃塞俄比亚老板群) with 433 members.

This software enabled me to observe the discussions on Chinese enterprises' daily running, opportunities and challenges in the host countries and sometimes participate in their conversations, and hence to obtain first hand information. Since they are free to talk about any issues raised in their life and work, it was more likely to reveal the real occurrences of Chinese activity in Africa, which could then be used to compare with Beijing's official African policy.

Bulletin Board System (BBS) is another common tool, which gathers people who have similar interests or needs to discuss their daily or specific issues. BBS, which is different from an instant message tool, is a public or private space (board) for members to post their articles. Every board will have a specific subject, and the manager of this board manages the range of discussion; members can use these boards to discuss or share their thoughts or experiences on any given subject. The articles on BBS are more systematic than QQ group chats. I observed the following ones:

Chinese in Nigeria BBS: www.nigeriabbs.com/bbs/South-Africa Chinese BBS: www.nanfei8.com/
Ethiopia Chinese BBS: www.ethiopianbbs.com/bbs/portal.php

The data collected from participant observation of QQ chat group and BBS is anonymous. On the one hand, people are more likely to express their real feelings without few constraints, even if on sensitive topics. However, as the informants are not required to be responsible for their opinions, the authenticity of their articles needs to be evaluated by the researcher on the basis of other, more reliable sources – such as documentary evidence, papers and books.

2.2.3 Documentary and archival analysis

It is very important for a political researcher to use essential documentary and archives when conducting a research project. There are three categories of documents and archives: primary, secondary and tertiary (Burnham et al., 2004, p. 166; Lichtman & French, 1978, p. 18). Primary documents or archives are directly related to the research topic and can be materials that still need to be studied. Secondary documents refer to materials which are related to the research topic or were written or recorded just after the research events. Tertiary materials are written or recorded after the event and attempt to reconstruct the facts of the event (Burnham et al., 2004, p. 166; Lichtman & French, 1978, p. 18).

Normally, as a researcher, primary documentation is the most valuable material because these materials detail facts of events. However, these materials can be hard to obtain (Burnham et al., 2004, pp. 166–169; Frankfort-Nachmias & Nachmias, 1996). When using secondary materials, there are certain limitations related to the reliability of the materials. Therefore, government documents, international organisations' official archives, United Nation's publications, respected newspapers and magazines would be considered reliable documents and archives (Burnham et al., 2004, pp. 171–172). Official documents on China-Africa are not transparent, and the bilateral data is hard to access. Therefore, most of the evidence contained in the case studies was acquired from local, respected newspapers. Notably, the Sudan Tribune of Sudan; Vanguard and allAfrica of Nigeria; the Mail and Guardian of South Africa; and the Ethiopian Herald of Ethiopia.

In summary, the best research utilises a combination of methodological approaches in order to deepen the research findings (Hertz & Imber, 1995). The qualitative methods have been aligned with an interpretive epistemology that stresses the dynamic, constructed and evolving nature of social reality, while other sources and techniques – such as archives, materials on the internet, and discourse – all could be utilised to check the rough data. Elite interviews and focus-group observation will be used to collect original data, and the interpretation of the data will be conducted through both individual case and comparative design. One advantage of approaching a research question comparatively is that doing so has the potential to improve the classifications we use to impose some sort of order on the diversity of the political world. In terms of a diversified Africa, it helps to find the general trends and approaches to China's involvement.

Part 1
Framework part

3 International responsibility

The concept and its implications

3.1 Introduction

The notion of international responsibility derives from the dilemma that, on the one hand, "state sovereignty has long been regarded as the pivotal structural paradigm of international law" (Payandeh, 2010, p. 469), while on the other hand, the emergence of different kinds of global issues require states, living in the international society, to not only meet the demands of their people but also to be bound by rules imposed on them by external forces, and to bear obligations beyond their borders and people's needs. As an emerging political concept, the word "responsibility" can be easily found in political discourse, diplomatic documents and speeches, such as: "to be a responsible great power", "responsible stakeholder", "responsible sovereignty", "responsibility to protect", "irresponsible behaviour", "power and responsibility", "special responsibility", "global responsibility", "regional responsibility", and so forth (Breslin, 2010, p. 53; Etzioni, 2011, p. 539; Küng, 2004; Slim, 2010, p. 156; Stedman, Jone, & Pascual, 2009; Teitt, 2008, p. 4; Y. Zheng & Chen, 2006, p. 11). However, the conception of this term is incomplete, and the international community is far from reaching a consensus on a complete definition. Additionally, it is still a flawed concept, since the evaluation of "responsibility" is ambiguous. This chapter intends to demonstrate the existing interpretation on "international responsibility" and to develop the criteria to evaluate this term and then to locate it within China's political context, in order to further assess its implication for China's African engagement.

This chapter starts with a discussion of "responsibility" and summarises five criteria to judge "being responsible or not". In the second section, it introduces "state" as the subject, and explains "international responsibility" on the basis of two theories from the English school (pluralism and solidarism). Then it analyses the defects of the term (incomplete and flawed). This chapter complements the term through China's and Africa's interpretation and develops the criteria of "responsibility". Finally, it sets five criteria with which to assess a state level of responsibility. In the third section, it looks at the term from the context of China's politics, and answers the question, "What is the proper international responsibility for a state like China?" This chapter aims to establish a reasonable standard for state's responsibility which would lay a conceptual foundation and scope for further argument.

3.2 Conceiving international responsibility

3.2.1 Responsibility

In order to determine what "international responsibility" means, and what its implications are, we must start with the word "responsibility". According to the Longman Dictionary, "responsibility" refers to "a duty to be in charge of someone or something, so that you make decisions and can be blamed if something bad happens".[1] For Adam Watson, "responsibility implies accountability for one's actions, for their consequences" (Watson, 1997, p. 95). Others look at responsibility in two dimensions: the first is "accountability, answerability and liability look backwards to conduct and events in the past", and the second is, "roles and tasks look to the future" (Cane, 2002, p. 31). Following these definitions, "responsibility" could be interpreted two different ways: an obligation, duty and task one should fulfil, and the accountability for the consequences of one's actions or inactions. Similarly, Lucas has categorised responsibility as having both a positive and negative angle. He argued that responsibility could be seen from a negative perspective, in contrary to the positive responsibility. The former refers to "bear[ing] the consequences for their misconduct", while the latter one means "fulfill[ing] the requirement" (Lucas, 1993, p. 53). These explanations bring about two questions – specifically, "What it means to be responsible?" and "What are our responsibilities?" (Kramer, 2004, p. 133). There arises a dichotomy from these distinctions. One is the bottom line to shoulder a consequence, while the other is the high line of fulfilling a requirement. Cane has interpreted it from a legal and moral perspective. According to his view, the law is the bottom line to be responsible, while moral standards shape the range of "what our responsibilities are". However, it is worth noting that "moral" is an equally ambiguous and conditional term which depends on one's perspective and situation. Cane suggests that there are three issues that should be considered with regards to assessing responsibility: (1) the conduct and mental life of agents;[2] (2) the consequences of conduct and their impact on others; (3) what our prospective responsibilities are (Cane, 2002). The three issues imply that the judgment of responsibility could be made from three perspectives: the subject's motivation and strengthen the impacts on the object, and external expectations.

The debate on the high line of moral responsibility has drawn the attention of a large number of philosophers. Wolf and Wallace assume a responsibility that goes beyond "moral character" is not casual (Wallace, 1994, p. 52); historically it relied upon two aspects: "the merit-based view"[3] and "the consequentialist view".[4] The former presumes that being responsible should be a condition of "metaphysical freedom", the latter assumes the agent could be "influenced through outward expression of praise and blame in order to curb or promote certain behaviours" (Bivins). The merit-based view echoes Cane's evaluation criteria of a subject's strength and capability, while the consequentialist view introduces the consideration of outward expression. Later, Strawson pointed out that both of these interpretations have defects, according to his "participant reactive attitudes" theory, "the justification refers back to the reactive attitudes". That is, the internal role in the relationship, not theoretical conditions. This judgment highlights the importance of a participant's attitude. Generally, responsibility could be understood by attributability or accountability. When it came to responsibility as attributability, the assessment of the agent itself should be measured, which brings the agent's ability into consideration. Meanwhile, when it comes to "being responsible" in the sense of accountability, Strawson developed his theory by proposing the influence of external expectations (a branch of reactive attitudes) to holding responsibility (Stanford Encyclopedia of Philosophy, 2011).

Recognising of diversity of discussion in interpretations of the word "responsibility", the criteria for judging "responsibility" can be summarised thus: (1) liability and accountability to the subject's behaviours, this could be judged by legal and widely accepted normative norms, which is the basic standard and foundation of being responsible. The following four criteria are viewed from the perspective of "tasks in the future", which, in contrast, lack regulations or rules: (2) the agent's physical and mental condition, which refers to the subject's strength and capability as well as attitudes towards the object. This standard is viewed from the subject's perspective and explores the inner motivation of being responsible. (3) The subjects' behaviour, which includes action and inaction, the main components of responsibilities. (4) The consequences and impacts, the influence could be positive or negative, which is judged from the objective's perspective; (5) judgment and feedback of the behaviour, censure or praise, sanctions or rewards. This feedback is viewed from the perspective of public opinion, which provides a third-party perspective alongside subject and object.

As discussed earlier, for the first dimension, different kinds of laws and regulations clearly describe the primary range of retrospective responsibility. Blame or praise, sanctions or rewards mostly come out of the consequences and impact of the agents' actions or inactions. By contrast, the perspective of responsibility does not always have clear instructions – that is, what means to be responsible seems ambiguous. Some moral standards, common and acknowledged items have partly shaped "responsibilities", but the evaluation of them is difficult. The four criteria introduced in the previous paragraph help to judge behaviour as responsible or not. The second criterion of a subject's physical and mental condition could be added to the subject's general capability and identity, as well as its willingness and its own interests. The fifth criterion talks about the pressures from public opinion, which form an expectation for the subject to act in a specific way. It should be noted that public opinion is a general term, shaped by various voices. Not all voices enjoy the same position or influence in an evaluation. As shown in Figure 3.1, below, "expectation and demands B" is considered to have a bigger influence than others. Following Strawson's logic, expectation and demands B comes from the participants and is more like the receiver.

As shown in Figure 3.1, employing the five criteria to make a judgment of responsibility or not, the subject, object and third party (external) expectations of behaviour works in a dynamic way. Laws and rules serve as the foundations for being responsible; while the subject's capability and external expectations influence the subject's identity. The subject's identity, its own interests towards the object, and its willingness to be responsible finally determine the "responsibility".

The explanation above draws a general boundary for responsibility from individual and social perspectives. When it comes to state level, the only authoritative definition of "international responsibility" rested on international law. Generally, "every internationally wrongful act of a state entails the international responsibility of that state in the international law" (Yearbook of International Law Commission, 2001). It provides a baseline and lowest standard of international responsibility. However, this definition only provides a rough idea of retrospective responsibility and does not explain perspective "international responsibility" in political discourse. Since this book focuses on bilateral and multilateral responsibility

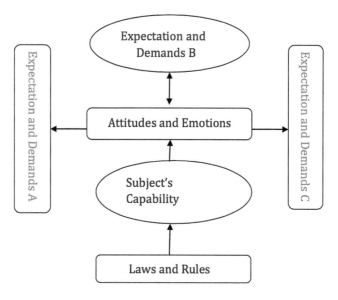

Figure 3.1 The Dynamic influential factors of "responsibility".
Source: Author.

between China and African states, the following section will investigate what "international responsibility" means in political discourse, through a discussion of "responsibility".

3.2.2 International responsibility

Historically, states have developed a sovereign border within which the government takes charge of the behaviour of the state in bilateral and multilateral dealings. These states, as units with various political, cultural, economic, religious, and ideological backgrounds exist in an anarchical system. As Bull described, "there is no higher level of authority over states" in international society, "each state has ultimate sovereignty over its citizens within its borders" (Bull, 2002, p. 25). In practice, states form an international society with some basic values established through international laws, the balance of power, diplomacy, war, and the impact of great power. Therefore, shared rules and international norms provide order to the international arena. The emerging political norm of "international responsibility" stems from such an international society, where states are the main subjects of "being responsible". Different from the "responsibility" of individuals, a state's international responsibility inherits the legal, political and moral traditions of each state. It is useful to consider these three aspects to evaluate a state's responsibility.

International regulations and rules define the legal obligations of states in terms of retrospective responsibility; clarifying what laws constrain their actions, and what consequences they would be subject to if they broke these laws. However, the International Law Commission reveals that the notion of international responsibility is one of the most difficult issues under international law, and concluded that two elements are required to ascertain a state's responsibility: "an illicit act under international law and that the act is attributable to the State". However, "International law has followed with excessive slowness and lack of reaction to the changing environment of international relations" (Solla, 2004, p. 1). For instance, in the past, only states were subject to international responsibility. But, in the current international system, even though states still play a dominant role, the impact of non-state actors cannot be neglected. They include international organisations, multinational corporations, some NGOs (such as in the field of human rights, environment and development), even certain individuals who have a great influence in international affairs. It is unrealistic to bestow all relevant actors with the same status as states in the framework of legality in the short term, but it cannot be denied that disputes arising from the actions of non-state factors sometimes need to be solved at the state-level, which has created a dilemma that, on the one hand, states are trying to avoid being constrained by international law, while on the other hand, interaction and communication between states are more complex than interstate disputes, and cannot fully be solved without the intervention/involvement of international institutions. That is to say, some impacts and consequences of a state's behaviour are surely felt beyond the state itself. Indirect responsibility can arise beyond the immediate cause-and-effect actors. It is inevitable that non-state actors must be taken into consideration in terms of international responsibility. As a result, when evaluating a state's responsibility, the subject of "responsibility" is the state in most of the situation, but in reality, various other actors have/can become involved in the process of being responsible (or irresponsible).

Furthermore, as international laws are generally regarded as soft laws, the political choices of states to abide by the laws and to use their discretional power under the common legal norms, or in cases where such legal norms are totally absent, is of great importance to the interests of other states and actors (Z. Chen, 2009, p. 9). Jackson considers this discretion-based responsibility as political or prudential responsibility, as opposed to the legally-based procedural responsibility (Jackson, November 1998, p. 5). International political responsibility requires states to avoid the possibly adverse consequences of prudential decisions, policy or action (Z. Chen, 2009). When contemplating foreign policy, national leaders are usually responsible for not only domestic requirements, but also the influence and impact of other authorities – for example, to allies, to partners, to neighbouring countries, and to international society as a whole. The political responsibility is determined by a state's rightful membership and status in the international society. It should be noted that for those leaders of great powers and major powers, not only their inner policy will have a global impact due to their strong economies and militaries, but also their values and ideology are mainstream and distinguished from those who are on the periphery. They are the rule-makers of current international society. This means, the great power the state enjoys, the greater the responsibility it should exercised. Since most states have their own cultural traditions, ideology and ethnicities the evaluation of political responsibility has various interpretations. Therefore, the impact on the host country and the feedback from international society will be used to adjust the assessment.

Finally, legal and political responsibilities have shaped States' moral responsibility, an obligation without a formal mechanism for enforcement, but determined by its own capability and awareness. Moral responsibility does not require states and other international actors necessarily to abide by laws, rules or regulations, nor to obey a certain government in the international society, but for the application of certain common values. It is like international ethics that focus on moral issues. Here the moral responsibility assumes that international security, stability, peace and common prosperity are a basic value shared by all members in the world. Judgments will be made from external expectations, internal identities, capabilities and motivations rooted in these values. As a higher responsibility, moral responsibility should be accomplished based on and cohered with former two. Following the discussion of "responsibility", there is also a dynamic relationship between a state's identity and external expectations. Each state will conceive its own definition of "being responsible" according to its national interests, capabilities, values and developmental stage. It interacts with international expectations and, when operating abroad, a host country's demands. The following section will discuss different types of states and their respective political agendas, and different understandings of what responsibility entails, and answers the question of what criteria each state may use to judge another nation as acting responsibly or not.

I Western interpretation of international responsibility

The international consensus regarding the criteria of what constitutes "being responsible" has always been in flux. The emphasis, on the principle of sovereignty, national diversity and non-intervention, has shifted towards mutual dependence, cooperation, and increasingly towards attention on human rights and humanitarian intervention.

Two international relations theories are concerned with the dilemma between national interests (such as sovereignty, diversity values) and international responsibility (widely considered as global interests, such as humanitarian intervention and development finance): realism and liberalism.

Liberalism, based on a belief in the inherently good nature of all humans, rests on the law and stable institutions. Liberals believe that political activity should be framed in terms of a universal human condition, rather than in relation to the particularities of any given nation. They place norms and laws at the forefront of their national interests and power. Inferred from their assumption, an open international and a competitive market will help to solve economic problems and to allocate recourses effectively. On the other hand, Realism emphasises the importance of states, claiming that International relations are motivated by national interests and driven by power. Although realists accept the importance of morality, they insist that morality is shaped and judged in terms of power (Stering-Folker, 2004, pp. 341–343). Guided by this principle, narrowly focusing on the national interest leads to weaker attention to the greater panorama of international relations. The pursuit of maximised national interest has relegated international responsibility to a place where it may or may not be needed. Self-interest serves as the yardstick for whether or not to bear responsibility, and to what extent should it fulfil the commitment.

As for the question of "How can we judge a leader's action?", utilitarianism suggests a consequences-oriented answer, while cosmopolitanism makes a judgment from a deontological perspective. Utilitarianism emphasises the greatest good for the greatest number. However, "the greatest good" is vague and has a risk of sacrificing some for the benefit of others. Cosmopolitanism argues that relevant community is global – since we interact with people in other countries, we have a duty to treat them morally – but there is a lack of law or regulation for enforcement, and there is also an imbalance between stronger and weak states.

These four approaches provide two dimensions from which one can understand a state's responsibility: the gap between national interests and global interests, the political decisions from consequence and deontology. Recently, IR scholars of the English school have delivered more moderate explanations and provided more reasonable and practical suggestions for addressing the dilemma of national-vs.-global interests. They emphasise the normative norms and system establishment in international society, which provides a theoretical foundation for further exploration of the boundary of a state's responsibility. Although pluralists and solidarists still argue about the priority of sovereignty and non-intervention or intervention, the debate between them has shaped the theory and practice of humanitarian intervention (Bellamy, 2003).

Pluralists argue that states do not share substantive goals and values. Instead, they recognise that they are legally and morally bound by a common code of co-existence (Wheeler & Dunne, 2002, p. 95). Hence, the most crucial recognition is a respect for sovereignty and the norm of non-intervention for the basis of a 55

> responsible government. The great strength of pluralism is that it enables states with different conceptions of justice to provide for minimum interstate order, but crucially the moral value of a pluralist society of states has to be judged in terms of its contribution to individual well-being, and Bull makes this the ultimate test of any ethical position (Jackson, 1990, p. 267). First of all, pluralism emphasises the rights and duties of states, which are considered to be the foundation of a state's responsibility. Second, it recognises an interstate order of cultural heterogeneity. It suggests protecting individuals' rights through the cooperation and protection of sovereignty of countries in an orderly world. As for the establishment of an international justice order, Bull held that great powers have responsibilities in providing for international and world order. However, against the background of the Cold War, Bull was pessimistic about the role in international order of the then-Great Powers, the USA and Soviet Union. Later, Jackson argued that international pluralism weakens the responsibility of great powers, and deliberately seeks to do that through diverse standards of morality and ethics, as well as relative values. They consider ethics of statecraft as a situational one, thus, "responsibility is the alter-ego of power in world politics [and] the responsibilities of states people cannot everywhere be the same because the military and economic power available to them definitely is not the same."
>
> (Jackson, 2000, p. 141)

Pluralism recognises the diversity among states, and that it contributes to problems of international order and justice. Vincent compared international society to an egg-box (Vincent, 1986, pp. 123–124), where an egg was a state and the box was international society. A smooth international order will separate and relieve the conflicts between eggs, that is to say, nations, groups or individuals could appeal through states rather than through direct, joint intervention. The emphasis on the sovereignty of a state on one hand demands a legal and political responsibility of policy makers. Only in an international society with responsible states can establish the expected international order. While on the other hand, it lacks realistic suggestions on how to regulate states and motivate them to become responsible. It recognises the importance of international organisations' concerns for human rights and humanitarian intervention along with the increasing interdependence of states, and argues that this process is not meant to undermine state's sovereignty (Neumann & Waever, 1997, pp. 47–49). However, when faced with a serious humanitarian crisis or disaster, it is unrealistic to protect the human rights as well as maintain an irresponsible government's sovereignty. A great power's motivation and capability of intervening is also doubted. As a result, pluralism has a high requirement of a state's responsibility, but it does not provide a solution to or suggestion for dealing with the dilemma between the realisation of international justice and the protection of international order.

Based on pluralism, solidarists go deeper to solve the problem of sovereignty and international responsibility. Solidarism posits that international society is a society formed of states and sovereigns, whose position is secondary to that of the universal community of mankind (Bell & Thatcher, 2008, p. 21). Vincent holds that, despite sovereignty and non-intervention playing a significant role in maintaining international order, it does not mean that a sovereign country will always be the basic political unit in international society, nor that laws do not apply to international society (Vincent, 1974, p. 349). It requires a middle way between a state's practice and the protection of individuals. Furthermore, Vincent suggests that there should be a minimum standard for the protection of human rights (Vincent, 1986, p. 125). The central assumption of solidarism is "that of the solidarity, or potential solidarity, of most states in the world in upholding the collective will of the society of states against challenges to it". (Bellamy & Wheeler, 2006) It implies that a state does not only have the responsibility to protect human rights domestically, but also when it fails, the international society has responsibility to protect it on the basis of moral boundary. Later, Deng introduced the concept of sovereignty as responsibility, in 57

> 1993, which helped to "redefine sovereignty away from the then (current) interpretations based on strict non-interference in the domestic affairs of states" (Stedman et al., 2009). Deng's work has emphasised the link between sovereignty and responsibility. For him, the crux of the protection's conundrum was to determine how to move beyond the obstruction of national authorities rebuffing international assistance and offers of aid in situations where the state is unable (or unwilling)

to fulfil its own responsibility (R. Cohen & Deng, 1996). In summary, solidarism does not only reconfirm the assumption of pluralism's perspective on a state's responsibility, but also makes a breakthrough for pluralism and emphasises the responsibility and obligation of states in international society, which therefore provides a normative standard for shouldering responsibility beyond boundaries/borders.

The English School has made contributions to the exploration of state responsibility. It not only analyses the possibility and limitations of a state responsibilities to its domestic population and international society, but also discusses the developmental trends towards concern for human rights in international society. However, the genocide in Rwanda, where thousands of Rwandans were killed with no international intervention reveals the lack of methodology for protecting civilians in developing countries (UHRC, 2012). This tragedy encouraged the legitimacy of international intervention when Responsibility to Protect (R2P) principles were introduced by the US in order to prevent future mass atrocities, that were later adopted by the UN at the United Nations World Summit in 2005. It clearly declared that the state has a responsibility to protect its people from genocide, war crimes, ethnic cleansing and crimes against humanity, and also from their incitement. When a state fails to provide such protection, UN member states have the responsibility to respond in a timely and decisive manner, and to assist failed state to meet these obligations (Teitt, 2008). Recently, the crisis in Libya has shown progress in implementing the R2P through diplomatic, humanitarian, and coercive means. The endorsement and practice of this principle has impelled a new interpretation of traditional sovereignty and humanitarian intervention. The R2P principle avoids the limitations of traditional sovereignty and places human rights as a basic value to protect. At the same time, it legitimised the right of international intervention.

In general, most states in international society have shown a willingness to accept the concept of "human rights beyond sovereignty". The traditional interpretation of sovereignty has given way to a new consensus in response to this conceptual change, and some researchers have argued that the "national sovereignty" of the twentieth century must develop into "responsible sovereignty" – a principle requiring nations to not only protect their own people, but also to cooperate across borders to safeguard common resources and tackle common threats (Stedman et al., 2009). Both international trends and practice show that sovereignty can no longer be used as a shield to protect a government from bearing responsibility for their actions and shouldering internal and external accountability. It also implies that major powers have obligations to intervene and assist weaker states.

In practice, stable improvements in human rights conditions usually require some measure of political transformation and can be regarded as one aspect of liberalisation processes. Enduring human rights changes, therefore, go hand in hand with domestic structural change (Donelly, 1998).

Further to this, the external legitimacy of a state depends increasingly on how domestic societies are ordered (Hurrell, 2007, p. 143). Human rights and democratic entitlements serve as a "test for fit membership of international society" (Clark, 2005). Other elements extending from human rights include the actions relating to refugees, women's employment and equal rights, a ban on landmines, the protection of property rights, and climate change (Zhang, 2010). Additionally, democratisation is a broad system that involves free media, an independent judiciary, the rule of law and full respect for civil rights (Clark, 2005). All these requirements shape the western scholars' perspective on state's responsibility and the "entrance ticket" of international society.

However, even if human rights protections have already become a common goal on the world stage, Western scholars did not offer/suggest a tangible way for the majority of developing countries to implement these goals, nor to distinguish interests or values in shouldering responsibility. They do not clarify the possibility of conflicts of interest between individuals. The employment of Western standards in other countries is often limited.

In conclusion, Western standards for being responsible have become the new international norms that have linked responsibility with sovereignty. That is, the criteria for legitimate sovereignty is an entrance ticket for the world stage, and bedrock of international order. In practice, Western scholars have argued that there can be no neutral definition of human rights, and that human rights cannot be logically disengaged from comprehensive notions of what constitutes a good society (Hurrell, 2007, p. 143, this volume), and that accepting assistance in terms of human rights does not weaken sovereignty, but rather preserves it (Sofaer & Heller, 2001). On the other hand, they acknowledged that reality is that these requirements have become stark symbols of division and confrontation, rather than well-institutionalised reflections of a shared humanity (Hurrell, 2007, p. 143). Since currently the extent to which outsiders can alter a sovereignty country is limited, it is unrealistic to implement these Western requirements without the cooperation of host countries; it is essential to have a better understanding of "other" countries' perspectives to complement the theory of "international responsibility".

II China's interpretation of international responsibility

In the early 1990s, few researchers were concerned about the term "international responsibility" with regards to China. On one hand, this emerging concept was quite different from the Chinese government's Five Principles of Peaceful Coexistence and Chinese leader Deng Xiaoping's foreign policy guideline "keep a low profile" (tao guang yang hui 韬光养晦). On the other hand, either "international distributions of power" (guoji geju 国际格局) or China's international role and identity at that time required China to shoulder responsibility for other countries, since the country was still a large recipient of foreign aid. In short, whether to be a responsible stakeholder or not was not a salient issue for both the Chinese government and academia. Only a few scholars mentioned responsibilities generally. Pioneering awareness included: China, as a member of UN and other international organisations, should develop into a "responsible state of great importance", have a global vision and a spirit of international cooperation (Y. Wang, 1995); national interests include external responsibility, and specifically "playing a greater role in international affairs serves as a significant element in China's national interests" (Yan, 1997); based on experiences of former great powers, some researchers suggested that "obligations came along with power is an inevitable strategy for China's rising" (G. Zhou, 2009). Some have gone further and categorised international responsibility as internal, regional, and global duty, and divided states into three sets too: general states, regional powers and great powers. He argued that each set has to fulfil its own responsibility (see Table 3.1). His argument revealed that most Chinese researchers believed responsibility should be conducted based on national strength.

Although calling on China to be a "responsible world power" began during the Clinton administration,[5] it was during the George W. Bush administration that then-Deputy Secretary of State Robert Zoellick called for China to act as a "responsible stakeholder" in 2005. Zoellick's words drew the Chinese IR field's attention to the term "international responsibility". Initially, most of the debates were about whether China's international responsibility was another Western Trojan or not; and what China's responsibility should be, rather than an analysis of the term itself in the international arena. Against this backdrop, they viewed responsibility in a more practical way. A definition was arrived at, which translated international responsibility as "obligations that a member of international society should undertake in relation to the external world in the fields of the economy, politics, security, morality and so on, reflecting the contributions a country should make to the external world". International responsibility is a derivative attribute of a

Table 3.1 The comparison of responsibility among three sets of states

	Internal responsibility	*Regional responsibility*	*Global responsibility*
General state	Pursue internal security and general prosperity	Strategic border	In general
Regional power	Internal security and general prosperity	A safety zone	Pursuing
Global power	Security and wealth	Influential orbit	Be responsible for global order

Source: Author (raw material: Kong, 2011).

member state of international society. Countries, big or small, should bear certain international responsibility (G. Wang, 2008, p. 26, this volume).

Compared to Western scholars, the Chinese interpretation of "international responsibility" has experienced a change, from a passive and cautious response with doubts to an active acceptance of the norm. The Chinese definition is given on the basis of its national strategy. First, it emphasises the connection between national strength and capability in shouldering responsibility. They argued that bigger countries have greater responsibilities. But they did not clarify the bottom line of small countries' responsibilities, nor what international society could do if a country fails to be responsible. Their understanding of being responsible is different from the Western counterparts. Shi holds that the primary task of promoting international obligations and responsibilities is China's domestic long-term healthy development and China's strategic security (Shi, 2008). This implies that China considers domestic stability, security and development as the fundamental elements for becoming responsible. Following this logic, China's perspective on "international responsibility" focuses on a more practical approach. China believes that states at different developmental levels have different criterion for being responsible. Witnesses 1, 4, 22, and 23 all held that survival and development rights are primary human rights. Hence, their concerns for developing countries mostly come out of economic performance rather than their political systems or good governance.

III Africa's attitude towards international responsibility

From the genocide in Rwanda in 1994, to the crisis in Darfur since 2003, and the civil war in Libya, many African governments are not capable of maintaining the stability and economic growth in their own countries, nor to shoulder responsibilities to international society. "In a good many African countries, power is a patrimonial power not a representation of the sovereignty will of the people". (Taylor, 2009, p. 9) Hence, in a continent plagued by war, poverty and disease, Africa has become the largest recipient of humanitarian intervention, aid and assistance from international society.

Africa's attitude towards international responsibility results from its position as recipient countries. In terms of intervention, the African Union and the continent's key regional organisations – the Southern African Development Community (SADC), the Economic Community of West African States (ECOWAS), the Intergovernmental Authority on Development (IGAD), the Economic Community of Central African States (ECCAS), and the Arab Maghreb Union (AMU) – have increasingly taken leading roles in implementing Responsibility to Protect (Sarkin & Paterson, 2010). Theoretically, most African countries support the concept of Responsibility to Protect. When R2P was endorsed by the UN in 2005, 53 African governments also adopted it. The African Union has even included the policy into its constitution. Some African countries went even further, and reached an agreement on the regional organisations' intervention in conflict. However, if we look at each individual state, many African leaders still remain cautious and suspicious of interference in their domestic affairs due to their colonialism histories and the Cold War. They prefer intervention from regional organisations, rather than from the UN or US-led organisations. Many African scholars do not favour humanitarian intervention on this continent where the majority of conflicts and human rights violations occur. They are more concerned about the following phase – that is, the post-conflict peace and rebuilding, reconstruction and economic assistance. Some have suggested that local communities should play a bigger role by cooperating with international organisations, which will ensure that adequate resources are channelled into peace efforts in Africa (Sarkin & Paterson, 2010). Some researchers from more-developed countries have emphasised their own countries' significance in the continent. For example, South Africa and Nigeria in Western Africa, believe they should have a greater role in the implementation of responsibility in this region. One could say African scholars' perspectives are far from forming a unified voice on the world stage. However, they do represent a Third World opinion of the term, that is, "security depends more on state building and economic development than protection against military threats internal and external". (Keller & Rothchild, July/August 1997).

IV Defining international responsibility

Inspired by Western scholars, China's and Africa's interpretations of the term suggests we can infer that the majority of countries have reached an agreement on whether or not a state should be responsible domestically and internationally. A state's primary responsibility lies at home, and the international society has a responsibility to intervene when a state fails to fulfil its obligations. To be specific, states need to shoulder the consequences of their misbehaviour or inaction, to comply with relevant international laws, regulations and international norms, and to address the obligations and responsibilities of international society with its own capability. But, in terms of what the criterion are for "being responsible", different perspectives have arrived at different answers. Western researchers are dedicated to viewing responsibility through the lens of a democratic system and human rights protection. These trends form an international mainstream consensus and an entry ticket for states to be accepted by the international society. While Chinese scholars consider a state's capability in undertaking responsibilities, and African scholars' interpretation is based on the demands of recipient countries.

The evaluation on the term "responsibility" lays a foundation from which to further explore the idea of "international responsibility". Combing the discussion of International relations theory and the thoughts from developing countries, the five criteria established for how judging "responsibility" could be developed for the state level are as follows:

1   Good governance: this criteria looks at retrospective responsibility.

    Regarding the state-level, it refers to the basic requirement that any state has to fulfil its legal responsibilities and abide by multilateral and bilateral treaties and agreements, to bear the punishment and consequences if they fail to do so. In theory, this contractual responsibility should be abided by any state, no matter its size. According to the English School's advocation of "responsible sovereignty", this criterion serves to assess the legitimisation of a sovereign state. If any state violates its legal responsibility, the international society has the right to intervene or punish in order to stop any illegal behaviour.

    The second to fifth criteria look at prospective responsibilities:

2   Expression: this criterion refers to policy and foreign strategy. Even if a state's foreign policy and motivation are designed on the basis of its own interests, it is necessary to compare the subject's expression with external demands, and to see the extent to which they are compatible with each other. Inspired by the evaluation of "responsibility", three influential factors have shaped the state's responsible (irresponsible) policy – that is, a state's motivation, the recipient countries' demands and international expectations. In terms of a state's capability, it refers to a combined consideration of the state's identity, national strengthen, national interests, and its relations with the recipient country. The African perspective has made a contribution by clarifying recipient countries' demands, while the Western perspective has shaped the international mainstream expectation.

3   The subject's capability: this criterion echoes the Chinese scholar's argument for combining national strength with international responsibility. It implies that bigger states have greater responsibilities, and some particularly influential states bear additional responsibilities due to their significant position. For Bull, "A great power cannot ignore these demands, or adopt a contrary position in the way that lesser powers can do; its freedom of manoeuvre is circumscribed by 'responsibility'". (Bull, 2002, pp. 199–222) It is unavoidable that states will shoulder responsibility according to its current development status and capability. This criterion provides higher standards for those more powerful states, and tolerance for those less-developed states. But it is worth noting that the consideration of capability is not an excuse for not being responsible, or ignoring responsibilities. The following criteria from recipient countries and international society's perspective could be used as an adjustment to avoid this problem.

    The subject's behaviour: Basically, the state's behaviour has three responsibilities, as discussed in earlier sections: legal, political and moral. The subject's behaviour is closely connected to the subject's capability. This criterion is employed to compare with the expression.

4   The consequences and impacts: this criterion is viewed from the recipient country's perspective. African researchers have offered a series of analyses on the efficiency of helping recipient countries. But "recipient countries" is a very general term. Take Africa as an example: the continent is made up of diverse countries with their own interests, priorities and agendas. In each country, the interests among different groups, levels and even individuals may be different and sometimes conflict. As a result, the evaluation of a state's impact on recipient countries should be analysed on a case-by-case basis.

5   External Expectations: This criterion is viewed from the perspective of international society. Currently, the international society has reached agreement on protecting its people from genocide, war crimes, ethnic cleansing, and crimes against humanity, to develop in favour of the welfare of their people, to maintain an open, transparent and incorruptible government, to create economic prosperity, and to diminish the risk of mass emigration. Differences lie in when a state fails to accomplish these tasks, to what extent should the international community get involved and through what means? Who could mandate such an action, and which members of the international community can participate in this action? As for the major powers, the international society tends to have expectations for foreign assistance in terms of financial aid, technical support, peacekeeping, and so forth.

In short, the assessment of international responsibility has inherited these criteria for "responsibility" and is divided into three layers, and includes internal, regional and global responsibility. In terms of content, it includes legal, political and moral responsibility. The relationship between the three layers is showed in Figure 3.1 (below) – the lowest responsibility is mandatory, while the highest one is conducted based on a state's capability. Judgment of international behaviour should be made based on the five standards listed above. That is, (1) good governance; (2) expression; (3) the subject's capability and behaviours; (4) consequences and impact, feedback; (5) international expectations. These five standards enjoy equal importance due to the dynamics between them.

There are certain misunderstandings that need to be addressed, and are detailed in the following section.

International responsibility is not "great power responsibility". Although great powers have a significant impact on maintaining order, peace and stability, as well as ensuring the international system and some basic values, each international actor should share its responsibility based on its own identity and capability. On one hand, as the integration of the global economy and the dynamic distribution of power, superpowers or power allies can hardly deal with the ever more complex and diverse issues. Negative issues that would need addressing include terrorism, disease, poverty and regional conflicts; and positive issues include international-cooperation,

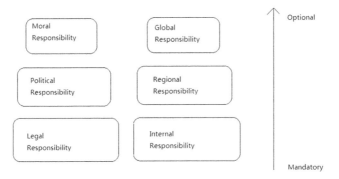

Figure 3.2 Subcategory of state's responsibility.
Source: Author.

communication, foreign investment and foreign aid. Bull has advocated that great powers should provide for international and global order (Bull, 2002, p. 200). But order relies on the joint efforts of all states in international society. On the other hand, according to the English School's interpretation of "responsible sovereignty", all states have basic responsibilities to their people and international community, otherwise its sovereignty will not be recognised by the international community. At the same time, developing countries are wary of great power responsibilities, as they are concerned that international society relying excessively on select great powers may increase the distance between states, and can even sometimes be used as an excuse for violating sovereignty (Kang, 2012). As a result, the following chapter will argue that each state as a member of the global community has respectively responsibility according to its capability. Differences would be reflected by their scales and capabilities decide the level of responsibility.

International responsibility is not the same as state responsibility. Alongside economic globalization and integration, more and more factors have begun to have an impact, sometimes powerful/considerable, on the development of the host countries – both positively and negatively in terms of their politics, society and economy. However, the rules and regulations for multinational corporates (MNCs) and other non-governmental international actors' responsibilities to host countries are lacking and slow to respond to the changing situation. Currently, most overseas companies and organisations are regulated by Corporate Social Responsibility for the protection of local labour rights, safety, welfare and the environment. Some leading companies go further, and concern themselves with the welfare of the local population and communities. But, in practice, due to their interest-driven nature, companies' awareness and activities in shouldering responsibility are constrained by their pursuit of profits. As for medium and small companies, their pursuit of profits often sacrifices the interests of their host country. Their misbehaviour and mistakes in the host countries do not only affect their own reputations, but also the image of the state from which they originate.

International Responsibility is not merely "responsibility to protect" (R2P). The principle of R2P adopted by UN in 2005 has been endorsed by the majority of UN members, and it officially solves the dilemma between crimes against humanity and sovereignty and domestic jurisdiction. However, as an emerging norm, doubts still persist among supporters and sceptics; for example, the alternatives to military intervention (Teitt, 2008, p. 17). On one hand, the norm is incomplete in reflecting the fact that states have responsibilities beyond combating human rights violations; and on the other hand, it is not clear where, when and who is to intervene. Therefore, this book categorises the R2P as a kind of obligation applied in extreme cases, and a commitment to promote the legitimacy of international responsibility.

International Responsibility is not the same as international ethics. International ethics are concerned with the extent and scope of ethical obligations between states in an era of globalization. It is more like moral responsibility discussed in an earlier section. International responsibility addresses legal, political and moral aspects. It also considers domestic situations as one of the criteria with which to evaluate whether responsibility, and argues that domestic responsibility is the foundation for being responsible on the international stage.

3.3 Framing China's international responsibility

3.3.1 External expectations and demands on China's international responsibility

Since 1997, the concept of great power responsibility has come to the fore, against a backdrop of warnings of the rising "China Threat" (Buzan & Foot, 2002, p. 52). Zoellick, former deputy secretary of state, a well-known advocate of China's international responsibility, has urged China to become "a responsible stakeholder". In his speech, China's "responsible stakeholder" covered "a wide spectrum of faster political reform, stronger IPR protection, looser control over RMB exchange rates, higher military budget transparency, bigger contributions towards post-war reconstruction in Afghanistan and Iraq, etc". (H. Niu, 2007).

Zoellick's demands of China's responsibilities are well tailored to the US's own interests, and the European Commission's expressions reflect the EU's expectations. The European Commission issued its China policy paper, entitled "EU-China: Closer Partners and Growing Responsibilities", which called for a greater emphasis on Beijing's part on democracy, energy efficiency and environmental protection, trade and customs and international cooperation in East Asia (EU Commission, 2006). Especially in the political realm, Europe has advocated for China to engage with the international community through constant encouragement to step up its reforms, adopt internationally accepted norms and values, and improve its domestic human rights situation (G. Wang, 2008). Japan, for its part, demanded that China pay higher UN membership fees. In short, all these developed countries expected China to become deeper involved in the international system, and join their global efforts for greater common prosperity (H. Niu, 2007). They particularly wished China to avoid being a free-rider on the world stage while enjoying the economic benefits within it, to open its domestic market and offer them new market opportunities, and also to promote human rights and democracy. In contrast, developing nations mostly want Beijing to promote their interests in the international community and to raise development aid and foreign investment as an alternative source to the US or EU. In other words, to "represent the developing countries to play a bigger role in world stage" and provide development finance (Yongnian Zheng, August 8, 2007). Generally, the external demands on and expectations for China's responsibilities range from security, political and governmental reform, to economic development and international order. All of the requirements are designed to satisfying other nation's needs and interests, some of which are consistent with China's interests and principles but some may not be; some are reasonable and some may be beyond China's capability. In response to these various demands, the Chinese political elites have given different answers.

3.3.2 China's interpretations of international responsibility

I Responsibility and expectation

After Zoellick appealed for greater Chinese responsibility, Chinese academia and political elites given various responses, which can be divided into two main camps. The sceptics mostly came from party newspapers or government documents, and they argued that "China's Collapse", "China's threat" and the current responsibility theory are interlinked; one is the cudgel to death (bangsha 棒杀) and the other one is praise to death (pengsha 捧杀) (Chinanews.com, July 30, 2010). Similar explanations include: China responsibility, exaggerated and embroidered by the West, is defined by the Western world solely on the conditions of satisfying their own needs and interests. This is literally evaluated by how much responsibility China has assumed for the West (H. Li, 2009). Urging China to become a responsible stakeholder implies China is not yet a responsible state (Guo, July 27, 2010), and this statement masks a strategic conspiracy to set a trap for China (Lin, June 2007) and suggests they are eager to capitalise on China's strengths in order to shake off their own troubles, and also constrain China's development by making it bear responsibilities beyond its capability (Wen, July 31, 2010).

The supporters mostly come from research institutes or universities. They believed that this concept conveys a message that China is accepted by the Western-dominated international system, and that its international status and influence has been recognised by the traditional powers. To undertake greater international responsibilities is a useful way to eliminate the "China threat" fallacy, and to improve China's image internationally (Y. Wang, 2007). If China turns a deaf ear to the responsibility expectations, it would be easier for the traditional powers to doubt China's peaceful rise, peaceful development, harmonious global foreign policy. At the same time, developing countries could feel disappointed by China's behaviour, which would lead China to be isolated on the world stage (J. Liu, March 6, 2008). Since the government has put forward a harmonious world theory, it is time that China takes its responsibilities to safeguard this international system in which much is also at stake for China (J. Niu & Wu, 2011).

China's rise has been more rapid than many expected. As a result, the state appears slow in responding to external expectations (Zhu, September 2010). As the concept of "international responsibility" gradually becomes more accepted in China, the extent to which China should shoulder responsibility has become a concern in Chinese society. An article entitled "What international responsibilities should China take", published in the People's Daily, gave a threefold answer: (1) to address China's problems well; (2) to fulfil the duties and responsibilities imposed by the U.N. Charter and more than 300 international conventions China has joined; (3) to the two major issues of the world: peace and development (People's Daily, February 16, 2011). Comparing China's interpretation of its responsibilities to those requirements from the US, EU, Japan and developing countries, even the researchers who favour the responsibility theory have agreed that external interests might contradict China's own interests (Z. Chen, 2009). This creates a gap between China's conceived responsibility and international expectations. Further to this, it raised the question of how should China balance its domestic development agenda with foreign demands? Apparently, it is unrealistic for China to try everything simply to meet the high demands of others, and also to ignore the feedback from host countries and international society. On one side of the coin, high external expectations will help enhance the awareness of responsibility on the part of the Chinese leadership and people (J. Niu & Wu, 2011); on the flip side, a proper balance should be made between the consideration of China's identity, national interests, foreign policy principles, and capabilities.

II *Responsibility and foreign policy principles*

Contrasting attitudes to international responsibility reflect China's debate on traditional foreign policy principles and the introspection of them. Launched in the mid-1950s, the Five Principles of Peaceful Coexistence have had a profound influence in China's foreign policy, and guided China's diplomatic agenda ever since. These principles cover the claim of national sovereignty and territorial integrity, non-aggression, peaceful coexistence, non-interference in other countries' internal affairs, and equality and mutual benefit. Of these, advocating for "non-interference" conflicts with the idea of being a responsible state because it requires the "right (and indeed the obligation) of the international community to infringe on the autonomy of the nation-state to protect or advance considerations" (Harding, 2009). However, adherence to "non-interference" does not necessarily mean China could escape from shouldering its international responsibilities. Along with its expansion into world stage, the Chinese interpretation of "non-interference" has experienced an evolution according to a changing political strategy.

The five principles were introduced at a time that China's foreign policy had "the tendency to regard social system, ideology, or the concept of values as inevitably determining the relationship between nations" (Harding, 2009). China has a strong motivation to safeguard national sovereignty, which reflects a different ethical judgment tradition and produced very different approaches for dealing with today's international problems.

In the 1990s, then-Chinese leader Deng Xiaoping laid out a guideline for Chinese foreign policy: "keep a low profile, and achieving something". For more than a decade, Chinese foreign policy was generally grounded in the principle of "keep[ing] a low profile", concentrating on creating a favourable external environment for economic development at home. Also Deng Xiaoping's theory for China's domestic development implies that China should "be navigating along the middle course and concentrate on more practical things rather than seek leadership or hegemony" (H. Li, 2008, p. 2). Deng's reforms brought China dramatic economic growth. At a time when China has accumulated certain economic achievements, the debate on whether China should continue to "keep a low file" has grown louder. Some researchers have argued that "the present international distribution of power has not undergone substantive changes, compared with what prevailed when Deng first put forward this idea" (Feng, 2005). It is a long-term strategy in order to "strive for the realisation of a harmonious world, and the image that a confident and modest nation shows to the outside world" (S. Zhou, 2008).

Evidence from both diplomatic practice and governmental doctrine has suggested that policy-makers have made some subtle adjustments in exercising these traditional principles. China has endorsed Responsibility to Protect at the UN at the World Summit in 2005. In 2007, Hu Jintao said in his report to the 17th CCP Congress: "We advocate that the people of all countries should cooperate in efforts to promote the construction of a harmonious world of lasting peace and common prosperity. To this end they should adhere to the aims and principles of the United Nations Charter, consult on the basis of equality, abide by international law and the commonly accepted norms of international relations, and advance the spirit of democracy, harmony, cooperation, and common gains in international relations" (Xinhua News, October 24, 2007). In August 2008, China was contributing more engineers and civilian police personnel to UN peacekeeping missions than any other permanent member of the Security Council (Gill & Huang, February 2009). These actions demonstrated that Beijing exhibited some flexibility on their traditional principles. Also, there are examples of China using its influence on other regimes, like North Korea, Myanmar, and Sudan by sending special envoys for negotiations. In 2009, an official Outlook magazine article, "Hu Jintao's Viewpoints about the Times", proposed a concept of

> "shared responsibility", which set forth two important parameters for Beijing's international responsibility. First, China's contributions to the global commonwealth cannot adversely affect China's core interests. Second, China's international commitments are conditional upon the inputs of other states, especially developed countries and regions such as the United States and the European Union (Xinhua News, November 24, 2009). In 2011, China abstained rather than vetoed the UN Security Council resolution to impose a no-fly zone over Libya, and measures to protect civilians from attacks by forces led by Gaddafi (IBtimes, March 17, 2011). This suggests that Beijing has gradually abandoned its commitment to standing out of other countries' domestic affairs, slowly evolved from its traditional interpretation of "non-interference" and became more active and cooperative in solving international crises.

It is worth noting that China's engagement in international affairs does not signify a top-down, radical shift. Concerning the debate on whether or not China needs to still "keep a low profile", Chinese scholars have other suggestions. Some researchers argue that China "needs to be more bold and assertive in international affairs in a way that matches China's newfound status as a major world power" (Yan, March 31, 2011). Others have tried to find a balance between "keep a low profile" (taoguang yanghui 韬光养晦) and "achieving something" (yousuo zuowei 有所作为), and suggested that "doing something in the lights of general trend" (shunshi erwei 顺势而为). This is not a passive or reactive policy, but one aimed at defusing the pressures of responsibility. Instead, it is a proactive approach, which combines China's development strategy with a peaceful cooperation in the current international system (X. Zhao, 2010). In short, Chinese policy makers have recognized that the principle of "keep a low profile" and "non-interference" were not always compatible with China's current expansion and influence. And the country has undergone a stop-and-go process in order to demonstrate a responsible role to the world. Chapter 4 will further discuss the relationship between China's international responsibility and its foreign policy.

III Responsibility and national interests

Zhou argues that China must act as a great power and shoulder its responsibility in keeping with its peaceful development strategy. Furthermore, as its global influence expands, this would also benefit its external interests and improve its image (G. Zhou, 2009). Zhou's argument connected "being responsible" with national interests (image). The majority of researchers agree that interests are composed of two aspects, both hard and soft interests – the former refers to a peaceful and stable international system, the latter indicates a peaceful power image (Wu, 2010). According to this category, international responsibility is compatible with soft interests and is not always compatible with hard interests.

Chinese scholars have emphasised that China's international responsibility should be defined by its own national interest. This could also be reflected in China's interpretation of "international responsibility". As for the foundation of international responsibility, Chinese researchers hold that "as the world's most populous country, China's primary responsibility should be to provide for its citizens, who account for one fifth of the world population, and ensure them a better life. This is not merely a domestic affair, but also one of international significance". (Hu, 2007) Based on this reorganization, a peaceful international environment, international cooperation and communication are for China's own interests.

Therefore, some Chinese researchers advocate viewing international responsibility as a win-win situation between China and a host country, rather than a burden. They suggest states undertake international responsibilities based on their own interests, which is why the great powers with the broadest interests have always been the most active in acting on international responsibilities in the past (Yan, 2011). As China's economy continues to grow, its trading partners expanded across the world, which brought its attention to previously ignored countries, such as Africa, Latin America, and in the Middle East. The political and economic situation in those countries is connected to China's interest. This understanding has brought a broader interpretation of China's national interests, and advocates a "mutual benefits" situation between China and a host country. Even considering "win-win" situation are mostly come out of political rhetoric, it cannot deny the fact that national interests are not necessarily identified in accordance with international expectations, nor do they necessarily contradict them. Like many other countries, China's responsibility is a combination and comprise between national interests and external expectations. The second section of each case study chapter will further discuss the dynamic interaction between national interests and external expectations.

IV Responsibility and capability

If legal and political responsibility is seen as the base line of international responsibility, then moral responsibility could be interpreted as the highest standard of the three layers. Many Chinese researchers insist that China should do what it is able to do, no less and no more(Zhu, September 2010). To figure out what China's proper obligations are, it is necessary to keep an eye on its capabilities.

China's capability is an ambiguous term, that depends on from what perspective you are looking at this country. One may conclude China as a strong economy power if we consider the figure that since 2006, China has held the world's largest foreign exchange reserves for four years, from 1.066 trillion US dollars, to 2.399 trillion US dollars by the end of 2009. Up to 2009, China followed the US, France, Japan and Germany, ranked fifth with 565.3 billion US dollars in foreign direct investment. In 2010, China's GDP surpassed that of Japan and become the world's second largest economy; however, one may also categorise China as a weak state when considering China's domestic problem on governance, wealth gap, pollution and corruption. The United Nations Development Program (UNDP), which calculates a "human development index" for each country based on three indices – average life expectancy, education and living standards – ranked China 89th in 2010, and categorised it as a developing country with "a medium level of development". Of the 12 indices examined in the Global Competitiveness Report of 2009–2010 issued by the World Economic Forum, China ranked 79th in the world in the maturity of its science and technology (Qu, February 18, 2011). It could be say that China has made a great achievement in boosting its economy, but over-rapid growth has brought about an imbalance, which can be seen in its social development, education, health, science and technology, legislation, modernisation, and so forth. According to the World Bank and IMF, China remains a lower middle-income country. The dual interpretation of China's capability has created a gap, between China's expected national power versus that of its practical power; the potential strength and its influence, versus its current international capability; limited resources for domestic development versus international demands. Much of Chinese political discourse recognises this gap, and concludes that China is the world's largest developing country, with a large population, a poor foundation and uneven economic development. Hence, it should not assume responsibilities out of proportion to its strengths and development phase (Zhu, September 2010).

Meanwhile, when discussing China's responsibility in Africa, China's place is as a donor and Africa as a recipient. Ostensibly, the relationship is asymmetrically in favour of the donor. And it seems that the donor has maintained the decision power while the recipient is in a passive position. In practice, however, foreign assistance from China is neither military nor economic intervention. Instead, it is the transfer and exchange of resources, which could not be achieved without the cooperation from the host country. Therefore, the recipient has a capability that 80 is not consistent with its national strength. China's capability in the host African countries is constrained by the political and economic situation therein. The host country has the ability to affect China's implementation of its African strategy. The third section of each case study chapter will analyse China's limitations for implementing responsibility in the host countries.

In response to the three levels of China's international responsibility, the proper responsibilities can be summarised thus:

1   Domestically
    Premier Li Keqiang, said in Davos in the summer of 2013, that "China is still a developing country. According to international standards, we have more than 100 million people who live below the poverty line. China's modernisation has a long and arduous way to go, its international responsibility and obligation should be in accordance with its development status". (Xinhua News, September 13, 2013) Excessively undertaking responsibility is unsustainable and a long-term internationally responsible role depends on domestic sustainable development. Witness 3 said:

> China should not shoulder international responsibility beyond its capability. In a transitional period, it has the problems of social justice, environmental protection, three rural issue and population aging. As Premier Wen Jiabao said, solving our own problems is the largest responsibility to international society. Because in a time of globalization and regionalisation, China's domestic problem has a great impact worldwide, a peaceful and sustainable developing China is a kind of Beijing's responsibility to the international society. Only with a growing China, can it have more capability and strengthen to fulfil its international responsibilities.

Chinese officials' comments reflect the importance of China's domestic affairs as the foundation of 'being responsible' internationally. This indicates the fact that the stability and development of the state, especially a large state, benefits the world. However, the Chinese officials tend to consider economic performance as the only way to evaluate 'being responsible' and to neglect many other important aspects, such as good governance and the protection of human rights. Without these normative measures, the state could never be considered as fully responsible and accepted by international society.

2   Regional power
    Retrospective responsibility (which concerns China's increasing influence and presence in this region, and the threats to its neighbours that come with it) requires China to be very prudent about its policy-making, and avoid the negative consequences and the potential conflicts within this region. Additionally, like any sovereign state in the world, China has to fulfil certain duties and responsibilities imposed on it by the U.N. Charter and more than 300 international conventions it has joined (People's Daily, February 16, 2011), especially at a time when China gains membership of more and more treaties and organisations.

Chinese political elites and researchers all agree that international responsibility should be undertaken based on the United Nations Charter and the existing international system and order.

In terms of prospective responsibility, as an influential power in Asia, where about 80% of its FDI goes, China considers its responsibility set/clear in this area, as currently China's national interests are concentrated around Asia where hot-button issues and great powers' involvement jointly impact its stability and development. Safeguarding peace and security in this region, advocating for regional or sub-regional dialogue on security, and taking steps that would help to increase national confidence and assuage doubts while promoting the establishment of a security mechanism that conforms to the interests and wishes of all countries in this region, all of these are key elements of China's responsibility (Y. Wang, 2007). Meanwhile, China should shoulder greater responsibility in promoting Asian economic development, enlarging common economic interests among Asian countries, and enhancing the common prosperity of the region.

3 Globally

Whether or not China is a global power remains a controversial topic. However, as one of the five permanent members of the UN Security Council and a leading economy, certain corresponding responsibilities are unavoidable. For example, UN peacekeeping operations, and financial assistance. Some researchers from developing countries' have suggested that China should make the effort to address the imbalance between Northern and Southern states, to promote South–South dialogue and cooperation, (He, 2008) and to provide them with more aid and multilateral cooperation opportunities. Some writing from the development viewpoint advocated that, along with expanding overseas interests, it is China's responsibility to safeguard the stability in those areas in order to secure its economic interests, including the safety of energy supplies, major strategic areas and transportation hubs (G. Zhou, 2009). By doing this, it is China's shared responsibility to cope with international terrorism, relational extremism, crisis and military conflicts.

In conclusion, Chinese scholars believe that China's responsibility is not what is imposed by western powers (Sun, 2008), but rather the inevitably responsibility China should take in line with its own capability and practical national conditions. The following chapters will answer questions relating to the compatibility of China national interests with external (African and international) demands.

3.4 Conclusion

This chapter has reviewed different interpretations of "international responsibility", and has established five criteria to assess state responsibility.

In addition to a country's foreign strategy, it acknowledges the importance of comments from international society and feedback from host countries in shaping a state's responsibility policy. At the same time, it emphasises a state's capability in implementing responsibility in practice. Based on the five standards, it further explores what kinds of responsibility should a state like China take domestically, regionally, and globally.

After reviewing the relationship between China's international responsibility and national foreign policy, interests and capability. It recognises that China's foreign policy agenda and national interests are not always contradicted by China's international responsibility, because a responsible international reputation is of significance to Beijing's soft interests, and a stable Africa is also in China's interest. However, China's capability of being fully responsible in the international society is constrained by China's domestic developmental status on the one hand, and the diversified demands and limitations in the host African countries on the other. The following two chapters will discuss China's international responsibility in Africa from the policy and implementation levels, respectively, and explore to what extent international responsibility is compatible with China's national agenda.

Notes

1 The Chinese authorised dictionary defines the word in the same way.
2 Unlike conduct, mental states cannot be observed directly, but Cane believed that it rested on an interpretation of what the agent said or did – viewed against a background of relevant circumstances – as manifesting or not manifesting the mental state in question.
3 According to which praise and blame would be an appropriate reaction toward the candidate if, and only if, she merits – in the sense of "deserves" – such a reaction.
4 According to which praise and blame would be an appropriate if, and only if, a reaction of this sort would likely lead to a desired change in the agent and/or her behaviour.
5 During the Clinton administration, Secretary of Defense William Perry argued that engagement was a strategy for getting China to act like a "responsible world power", and Secretary of State Madeleine Albright called on China to become a "constructive participant in the international arena".

4   China's policy analysis

4.1 Introduction

Chapter 3 has set the criteria for "being a responsible stakeholder" in international society. Among the five standards, it included "expression" as an index to evaluate responsibility. On the state level, "expression" refers to policy and the foreign strategy behind it. Thus, it is useful to find out what China's African policy is, in order to assess its responsibility in Africa and further to test hypobook II, "are China's motivations and African requirements incompatible?" This chapter will concentrate on the policy level and explore whether China is responsible in Africa based on this criterion discussed in Chapter 3.

4.2 China's African policy and its trends

China's Africa policy serves Beijing's diplomatic strategy and trends as a whole. Its development reflects China's evolving foreign policy. From the founding of the People's Republic of China (PRC) in to the introduction of Reform and Opening-Up in 1978, and further to the establishment of Forum of China-Africa Cooperation (FOCAC) in 2000, China's African policy is a miniature version of Chinese national political agenda as a whole. For more than half a century, China-Africa relations have been conducted under the "Five Principles of Peaceful Coexistence", which are the foundation and guidelines for China's foreign strategy, as well as an important element of China's "independent foreign policy of peace". Even when China shows flexibility in international affairs, this principle has still been advocated by Chinese politics as the foundation for China's relationship with all other countries, according to China's Foreign Policy released by Ministry of Foreign Affairs (MOFA), of the PRC, and updated on November 26, 2013.

Since the establishment of the PRC, China has always referred to African countries as brothers to emphasize its identity as a developing country and belonging to the developing world. Initially, China and Africa shared similar experiences of grievous colonial history, civil war, poverty and domestic chaos. However, whether China considered these "brothers" equal or not is open to question. Even at a time when China itself suffered from famine and domestic chaos, it still sought to become a leader of these "brothers". Following this logic, aid from China to Africa has been generous and forthcoming since the founding of the PRC. In order to develop diplomatic support from Africa, China has to provide official aid to African countries continuously. It actively maintains the relationship with African countries who share a similar interpretation of socialism. In return, the African governments recognize the PRC as "China", rather than the Republic of China (ROC) in the international arena. A notable fact is that African countries voted for the restoration of China's lawful seat in the United Nations (UN) in 1971, leading Mao Zedong to say that "it was our African brothers who carried China into the UN".

The "Five Principles of Peaceful Coexistence",[1] the foundation of China's relationship with other countries, was introduced by Premier Zhou Enlai during his negotiations with Indian delegations, in discussions on the Tibet issue. The principles have been adhered to by Chinese governments for more than six decades. China-Africa relations are no exception. Thirty-Eight African countries have incorporated the Five Principles of Peaceful Coexistence into their joint communiqués with China and was included in the declaration of many Afro-Asian conferences as well-for example, the Final communiqué of the Asian-African conference in 1955; the Afro-Asian People's Solidarity Conference in 1957; Organization of African Unity Charter in 1963; and the non-aligned movement. Premier Zhou Enlai explained the five principles in a press conference in 1954,

> All world countries big or small, strong or weak, no matter its social system should coexist peacefully, all nations should have rights to choose their own system and way of living without external interference.

His explanation implies that the core concept of the "Five Principles of Peaceful Coexistence" is that a state's independence should not be infringed upon. At that time, the "Five Principles of Peaceful Coexistence" was an ideological claim, but it provided a foundation for China's future foreign policy. It shields China from international pressure on the improvement of human rights protection and humanitarian principles implementation on the one hand, and international expectation of China shouldering responsibility beyond its border on the other. Due to its ambiguity, China has sometimes provided different interpretations of this principle in relation to its foreign strategy and priorities. Taking "non-inference" as an example, China didn't present a boundary or range for the meaning of "without external interference". For example, whether larger foreign economic involvement could be a kind of interference, or whether interference can be justified if there is a serious human right crisis.

In the early 1960s, when Beijing broke with Moscow, the Third World and non-aligned movement became more important for China to gain international support to survive in a bipolar world dominated by the United States (US) and the Soviet Union. Premier Zhou Enlai visited ten African countries between December 1963 and February 1964. During this tour, he announced five strands[2] of China-African Relations and eight principles[3] of Chinese African aid. These radical strands were accompanied by generous debt relief and large-scale economic aid and improved China's reputation on the continent, but also exceeded its capability to shoulder burdens at home. In the 1960s China's foreign aid to Africa has been US$46 million, which is ten times that of the 1950s. However, the average GDP increased less than double, let alone per capita Gross Domestic Product (GDP). Despite domestic poverty and famine, this figure has dramatically increased to US$319 million from 1970 to 1975, which accounted for over 5% of GDP in the corresponding period. Meanwhile, in the early 1950s, the main recipient countries of China's aid were in Asia. After 1955, the recipients of China's foreign aid expanded to include some African countries. By 1970, China had donated more aid to Africa than its foreign aid to its neighboring countries. Africa became a major destination for Chinese aid flows after that (H. Liu & Huang, 2013). The continuous donations are far beyond China's ability, which has faced the state's foreign assistance with a dilemma. Without considering the economic benefits, China agreed to take on the Tanzania-Zambia railway project, which has been rejected by the World Bank and great powers due to its impracticality and cost – almost 10% of China's foreign reserves at the time. The completed flagship project was handed over to local operators in 1976, but it was not the end, and the Chinese have had to stay in order to ensure its continued, efficient running while also continuing to provide loans for spare parts and maintenance (Brautigam, 2011).

Enduring a famine for more than a year, China nevertheless still donated ten thousand tons of rice to Guinea in 1960. At the same time, China has implemented its economic and technological cooperation agreement with Guinea by constructing a Cigarettes & Matches factory near Conakry – a first completed project in Sub-Saharan Africa. The Chinese staff overcame the temperature, malaria, language and clean water problem, and finished the factory – "a pearl of Conakry" as one local newspaper called it – within one year and eight months.

Then-president Ahmed Sékou Touré cut the ribbon himself at the completion ceremony (People's Daily, October 29, 2006). However, China subsequently broke its relationship with this country because of its pro-Soviet position. The same situation happened with the South African Communist Party, Independence of Cape Verde Party, Mozambique National Liberation Front, and others, and China also refused to cooperate with Congo's Party of Labour as a result of its non-communist identity. Despite that, from 1956 to 1977, China provided more than US$2.4 billion in economic assistance to Africa, which accounts for 58% of its foreign aid and twice that of the Soviet Union's during the same period, the late of 1970s, only the Ethiopian People's Revolutionary Party and several communist parties have interactions with CPC (Communist Party of China) in the continent (H. Liu & Huang, 2013). This over-capacity and inconsistent foreign aid experiences set off alarms for both Chinese academics and people nowadays. Along with China's expansion in Africa, Beijing is very careful to persuade the domestic audience that China is capable of providing the current scale of foreign assistance to Africa. According to a Chinese official report, China's foreign aid accompanies its increasing Gross National Income (GNI) and economic growth. The report indicates that China's annual foreign aid volume of 30 billion Renminbi (RMB) from 2010 to 2012 accounted for 0.064% of GNI (Luo, August 11, 2014), which is lower than the international standard of 0.7% and the Organization for Economic Cooperation and Development (OECD) donors' percentage (OECD).

In 1977, the leaders of the CPC authorised its International Department, Central Committee and Ministry of Foreign Affairs to jointly research China's relationship with the parties in Africa. Five months later, the Political Bureau of the Central Committee ratified the joint proposal. As a result, since 1978, Beijing has started to re-establish communications with some parties in Africa, and to receive visitors from Africa (A. Li, 2006a), which revealed that ideological export was no longer a priority in China's foreign policy. Soon after, the third session of China's Eleventh Communist Party Congress represented another important turning point for the CPC. Radical Maoism was gradually replaced by a more practical, open and economic-oriented policy. Consequently, foreign strategy has developed from one ideologically driven to that of more economic consideration. Meanwhile, the opening-up policy has considerably grown China's international trade and foreign exchanges. It requires China to rethink its identity and role in the world stage-hence its changing relations with Africa.

At the end of December 1982, then – Premier Zhao Ziyang visited 11 African countries,[4] seeking south-south cooperation and to promote a fairer international order. During this trip, he announced four principles of economic and technical cooperation with African countries: equality and mutual benefit (ping deng hu li 平等互利), stress on practical results (jiang qiu shi xiao 讲求实效), diversity in form (xing shi duo yang 形式多样) and common progress (gong tong fa zhan 共同发展). Zhao's redefinition of China-Africa relations was more reasonable, realistic and practical when compared to China's domestic situation at that time. It abandoned the constraints of ideology and brought forward the idea of "cooperation", rather than one-way aid flow to Africa. What's more, by emphasising "practical results", it introduced the consideration of economics and efficiency. Meanwhile, "diversity in form" enabled non-governmental communications (You, 2007).

The 1980s witnessed a transition of China-Africa relations. During this decade, both China and Africa underwent profound changes. After the Cultural Revolution, domestic difficulties made it hard for the Chinese government to solve the inner political chaos and economic crisis while also remaining involved in international aid in an enthusiastic manner. Also, past experiences led the state to think about re-establishing a systematic strategy with a clear agenda and a sober framework in its communications with Africa. When it came to Africa, the wave of national independence movements passed, leaving many with damaged economies and tremendous debt. New governments faced the challenges of "transforming national territories inherited from colonialism into viable political communities" and also economic development. In 1980, African leaders gathered in Lagos and passed the Lagos Plan of Action for the economic development of Africa, 1980–2000, through the Organization of African Unity. It called for a decreased reliance on raw materials extraction and global equality in trade relations (Eyoh, 1998). Later, many countries have implemented structural adjustments launched by the World Bank and International Monetary Fund (IMF). This period marked a watershed between China and Africa. China has concentrated exclusively on its economic development and modernisation, while the structural adjustment required African governments to pursue an austerity policy.

Despite each side developing its economy along a different path, the interactions have increased. By the end of the 1980s, not only had China strengthened relations with old friends, such as Tanzania, Zambia, Egypt, Mali Guinea, Zaire, Ghana and Gabon, but also was able to establish diplomatic relations with pro-Soviet or pro-US states including Angola, the Ivory Coast, Lesotho – thereby increasing the number of recognized countries from 44 to 47. Economically, although China has concentrated on domestic economic reform and sought to keep a low profile in international affairs, its foreign aid to Africa has steadily grown by US$274 million over the figure in the 1970s, while at the same time its aid to Asia and Latin America has sharply decreased (Brautigam, 2008b). At the same time, China also signed 127 agreements on financial support in more than 49 African states, which demonstrated China's preference for Africa (A. Li, 2006b).

A political breakthrough was made by Zhao Ziyang's authorisation that staying in African countries for management and technical support was not "interfering in internal affairs", which was a re-interpretation of the "non-interference" (A. Li, November 12, 2008). It enabled Chinese experts to stay on the continent after the completion of assistance projects, and those who chose to stay in Africa became the first wave of mainlander migrants to Africa. The flexible foreign policies enabled Chinese enterprises to seek business opportunities in Africa. The trade value during this decade fluctuated between US$0.8 and US$1.2 million. More than 150 business centers and offices were established, which attracted over 200 Chinese companies to the continent (A. Li, November 12, 2008). Additionally, the exchanges in the fields of science, education, culture and health between China and Africa became more frequent. More than 80 African cultural and arts delegations visited China, and over ten ensembles performed. More than 2,300 African students entered Chinese universities and over 100 Chinese experts and teachers were sent to teach in African schools (You, 2007).

Generally, this period witnessed a transformation from radical direct aid to a pragmatic and reciprocal strategy with the diversification of communication between China and Africa. It could be said that even if China had established close ties with the West due to economic needs, "its aid policy clearly continued to favor Africa over other regions" (Brautigam, 2008b, p. 52).

The 1990s witnessed new global waves of democracy and urged governments to rethink their bilateral relations. On the one hand, the protest in Tiananmen Square triggered political turmoil in China in 1989, after which Western countries responded by issuing sanctions and isolating China. On the other hand, African states experienced the shock waves of the multiparty democratisation movement; just between 1990 and 1994, 42 African countries accomplished multiparty elections. Also, Taiwan with its democratic identity and a boosting economy tried to buy back the recognition of ROC in the 1990s. Starting with Liberia, ten African nations broke diplomatic ties with Beijing and turned to Taipei in eight years. Beijing immediately responded to the challenge, beginning a competition of courting African countries for recognition in the 1990s (H. Liu & Huang, 2013).

In July 1989, soon after the Tiananmen Square Event, then-Foreign Minister Qian Qichen visited six African countries[5] to clarify its stance on the Five Principles of Peaceful Coexistence and its support for South Africa's anti-apartheid policy. His trip initiated a tradition that the Foreign Minister would visit several African countries in the January of each New Year (Q. Wang, 1999). This action has been viewed as China's reassessment of Africa's significance and a quick response to the international and domestic changes. After the breakdown of the Soviet Union, then-president Yang Shangkun made a trip to Morocco, Tunisia and the Ivory Coast, and put forward six principles[6] in response to the new international environment towards China. His speech emphasised the core values of the Five Principles of Peaceful Coexistence again, but the idea of Third World theory proposed in Mao's era was rarely present. This could reflect that Third World theory was ebbing while words such as "solidarity", "unity" and "jointly" came into view in China's African policy.

In the 1990s, Taiwan emerged as a significant economic power with weak diplomatic status. Therefore, dollar diplomacy became a major way for Taipei to find political recognition. The impoverished African countries keen for financial support rather than political ambitions were considered the targets for Taiwan's dollar diplomacy. At the same time, the "One China Policy"[7] was a great challenge to China-African relations because ten African counties broke relations with Beijing and established ties with Taipei-some of them, for example, Liberia and Central African Republic, have broken relations twice. The shift in political ties can hardly be interpreted as "the Africans care much who is the 'real' China or with whom official diplomatic ties should be established" (Taylor, 2002). But the competition for African recognition between Beijing and Taipei did benefit the African leaders in terms of financial resources. In 1991, Beijing offered a ten-year interest-free loan to Gambia. Just in the middle of this loan, the country turned to Taipei, and in return it received a US$35 million aid package. A similar situation happened with Sao Tome as well: four years after Beijing pledged an interest-free loan of RMB 20 million and a delay to debt repayments, the state chose to recognize Taipei for US$ 30 million in financial aid, in 1997. It sounds practical that African countries recognized the highest bidder, but for the impoverished and marginalized countries aid has a priority (Brautigam, 2010). This reorganisation wave reflected that looking beyond political rhetoric between China and its African counterparts, the link between Beijing and African countries are fragile and largely relied on continuous foreign assistance.

In 1996, then-President Jiang Zemin made a significant trip to six African countries[8] and systematically expounded China's African policy[9] in the new era. Also, in his keynote speech in Ethiopia, he put forward a five-point proposal[10] for the development of China-Africa relations. In Jiang's speech, he attached great importance to African countries by calling them China's all-weather friends. He emphasized the equality of China-Africa relations (MOFA, 2010), even if the bilateral economic strength has become more and more asymmetric. Jiang's visit revealed the significance of Africa to China's changing diplomatic strategy. After that, high-level visits to Africa became routine for China's top leaders. Then-President Jiang Zemin, Premier Li Peng and Vice Premier Zhu Rongji, Vice President Hu Jintao all set foot on Africa in 1997, 1998 and 1999 respectively.

In the 1990s, China experienced a transformation of its Africa engagement. The third generation of CPC leaders held a foreign assistance conference to reform its foreign aid in 1995 (Information Office of the State Council, April 2011). Thereafter, the government started to diversify the sources of foreign assistance with three new features: first, it combined national grants and loans with overseas aid projects. The Export-Import Bank of China provided medium-and long-term low-interest loans to other developing countries, largely enlarging the number of recipients and increasing the efficiency of the funds. In this way, it promoted China's exportation of equipment, materials and human resources. Second, it integrated recipients' funds and enterprises' investment. The government set up the Foreign Aid Fund for Joint Ventures and Cooperative Projects with parts of the interest-free loans repaid to China by developing countries. The fund was mainly used to support Chinese small-and medium-sized enterprises to build joint ventures or cooperate with the recipient countries in the production and operation spheres. It extended the fund's resources and the scale of the projects, as well as ensured future operation and management. Third, the governments signed contracts for financial or policy support while the companies from both countries jointly operated. The project helped recipients cast off the export of the raw materials and establish processing industries of small-and medium-sized companies. These instruments greatly encouraged Chinese enterprises entering the African market, which echoed with the "going global" policy and the idea of taking advantage of the domestic and international market and resources (liangzhong shichang liangzhong ziyuan 两种市场 两种资源). It resulted in a sustained growth of trade between China and Africa, which rose from US$0.1 billion in 1990 to US $6.4 billion in 1999 (A. Li, 2006a). In comparison with former African policies, the new approach is much more oriented in terms of the economy. However, on the one hand, this has created diversified financial sources and new investment motivation for the continent, but on the other hand, the involvement of Chinese companies has also brought a negative impact. The case studies section will further explore the negative aspects.

In the new century, with the rapid development of China's economy, bilateral relations have been raised to a new level marked by the successful hosting a Forum of China and Africa Cooperation (FOCAC) conference, including one summit attended by more than forty African leaders. The forum was initiated by China's third generation leaders to further "promote mutual cooperation and jointly meet the challenge of globalization and to seek for common development every three years" (FOCAC, April 9, 2013). This first forum was held in 2000 in Beijing and attended by 80 ministers from 44 African countries, representatives of 17 regional and international organisations, and people from the business communities of China and Africa. They broadly discussed joint efforts for the establishment of a new international political and economic order in the 21st century, and China-African economic cooperation and trade in the new international environment. The conference also charted the direction for the development of a new, stable and long-term partnership featuring equality and mutual benefit (FOCAC, April 9, 2013).

The second ministerial conference was convened in Addis Ababa, in 2003. The theme of the forum was pragmatic and action-oriented cooperation. At the opening ceremony of this conference, Premier Wen Jiabao put forward a four-point proposal[11] on how to further China-Africa friendship and cooperation, after the Addis Ababa Action Plan (2004–2006) was passed.

The Chinese government named 2006 the "year of Africa". The Summit and the third ministerial conference were held in Beijing, where the Declaration of the Beijing Summit of the Forum on China-Africa Cooperation and the Forum on China-Africa Cooperation Beijing Action Plan (2007–2009) were passed. The theme for this summit was friendship, peace, cooperation and development. The leaders jointly discussed "reducing debts, economic assistance, personal training and investment" (Taylor, 2012). President Hu Jintao announced eight measures[12] to help African countries accelerate their development while further promoting China-Africa cooperation in the following three years (Xinhua News, November 4, 2006). Furthermore, the white paper on China's African Policy, which was released in the same year, called for the establishment of a new type of China-Africa strategic partnership.

In 2009, foreign ministers from China and 49 African countries got together to review the implementation of follow-up actions after the Beijing Summit and proposed new measures and new ideas for agricultural and food safety, infrastructure construction, trade and investment, medical support, and more for the next three years. The conference passed the Declaration of Sharm El Sheikh of FOCAC and the FOCAC Sharm El Sheikh Action Plan (2010–2012). Premier Wen Jiabao addressed eight new measures intended to strengthen China-Africa cooperation.

Along with the regular ministerial-level meetings between China and Africa through the platform of the FOCAC, Beijing has developed a practical and systematic approach to its engagement with the African continent. The state council has released a white paper on China's African Policy, China's Foreign Aid, and China-Africa Economic and Trade Cooperation in 2006, 2011 and 2013 respectively. These were the first of its kind in Beijing's diplomatic history for the continent and were presented as being the key documents for framing China's relations with Africa (Taylor, 2012, p. 65). Generally, African participants and international commenters have provided positive feedback towards FOCAC. Many African governments are satisfied with Beijing's proposals on the forum. The IMF has reported that Africa's generally positive growth rate is partly due to increased commodity demand from China (Servant, 2005). Kaplinsky's research on China-Africa trade suggests that China's demands for oil, gas and other primary products have 'positive direct and indirect benefits on resource-exporting African economies' (Kaplinsky, 2007). However, there are also concerns in Africa on the form, content and future of FOCAC: for instance, limited interaction between African countries and China may lead to Africa's long-term dependency on China and the neglect of an African agenda. They have suggested a comprehensive interaction between African Union-FOCAC (AU-FOCAC) and New Partnership for Africa's Development-FOCAC (NEPAD-FOCAC), which could give more weight to the African side of the dialogue (Center for Chinese Studies [CCS] Team, 2010).

Based on the understanding of China's African policy trends and the motivation behind it, the following section will further analyse the information and data from these policy documents from the perspective of international responsibility.

4.3 The analysis of China's African policy

China's African policy is evolving on the basis of China's national strategy as a whole. In order to assess the compatibility of China's Africa policy and external expectations, this section will analyse the following two aspects: China's national interests and policy with Chinese characteristic, and then attempt to figure out the relationship between its policy and African demands and international requirements.

4.3.1 Responsibility and China's national interests

No matter how rhetorical the political documents are, one cannot deny the fact that international responsibility cannot contradict national core interests. Seeking to become a responsible player in Africa, China doesn't and shouldn't avoid its national interests and appeals to Africa, because that is the fundamental motivation behind China's engagement with this continent. Also, to assess China's responsibility at the policy level is not the same as exploring whether China's policy is beneficial or not, but rather what China's core interests mean to Africa and the rest of the world.

The latest national defense white paper issued by the State Council Information Office, the fundamental policies and principles followed by the diversified employment of China's armed forces, delivered a clear message to the world of China's priority, which was to "safeguard national unity, safeguarding the territorial integrity of heavy and arduous task of safeguarding the interests of development" (Information Office of the State Council, 2013b), which cannot be challenged. Meanwhile, it is the first time that China has included the protection of its overseas interests in a national defense white paper. It reveals China's growing expansion in international affairs, and its traditional interpretation of the 'non-interference' principle is a barrier for its expanding interests. Especially with its increased investment in pariah countries, China is no longer able to escape from protecting its assets and the criticism in these countries. Africa, as one of the largest Chinese investment and foreign aid destinations with a large number of pariah governments, has pushed Beijing to reconsider its traditional policy. At the same time, the international criticism of China in Darfur alerts Beijing to care about its international image and sends a clear message that China cannot be a free rider in Africa. China's fear of 'a backlash and the potential damage to its strategic and economic relationships with the US and Europe' prompts the country 'to put great effort into demonstrating that it is a responsible power' (Kleine-Ahlbrandt and Small, 2008).

In response to the changing international environment, China has shown flexibility in the interpretation of "non-interference", evidence of which can be seen from China's pressuring of the Bashir regime in Sudan and the abstention from voting on the UN's resolution to impose a no-fly zone over Libya. In the National Defence White Paper of 2013, it clearly included "international obligations" and pledged to "play an active role in maintaining world peace, security and stability" (Information Office of the State Council, 2013b). Thus, as a result of China's increasing influence in international affairs, the "non-interference" for Beijing has already evolved from inaction or avoidance into non-"military intervention" or non-"economic sanction". It is true that China is very cautious and prudent towards international intervention, largely because of its own domestic territorial problems. However, the effect of the West's efforts is questionable as well. As a Chinese commenter argued, changing a small country's regime through intervention is not hard for great powers, but the problem is what international military intervention will leave in its wake. Even if they stay for a while afterward, it is hard for intervening powers to protect the local civilians – as happened in Iraq, Afghanistan and Libya (Zhong, February 6, 2012).

As a result, China's adherence to the 'non-interference' policy arises more from domestic needs and does not necessarily shield the country from being responsible for Africa's security crisis. Stability and peace in Africa, even in the pariah countries who are China's economic partners, are consistent with China's own national interests, even in the pariah countries who are China's economic partner. The difference between China and the traditional donors lies in the way this aim can be achieved. The case of Sudan in Chapter 6 will feature the further discussion of China's interpretation of 'non-interference'.

According to China's African policy, Africa, as an important partner of China's "South-South Cooperation" and a supporter of "North-South dialogue", is significant for China's national interests in terms of trade, energy supply, and diplomatic and political support. Internationally, as President Xi Jinping said to South African President Zuma, China-Africa development has great significance to increase the strength of developing countries and to promote "international relations democratisation" (Guoji Guanxi Minzhuhua 国际关系民主化) (MOFA, February 17, 2013). Here, international relations democratization calls for a fairer international political and economic order. As former Foreign Minister Yang Jiechi specified, "China-Africa have maintained communication and coordination on peace and security, climate change, Doha development round (DDA) and the reform of the international financial system, protected the legitimate rights of developing countries and promoted the development of a fairer and more reasonable international political and economic order" (Chinanews.com, January 6, 2012). China's stance corresponded with President of Burkina Faso Compaore's advocation of "close connection of African and other developing countries in the international financial system reform" (Xinhua News, November 17, 2008). It is obvious that both China and Africa are motivated to call for multi-polar international relations, from which they can gain more benefits than from the current one. However, it is questionable whether China's conceived new order is similar to Africa's, let alone that a diversified Africa has different requirements which are far from unified. It is hard to conclude that China is responsible in terms of "international relations democratization", simply because both sides consider themselves to be as vulnerable as the other in the current world order. Nor could the reverse be argued, due to the fact that each of them has its own national interests. Currently, both sides need support on the world stage, but the assessment of responsibility needs to be analysed case by case in the following chapters.

4.3.2 Responsibility and Chinese characteristics

I Oil for infrastructure

Africa is an important energy supplier for China. For those oil-rich countries, China has conducted an "oil for infrastructure" approach to access the energy industry there, in return for infrastructure construction. Angola is considered to be China's most successful oil supplier on the continent; some researchers have called the Chinese way of "oil for infrastructure" the "Angola model"[13] (Corkin, 2011; M. Davies, Edinger, Tay, & Naidu, 2008). The expansion of Chinese oil companies into Africa's market has drawn attention from the international community, which is concerned not only because China is a competitor for Western oil companies, but also because of its impact on the African countries and their people. China has not been actively involved in African countries' public financial management and has not linked its loans to these countries' oil revenue disbursement. The doubts held by many Western policymakers are that China will undermine efforts by traditional donors and international financial institutions to regulate oil revenue management and reduce corruption. At the same time, partly due to large inflows of Chinese labour, the local job creation of Chinese projects in oil and infrastructure investment is limited. There is a risk that this "oil for infrastructure" relationship will result in resource extraction and that human capital development may be neglected (Collier, 2007; Zafar, 2007, p. 39).

First, the effectiveness of persuading African governments to accept Western good governance and transparency as requirements for loans is questionable, (R. I. Rotberg, 2008, pp. 121–124) because for oil rich countries, their governments have diversified sources for their survival rather than solely relying on either multilateral banks or China. And lacking the inner motivation to adopt the requirements, the contribution of these measures is always not as successful as expected. Second, resources do play an important role in China-Africa economic relations, but there is much more business beyond natural resources. According to the China-Africa Economic and Trade Cooperation, currently "over 2,000 Chinese enterprises are investing and developing in more than 50 African countries and regions" – some of these countries have oil or other resources, while many don't. The case studies chapters will make further comparisons between China's engagement with oil-rich and non-energy reserve countries to test this policy. Meanwhile, its cooperative fields "have expanded from agriculture, mining and building industry to an intensive processing of resource products, industrial manufacturing, finance, commercial logistics and real estate", which reveals that China's business exploration on the continent is not only 103 focused on resources, but on a broad range of industries. In recent years, China has improved its mechanisms for investment in Africa. By the end of 2012, China had signed bilateral investment treaties with 32 African countries and established joint economic commission mechanisms with 45 African countries. By the end of 2012, the China-Africa Development Fund, established as one of the eight pledges China made at the FOCAC Beijing Summit, had agreed to invest US$2.385 billion in 61 projects in 30 African countries and had already invested US$1.806 billion for 53 projects. According to preliminary statistics, the agreed-upon investment projects will bring US$10 billion worth of investment to Africa, increase local exports by about US$2 billion annually, and benefit more than 700,000 people. Thirdly, in terms of the

Chinese labour force's impact on African employment opportunities, the witnesses from both MOFA and State-owned enterprises (SOEs) have disclosed that central government and policy banks don't have requirements for hiring local people with the loans. It is up to the Chinese companies to make decisions on their human resources management according to the host country's law and their profits consideration. The main reason to limited local employees, nearly all the witness agreed, is the competence of African workers and their skills. In response to this problem, the Chinese government has launched a series of training programs. From 2010 to 2012, China held various training courses in 54 countries and regions in Africa; the courses involved a total of 27,318 officials and technicians, and covered topics relating to economics, foreign affairs, energy, industry, agriculture, forestry, animal husbandry and fishing, medicine and health care, inspection and quarantine, climate change, security, and some other fields. In addition, Chinese medical teams, agricultural experts and enterprises located in Africa have also trained local people in an effort to enhance local technological capabilities (Information Office of the State Council, 2013a). The Nigeria case in Chapter 7 will further discuss the approach of "oil for infrastructure".

II Aid with no-strings

China's official policy statement on its foreign aid, as the second feature, emphasizes "no political conditions", and China

> respects recipient countries' right to independently select their own path and model of development, and believes that every country should explore a development path suitable to its actual conditions. China never uses foreign aid as a means to interfere in recipient countries' internal affairs or seek political privileges for itself.
>
> (Information Office of the State Council, April 2011)

President Xi Jinping re-confirmed this principle during his African tour in March 2013, and said, "China will continue to offer, as always, necessary assistance to Africa with no political strings attached" (Reuters, March 25, 2013).

China's non-conditional aid has been seriously questioned by Western donors. First, its non-conditionality (i.e. aid without requirement on good governance, transparency or political reform) is said to support irresponsible regimes, thereby fuelling corruption and delaying necessary economic and political reform in African countries. Second, China's aid to Africa is considered to be driven by a/its domestic thirst for resources and the exploration of new African markets. Therefore, compared to traditional donors whose aid comes with political conditions, China is criticised for exporting its "growth at any cost" strategy at home to Africa (Condon, 2012, pp. 6–7). However, given that Chinese aid is offered in kind rather than cash, it might also be less prone to corruption (Brautigam, 2008b). According to a white paper about China's Foreign Aid, China offers foreign aid in eight forms: complete projects, goods and materials, technical cooperation, human resource development cooperation, medical teams sent abroad, emergency humanitarian aid, volunteer programs in foreign countries, and debt relief (Information Office of the State Council, April 2011). The assistance is tangible and often conducted by Chinese companies.[14] Different from international banks and traditional donors, the cash flow is always under the control of the Chinese government and Chinese enterprises, which limit the possibility of corruption in recipient countries. Second, as discussed in former section, the support of pariah governments contradicts with China's overseas interests protection and international image. The approach of "aid with no political conditions" is out of the weakness of Beijing rather than its intentional protection of dictators, because its domestic political situation gives China less voice to persuade African governments of good governance and human rights protection. Meanwhile, "political conditions" has an assumption that China has the capability to press its African counterparts, but in the case of Africa, China and its projects are largely constrained by local regulations and political manipulation. The country even cannot fully protect its overseas assets and citizens, how could it have the power to change local governance?

III China as a model

According to Witness 1, who was involved in the briefing meeting of FOCAC V, the biggest difference between FOCAC V and former meetings within this platform, is that it included "China and Africa will enhance the sharing of experience in governance" in the fifth ministerial conference of FOCAC Beijing Action Plan 2013–2015. However, little political discourse has mentioned what "experience in governance" China would like to share. Witness 3 interpreted it as "China's experience and model of rapid growth". In the Joint Communiqué of the Third Round of Political Consultations between Chinese and African Foreign Ministers, in 2013, it emphasised shared experience of "development". While in the Beijing Action plan 2013–2015, it said "two sides will continue to expand the scope and diversify the forms of exchanges between political parties, deepen political dialogue, consolidate political mutual trust, enhance experience sharing on governance and national development and promote practical cooperation" (FOCAC, July 23, 2012). In September 2013, the Central Party School of CPC held a seminar on "China-Africa experiences of governance and development" to further discuss the topic with 110 experts from more than 50 African universities and research institutes. Zhang Boli, the vice principal of the Central Party School has pointed out that, China-Africa's new strategic partnership should be established not only through political, economics and trade, but also dialogue and communication among people (FOCAC, October 9, 2013).

China's Special Representative to Africa Liu Guijin, emphasised that China just wants to share its own experiences with Africa, but not to force any African countries to accept it, because there is not a universal model that is suitable for every country (Xinhua News, September 25, 2013).

The Chinese government didn't give a clear explanation of what "governance experience" it would like to share with African countries. From the limited political documents, it has indicated that China's development path, which also echoed with African countries' expectation. As Senegal President Abdoulaye Wade said, "the Chinese model for stimulating rapid economic development has much to teach Africa" (Wade, January 23, 2008). Most African countries are interested in China's experience of lifting hundreds of millions of people out of poverty in a relatively short period of time. Thus, this book will assume that what China shares is an alternative economic development model, what Joshua Cooper Ramo named the "Beijing Consensus" (Cooper Ramo, May 2004). On the one hand, China's rapid economic growth was achieved through a high level of investment and concentration of exports. In recent years, many African countries' economic growth has also been spurred by China's investment in African commodities. The exportation of the Beijing Consensus could help to promote further and facilitate China's investment in Africa. On the other hand, China's economic strength is attractive to African political elites. Sharing experiences will enhance China's soft power in Africa. From the launch of the China-Africa Joint Research and Exchange Plan in March 2010 to the end of 2012, it had supported 64 projects in the form of workshops, subject research, 107 academic exchanges, and publishing works (Information Office of the State Council, 2013a). The project had also subsidised visits and exchanges for over 600 Chinese and African scholars. At the same time, China emphasised its respect for Africa's choice of its own development path. China did provide an alternative source of funds and a development model, but whether China's development model suits African countries largely depends on the situation and environment within the host countries. The Ethiopian case in Chapter 9 will further discuss China as a model for Africa.

4.4 Conclusion

China's Africa policy has experienced an evolution, from radical ideologically driven towards a more practical way and flexible interpretation. Notably, its non-interference principle has a different interpretation according to its changing national agenda. Currently, China has political, economic and diplomatic interests in Africa. And based on its own national interests of protecting overseas assets and citizens and a stable and peaceful international environment, China has a similar expectation with African countries with the continent and international society, and it is of China's own interests to become responsible to African's stability and development. The second part of each case study chapter will further address how the mutual requirements between China and its host country come out and their compatibility.

China has a different approach and philosophy towards its responsibility in Africa. On the international level, it advocates a fairer international order in favour of Southern countries' interests. In practice, this advocacy has manifested as mutual political support for each other in the international arena. On the policy level, China-Africa engagement has the following features: non-interference, oil for infrastructure and aid with no strings attached. These approaches were introduced for China's win-win situation with African countries, in order to provide African governments with a free environment to choose the way that fit their own development agendas and financial assistance for their infrastructures. And it also reveals China's limited capability in the continent. In practice, these approaches, may even have good will in mind, have brought Africa negative effects as well, such as overwhelming floods of Chinese labour and Chinese products. Hence Beijing launched various measures for the promotion of investment, debt reduction and relief, economic assistance and cooperation. In response to African countries' trade deficits, China has vigorously expanded its imports from Africa by enacting tariff exemptions and setting up exhibition centers for African products. Since January 2012, the 30 least-developed African countries that have established diplomatic relations with China have been granted zero-tariff treatment for 60% of their exported items. By the end of 2012, 22 of them had seen 910-million yuan worth of tariff exemption, involving US$1.49 billion-worth of goods (Information Office of the State Council, 2013a). In order to support African medium and small businesses, at the Fourth FOCAC Ministerial Conference in 2009, China announced the establishment of "a special loan for small and medium-sized African businesses". By the end of 2012, the special loan service had promised to offer loans totaling US$1.213 billion, with a contract value of US$1.028 billion, and loans granted worth US$666 million, providing strong support for the development of agriculture, forestry, animal husbandry, fishing, processing and manufacturing, trade and logistics, and other industries closely associated with people's livelihoods in Africa (Information Office of the State Council, April 2011). As for the complaints regarding the quality of Chinese goods, from December 2010 to March 2011, the Chinese took steps to crack down on the potential export to Africa of counterfeit and poor-quality products and commodities that violate intellectual property rights, which involved multiple measures, such as prior-to-shipment quality examinations for industrial products that were to be exported to Africa. These measures helped guarantee the quality of Chinese commodities exported to Africa (Ministry of Commerce of the PRC [MOFCOM], February 17, 2011). In terms of foreign aid, African countries accounted for 45.7% of China's total foreign assistance in 2009 (Information Office of the State Council, April 2011). And among the 123 of China's regular foreign assistance destinations, 51 are in Africa. All these measures were introduced to solve inequalities in the economic relations between China and Africa. The second part of each case study chapter will further analyse China's motivation in accessing different kinds of African countries.

In summary, China, even though it holds a different perspective, has shared similar aims towards a peaceful, stable and developed Africa. It provides tangible and efficient contributions to the continent. And the government also launches measures to reduce the negative effects in order to enhance Africa's capability for economic development. All the methods generally align with Africa's desire for poverty relief and economic development. As for the democracy and good governance advocated for by the traditional donors, China's policy does not support nor instinctively oppose these norms, because an African government with good governance is in the interests of China and Chinese enterprises.

Notes

1 The Five Principles of Peaceful Coexistence are (1) mutual respect for sovereignty and territorial integrity; (2) mutual non-aggression; (3) non-interference in each other's internal affairs; (4) equality and mutual benefit and (5) peaceful coexistence.
2 The Five Strands of China-African Relations refers to the following: (1) It should support the African people in the struggle against imperialism, colonialism and neocolonialism, and strive for national independence; (2) It should back African countries' peaceful, neutral policy of non-alignment; (3) It should support the African people's wishes to choose their own way to solidarity and unification; (4) It should encourage African countries to solve conflicts through peaceful negotiation; (5) It should advocate the respect for African countries' sovereignty from all nations, and be against all aggression and interference.
3 The eight principles of Chinese African aid refers to the following: it would be based on equality, mutual benefit and respect for the sovereignty of the host. (Principles of Peaceful Coexistence) Loans would be non-conditional, interest-free, or low-interest, and easily rescheduled. Projects would use high-quality materials, have quick results, and boost self-reliance. Chinese experts would transfer their expertise "fully" and live to the same standards as their local counterparts.
4 The eleven countries Premier Zhao visited were Egypt, Algeria, Morocco, Guinea, Gabon, Congo (Democratic Republic of Congo and People's Republic of Congo, Zambia, Zimbabwe, Tanzania and Kenya.
5 The six countries were Botswana, Angola, Zimbabwe, Zambia, Mozambique and Lesotho.
6 The six Principles of Sino-African Policy were: (1) It should support African countries' efforts in struggling against external interference and economic development. (2) It should respect African countries to choose their political system and way of development based on their national conditions. (3) It should encourage African countries' solidarity, unity for strength and solve the disputes through peaceful negotiation. (4) It should support African countries' efforts to jointly seek peace, stability and development, as well as the economic integration of the continent. (5) It should support African countries' active involvement in international affairs as an equal member. (6) It would like to develop friendly exchanges and various economic cooperation on the basis of the Five Principles of Peaceful coexistence.

7 The PRC automatically severs relations with any state that establishes diplomatic relations with the ROC.

8 The six African countries are Kenya, Egypt, Ethiopia, Mali, Namibia and Zimbabwe.

9 Its main thrust is to strengthen solidarity and cooperation with African countries and work together with them to contribute to the lofty cause of world peace and development. The guiding principle that China follows in developing relations with African countries in the new situation is: "to treat each other as equals, develop a sincere friendship, strengthen solidarity and cooperation, and seek common development". China's African policy in the respect all countries and treat them as equals, irrespective of their size, strength and wealth; to support African countries in their just struggle to maintain national independence, state sovereignty and territorial integrity and oppose foreign interference; to promote unity among African countries and advocate settlement of disputes among them, if any, through peaceful negotiation; to uphold justice and help safeguard the rights and interests of African countries in international affairs; to continue to new period mainly contains the following elements: to respect the choices of road to development made by African people themselves; to abide by the Five Principles of Peaceful Co-existence and non-interference in the internal affairs of African countries; to provide economic aid to African countries without attaching any political strings; and to stick to the principle of equality and mutual benefit in its economic cooperation and trade with African countries.

10 The proposal includes the following points: (1) to foster a sincere friendship between the two sides and become each other's reliable "all-weather friends"; (2) to treat each other as equals and respect each other's sovereignty and refrain from interfering in each other's internal affairs; (3) to seek common development on the basis of mutual benefit; (4) to enhance consultation and cooperation in international affairs; 5) And to look into the future and create a more splendid world.

11 The four point proposal included: (1) Continue to move forward the traditional China-Africa friendship through mutual support; (2) Promote democratization of international relations through intensified consultation; (3) Jointly meet the challenges of globalization through coordination of positions; (4) Turn a new chapter in China-Africa friendly relations through enhanced cooperation.

12 These measures included: (1) doubling China's 2006 assistance to Africa by 2009; (2) providing Africa with US$3 billion of preferential loans and US $2 billion of preferential buyer's credits; (3) setting up a China-Africa development fund worth US$5 billion; (4) building a conference center for the African Union in Addis Ababa, Ethiopia; (5) cancelling debt owed by heavily indebted poor countries and the least developed countries in Africa; (6) further opening up China's market to Africa by increasing from 190 to over 440 number of export items from the 29 least-developed countries in Africa that have no tariffs levied against them; (7) establishing several trade and economic cooperation zones in Africa and creating other measures to promote Sino-African cooperation in the socioeconomic field; (8) China has also pledged to support in the field of socio-cultural cooperation.

13 China Export-Import (EXIM) Bank's financing arrangement that ties a commodity (Oil) off-take agreement with the provision of infrastructure in the contracting African country are commonly referred to as the "Angola Model".

14 Here the argument of "Chinese side controls the cash flow" does not necessarily mean China is not corrupt. But as the book focused on the evaluation of China's impact on Africa, the tangible assistance at least is better than cash for African people.

5 A fragmented China in Africa with Chinese characteristics

5.1 Introduction

As discussed in Chapter 3, international responsibility is not the same thing as a state's responsibility, and instead many kinds of actors have become involved in the process of shouldering responsibility. The implementation of international responsibility is achieved in the political and economic contexts of the donor and host countries by the actions of various actors, as has been suggested in hypothesis III. In order to test this hypothesis, this chapter will investigate which branches or departments of government have been involved in the China-Africa policy implementation process, and also further explore which actors have a potential impact on China "being responsible".

It is common to see the phrase "fragmented authoritarianism" in Chinese studies literature, which refers to the idea that "policy made at the center becomes increasingly malleable to the parochial organizational and political goals of various vertical agencies and spatial regions charged with enforcing that policy" (Mertha, 2009, p. 996). Outcomes are shaped by the incorporation of interests of the implementing agencies into the policies themselves. Fragmented authoritarianism thus explains a policy arena governed by incremental change via bureaucratic bargaining (Mertha, 2009, p. 996). In a globalizing world, China's foreign-economic policies are put into practice by an increasingly diverse set of actors under pressure from a wide variety of interest groups and constituency demands (Taylor, 2009). For instance, China's overseas State-owned enterprises (SOEs) have to be sensitive both to general government policies and proclamations, and also to their profit motives (Taylor, 2009, p. 5), which implies that China's foreign policy implementation is a result of a compromise between actors through calculations of central policy, economic profits and other interests. As for the assessment of China in Africa, the following sections will discuss which actors have influenced China's activities in Africa from two major areas: foreign assistance and foreign investment. Additionally, it will provide an overview of China's foreign aid and foreign investment system, which is different from traditional Organization for Economic Cooperation and Development (OECD) countries' and is designed to test hypothesis III from China's perspective.

5.2 Explanation of China's aid system

5.2.1 An ambiguous number

Developed countries widely use official development assistance (ODA) as defined by the Organization for Economic Cooperation and Development (OECD) to measure international aid flows. The three largest OECD donors-the United States (US), European Union (EU) and France-have provided sub-Saharan Africa with US$7.6 billion, US$ 4.8 billion and US $3.9 billion, respectively, in the form of development grants and concessional loans in 2009 (Calculated from OECD website). By comparison, notwithstanding the lack of official statistics on its annual aid totals, Brautigam estimated that China probably disbursed US$1.4 billion in ODA in Africa during the same period (Brautigam, 2011, p. 211). However, Weston et al., Lum et al., Brautigam and Lancaster all agreed that the actual amount of Chinese foreign assistance in Africa has been understated if we use ODA as an indicator, because much of China's economic financing on the continent often doesn't fit the OECD's definition of development assistance (Lancaster, 2007; Lum, Fischer, Gomez-Granger, & Leland, 2009; Weston, Campbell, & Koleski, September 2011).

The lack of transparency perplexes researchers of Chinese aid studies. Although the government released a white paper on foreign aid in 2011, which was a substantial step towards making its foreign aid more transparent and systematic, people still could not find certain details of its foreign aid, such as annual aid data, nor the criteria used in calculating it. Why does such a goodwill issue have to be a "state secret"? (Weston et al., September 2011) The answer from Chinese officials is that they were trying to "avoid unwelcome pressure from many of those governments for more aid to keep up with the largest recipients" (Lancaster, 2007, p. 2) by not issuing the amount of bilateral aid. It sounds reasonable but does not satisfy all the concerns. There appear to be several other reasons, internal and external, for why the Chinese government is reluctant to release more details on its foreign aid.

First, it is hard to calculate. As mentioned above, much of China's assistance doesn't fit into the ODA definition of the OECD. According to the Foreign Aid White Paper, China has provided assistance to Africa through three types of financial resources: grants, interest-free loans, and confessional loans without clarifying whether the grants elements are less than at least 25% of the loans. At the same time, much of the official assistance doesn't qualify under the standards of ODA. For instance, "export buyer's credit", "export commodity-secured or 'mutual-benefit' credits", "official loans at commercial rates" and "strategic lines of credit to Chinese companies" in Africa (Brautigam, 2011). These kinds of aid are often provided as part of a larger package of investment or trade deals with local government and companies, which can hardly separate the amount of the ODA element from business expenses. Furthermore, based on the statistics estimated by the New York University (NYU) Wagner School, about 54% of China's foreign aid in Africa went to infrastructure projects and public works, which included transportation, communication, power supply, municipal utilities, civilian buildings, wells for water supply, conference centers, sports venues, culture venues, and facilities for scientific, educational and medical care purposes (Lum et al., 2009). Much of the workforce and technologies used in these projects were not included; as Witness 22 suggested, the technicians and specialists are the biggest advantages China can offer Africa because they have comprehensive procedures. In this way, how to quantify the Chinese human resource cost involved in these projects is another obstacle to ascertaining China's aid in the continent. In addition, if we did research on the basis of figures provided by the media or in pledges, there is a risk that some of the projects may not have been fulfilled or even be canceled. According to the data from the China-Africa Database, among all the projects China has conducted in Africa, 30 have been canceled. Meanwhile, some commitments that lasted for several years may be counted more than once (Brautigam, 2010). What's more, the bureaucracy in central and local governments has increased the difficulty in divining an exact number. Normally, five ministries (the Ministry of Commerce, Foreign Affairs, Finance, Health and Education), two policy banks (China's Export-Import Bank and Development Bank), as well as some state-owned enterprises would be involved in foreign aid, and none of them seem to be in charge of the whole process, nor responsible for providing more details.

Second, China, being categorized as a lower middle-income country by the OECD, who receives net ODA to the amounts of US$1.1 billion in 2009 and US$648 million in 2010, (Calculated from OECD website) may reduce the financial funds it could receive from OECD donors if it acted as a generous contributor itself. This concern could be reflected in the fact that the Chinese government frequently emphasises that it is still a lower-middle-income country and that its largest donor Japan has announced the termination of its government's Yen Loan to China, in 2007.

Third, "being a responsible power" has provoked a lot of domestic pressure. During the observation of Bulletin Board System (BBS) and quantile quantile (QQ) chat groups, lots of people complained and criticised the government by asking why China should prioritise other countries rather than their own people. They argued that mainland China's per capita Gross Domestic Product (GDP) was only US$4,382 in 2010, and ranked a lowly 92, even behind many of its aid recipients in Africa, such as Equatorial Guinea, Gabon, Botswana, Mauritius, South Africa and Namibia. According to per capita gross national income (GNI), China has long struggled to reach the bottom end of the upper middle-income countries as classified by the World Bank, which meant it was a lower-middle income economy until 2009. If using per capita purchasing power parity (PPP) as a criterion to avoid mistakenly categorising some countries with a lower living expense but a higher living standard, China still placed 96th, behind several African states. It is hard for people who witness the wealth gap as well as urban and rural developmental division, to feel satisfied with the government's scant investment in domestic education, health and social insurance, while generously financing people who turn out to be much richer than the Chinese themselves. Additionally, people with this kind of discontent would easily be suspicious of the West's promotion of China's commitments to the international community. The dual identity of China as the second largest economy and a developing country with a large number of people in poverty is inevitable to meet with pressure from external expectations and internal criticism. Against this backdrop, the Chinese government has always tried to veil the details of its foreign aid.

5.2.2 An aid system with Chinese characteristics

Many scholars of China-African studies argue that the amount of China's foreign aid might be understated without applying more flexible definitions. The research on China's foreign aid from the NYU Wagner School not only included grants, loans, debt cancellation or relief, but also state-sponsored investments, and in-kind aid when calculating the exact amount (Lum et al., 2009). Brautigam also paid attention to the official funds, such as export buyer's credit, and export commodity-secured credit (Brautigam, 2010). Apparently, the more types that are counted as assistance, the more actors that should also be considered. Take the Forum of China-Africa Cooperation (FOCAC) as an example: 27 ministries were involved in its implementation actions. And since there is not a special law similar to the Foreign Assistance Act in the US to regulate the aid system, each ministry might operate according to its own rules. Hence, some of China's aid was strategic-oriented, some was economic-driven, and some was just out of a sense of morality. The following section will attempt to ascertain who decides what.

I Management of aid to Africa

According to China's foreign aid, the decision-making power in China regarding foreign aid lies with the central government. However, agencies at various levels of the Chinese government are responsible for the management of foreign aid.

Ministry of Commerce (MOFCOM) is the major institution of China's foreign aid. The Department of Aid to Foreign Countries was broken off from the Ministry of Foreign Economic Relations in 1982 and is now affiliated with the MOFCOM. This department is responsible for the formulation of foreign aid policies, regulations, overall and annual plans, examination and approval of foreign aid projects, and the management of project execution. With three out of 13 divisions specialised in Africa, it is also responsible for promoting reform, organising foreign aid negotiations, signing agreements, dealing with intergovernmental assistance, and supervising aid projects. In addition, the Executive Bureau of International Economic Cooperation, non-profit entities (shiye danwei 事业单位)[1] affiliated with MOFCOM takes charge of the management and implementation of its completed foreign aid projects. It is mainly responsible for the pre-qualification documents of bidding for overseas completed projects, bidding for management, approval, monitoring and execution (expect exploration and design) of the projects. Meanwhile, it negotiates with the host countries for the implementation as well as inner supervision and estimation. It is also in charge of technical materials, personnel (experts), and project data. Other agencies include the China International Centre for Economic and Technical Exchanges, and Academy of International Business Officials, affiliated with MOFCOM are entrusted with tasks of managing the implementation of completed projects and technical cooperation, material aid and training programs (MOFCOM, March 8, 2009).

Foreign aid branches within MOFCOM have no overseas offices in Africa, nor do they have specialists on development and technology. Therefore, the related departments of the Chinese government keep in contact and cooperate with these agencies to provide foreign aid. In drafting foreign aid programs and foreign aid fund plans for each country, the Ministry of Commerce communicates regularly with the Ministry of Foreign Affairs, Ministry of Finance and the Export-Import Bank of China to seek their suggestions (Information Office of the State Council, April 2011). Some other ministries of the State Council are responsible for, or participate in, the management of foreign aid programs that require professional expertise, such as the Ministry of Education and Ministry of Agriculture. Additionally, the Exim Bank is responsible for the assessment of projects with concessional loans, and the evaluation of host countries' repayment capabilities, the allocation and repayment or relief of the loans. Chinese embassies or consulates abroad are in charge of the direct coordination and management of foreign aid projects in their host countries (Exim Bank, 2010). The local branches are required to cooperate with MOFCOM to deal with affairs related to foreign aid within their jurisdictions. (Interview from Witnesses 1, 2 and 3, who revealed their experience of such kinds of works.) In order to strengthen the coordination of the departments concerned, the ministries of Commerce, Foreign Affairs and Finance officially established the country's Foreign Aid Inter-Agency Liaison Mechanism in 2008. In February 2011, this liaison mechanism was upgraded into an inter-agency coordination mechanism (China's Foreign Aid, 2011).

Gathering information from Witnesses 1, 2 and 3, a typical foreign assistance project is achieved through the following procedures: usually, the foreign aid budget started at the Economic Counsellor's Office in Chinese embassy located at host state. The officers on the ground are responsible for collecting first-hand information and reporting the proposal of the African state's foreign aid budget to Beijing. When planning the project, Ministry of Foreign Affairs (MOFA) would collaborate with MOFCOM and Ministry of Finance (MOF) for control of the budget. Here is where the problems can arise: the protocols are designed for diplomatic strategy has been vetted by the ministries with economic benefits in mind. Even if no witnesses have revealed more information as to what extend the three ministries would coordinate together or undermine each other, Witness 2 believes that MOFCOM and MOF have a stronger voice than MOFA, because they control the money. As the criticism said, "most of China's aid is doled out by the Ministry of Commerce and the China Export-Import Bank (Exim Bank), whose central mandate is to strengthen China's economy" (Condon, 2012, p. 6), their commitment to African development shrinks.

As for the supervision of the projects, according to the responsibilities of each agency (listed on their official websites) involved in African assistance, the division and cooperation between them are not very clear. The monitor and supervisors for the projects are entrusted by the two branches from MOFCOM mentioned in the former paragraph. At the same time, Witness 3, who worked at China's embassy in Nigeria, described his working experience of monitoring and facilitating China's foreign assistance projects and coordinating with Chinese enterprises to make sure the project could finish on time. It reveals that the responsibilities overlapped between one ministry and another and reversely it may buck passing as well. Additionally, this mechanism lacks an independent agency with specialists to have a comprehensive evaluation of the projects, such as ecological impact, local capability and sustainability. It makes the Chinese sponsoring projects much more controversial and local unfriendly. China's foreign aid of grants (donations), interest-free loans pledged and disbursed by the Chinese government rarely have been implemented as a cash transfer, but usually as a completed project conducted by Chinese firms. On the policy level, this created a "win-win" situation in which African countries get the tangible projects in a short period of time while Chinese companies have the opportunities to access African markets. However, in reality, the Chinese enterprises, whether SOEs or private companies with their profit-driven natures, tend to complete the projects in the most economical way, sometimes sacrificing quality and local employment opportunities or environmental protection, which can have the result that the pledged assistance projects shrink in value. Meanwhile, comparing the official information with that from interviews and observations, we can see some illegal behaviour taking place in the host countries. According to the regulations of MOFCOM, the Chinese companies with foreign aid qualification would have a cipher code to access the Foreign Aid Tenders system under the Bureau of Foreign Economic Cooperation, and bid for relevant projects in terms of investigation, exploration and design, construction and supervision. However, during my interviews, Witness 16 from an SOE disclosed that her company had subcontracted the projects to other private companies in the name of cooperation and due to the hardships in African countries, but she has no idea if these private companies were qualified to work on foreign aid projects. Witness 15 from an SOE said that on-site managers and translators who belong to her company were always new employees or temporary contractors, rather than veterans in Africa, because the experienced technicians and managers prefer to work in Europe, America, and some Middle East countries. A lot of witnesses from SOEs admitted that the inexperienced Chinese employees don't get along well with African workers, due to the language barrier, and differences in customs, culture, and living styles.

What makes the process more complicated is one of the three key actors in China's aid system, alongside Ministry of Foreign Affairs and Ministry of Commerce: the China Exim Bank. Also known as one of the three policy banks that support the "going global" strategy, established in 1994, the bank is responsible for providing export buyer's credit, export sellers' credit, guarantees, loans for overseas projects and investment. It is also the only bank that provides concessional loans and preferential export buyer's credit. Researchers have various opinions on whether or to what extent the products provided by the Exim Bank can be categorised as foreign aid. The following section will talk address it specifically. But, there is one product that is considered in agreement: concessional loans. Although this type of loan is by its nature a form of aid, it is different from those of MOFCOM, because the Ministry of Finance would use the central assistance budget to cover the gap between a low, fixed rate loan offered by Exim Bank and the actual costs. In addition, the loans have a strict interest rate and terms, and it is unlikely to have a grace period or cancellation. The cycle for concessional loans is illustrated in Figure 5.1.

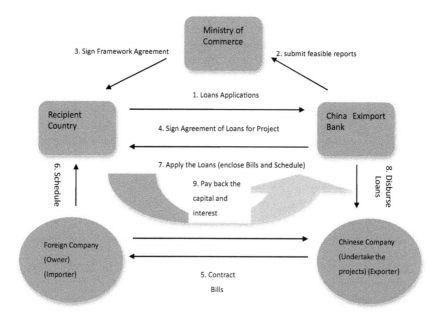

Figure 5.1 The cycle of concessional loans from Exim Bank.
Source: Author (raw material: The Export-Import Bank of China).

In contrast to the West, China doesn't have an independent aid agency, like the United States' Agency for International Development, which generally takes charge of economic support funds and development assistance programs. However, it has the same situation as that of the West, in which a variety of divisions and departments under the ministries and policy banks jointly have influence on its foreign aid decision-making system. And each of them to some extent has impacted the Chinese overseas companies, as well as the accomplishments of assistance projects.

II Forms of China's aid to Africa

China's foreign aid white paper included three types of financial resources-grants, interest-free loans, and concessional loans-as "aid". These categories reconciled with the definition of ODA if the funds were disbursed with an appropriate grant element. However, if we keep an eye on the forms of Chinese aid, they probably are not interpreted in the same way as ODA's definition. China has listed eight forms of its foreign aid: complete projects, goods and materials, technical cooperation, human resource development cooperation, medical teams sent abroad, emergency humanitarian aid, volunteer programs in foreign countries, and debt relief. It could be said that these forms of aid are equivalent to ODA, but they do not fully correspond to the concept.

"Turn-key-or complete-project" is the category that raises the most misunderstanding and concern, because it can easily be considered as state-sponsored economic cooperation activities, or be categorised as concessional loans if you neglect the fact that Chinese firms were fully involved. This approach reflected the Chinese aid philosophy as Witness 1 said,

> the meaning of China-Africa relations is not charity, it is aid for the poor, it is not humanitarianism, it is internationalism and international justice. We are a great power which has great power responsibilities, aiding Africa's development is part of our construction of a harmonious world.

Complete projects were conducted in terms of "mutual benefit", which is quite different from the Western donors, who "believe that a relatively well-governed country should be able to make its own decision about how to use foreign assistance" (Brautigam, 2010, p. 124) and therefore are focused on good governance and human rights protections. Instead, the Chinese preferred tangible contributions such as stadiums, government buildings, and other infrastructure. According to the white paper, complete projects account for 40% of China's foreign aid expenditure, widely distributed in the sectors of agriculture, public facilities, economic infrastructure and industry. By the end of 2010, China had accomplished more than 900 complete projects in about 50 African countries, which included 2,233 km of railway,

3,391 km of highway roads, 42 stadiums, 54 hospitals and 118 schools. It also promised to provide US$10 billion of preferential loans to Africa from 2010 to 2012. These loans are to be used to finance some of the big projects under construction, such as an airport in Mauritius, housing in Malabo, Equatorial Guinea, and the Bui Hydropower Station in Ghana (Information Office of the State Council, 2013a).

Along with food and medicine, goods and materials are mostly provided to support the completed projects, such as machinery and other relevant equipment, devices and transportation vehicles. Meanwhile, technical cooperation serves as a follow-up action to the completed projects. The Chinese experts would give technical guidance on production, operation or maintenance to ensure proper use and skill transfers. By the end of 2009, China had sent 104 senior agricultural technical experts to 33 African countries. One hundred and seven schools had been built in Africa with Chinese assistance, and 29,465 African students had received Chinese government scholarships to study in China. By June 2010, China had provided training programs for over 30,000 people from African countries, covering over 20 fields such as economics, public administration, agriculture, animal husbandry and fishing industry, medical care and public health, science and technology, and environmental protection (Information Office of the State Council, April 2011).

In Summary, the Chinese definition of aid explained in the white paper shares some characteristics with those of Western donors. Table 5.1 shows the similarities and differences between OECD defined ODA and Chinese aid. Even though they don't always fit in theory, they do provide benefits to the continent. Furthermore, many analysts preferred to apply more flexible measures to calculate Chinese assistance and therefore gave a higher number/value. Some estimated China had an aid scale comparable to that of middle-developed countries, such as Australia, Belgium or Denmark (Lancaster, 2007). The NYU Wagner School included government-sponsored investment as a kind of aid fund, which resulted in a 24% increase in the total value. Some European Scholars categorised China-Africa development funds provided by China Development Bank as in-kind aid as well (Welle-Strand, 2010).

Brautigam has clearly separated ODA from other kinds of official flows (OOF) to indicate international financial flows[2]. In this way, the export credits and guarantees, or funds with export facilitating purposes could be included. It also separated the funding sources from MOFCOM and those from the China Exim Bank and China Development Bank. Different from the traditional ODA donors, China's ODA funds to developing countries are lower than its OOF. The concessional loans for complete projects noted above actually accounted for a small part of the Exim Bank's products. By comparison, Figure 5.2 reveals that export credit is a major expenditure for the bank. The credit was paid out on terms of 2% interest, 10–15-year maturity, no grace period, and the Renminbi (RMB) as the debt currency. An

Table 5.1 The comparison of Chinese foreign assistance with OECD standard

	Government to government	Financing through development agency	Strong links to donor country economy	Concessional or favorable lending terms	Receives payment of debt in kind	Grant element of at least 25%	Private or corporate financing
OECD Aid Donor	Yes[1]	Yes	No	Yes	No	Yes	No
China	Yes	No[2]	Yes/No[3]	Yes	Yes	No[4]	No

Source: Author (raw materials: AidData; P. Davies, 2007; Foster, Butterfield, Chen, & Pushak, 2009; Lum et al., 2009).

Notes
1 Grants may be awarded to NGOs based in either the donor country or recipient country.
2 Aid is provided largely in the form of concessional loans administered by the Chinese policy lender, including China Exim Bank; China-Africa Development Fund; China Development Bank.
3 Some comments hold Chinese aid projects facilitate the export of natural resources and commodities to China, while some others argue Chinese enterprises in Africa turned to international markets and local labour resources for lower cost and higher profits.
4 The majority of Chinese aid projects have a grand element of more than 25%. Very few projects in Angola at the early period of China-Africa engagement has a grand element less than 25%.

OECD counsellor has calculated the grant element of this credit by ODA definition and has argued that it "carries a grant element of 40.81%", which is "high enough to count such concessional export as aid" (Reisen, 2007). Fitch Rating even estimated the China Exim Bank extended US $12.5 billion more in loans to sub-Saharan Africa in the past decade than the World Bank (M. Cohen, December 29, 2011). While Standard & Poor pointed out that the China Exim Bank extended 90% of its export credits to state-owned enterprises and large projects (Bosshard, 2007).

Another major OOF funding source came from the China Development Bank (CDB). The China-Africa Development Fund was announced as one of the Eight Measures to Africa by President Hu Jintao at the FOCAC Beijing Summit in 2006. Special loans for the development of African small- and medium-sized companies were also announced as part of the New Eight Measures by Wen Jiabao in 2009. Together, these have brought the policy bank into the spotlight.

Traditionally, the bank was focused on China's central western region and the northeast Old Industrial Bases inside China. Recently, however, it carries some of the responsibility for Chinese firms' "going global" strategy, supporting them in seeking markets and avoiding risks in Africa. In 2011, the bank supported several leading Chinese enterprises extending their overseas business – such as China International Trust Investment Corporation (CITIC) Group, China Three Gorges Corporation, Goldwind Science & Technology, and Chery Automobile – and provided loans to small-and medium-sized African companies from 29 countries (CDB, 2009). As the biggest investment fund to Africa, the China Development Bank (CDB) has launched US$1 billion loans at the beginning, in 2007, CDB Vice

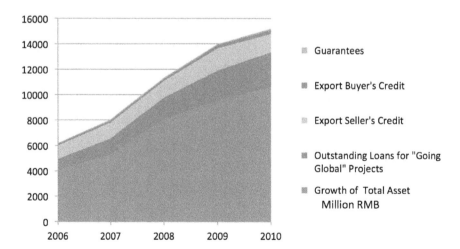

Figure 5.2 China Exim Bank expenditure.
Source: Author (raw material: China Exim Bank).

Chairman Hu Zhirong also promised to invest US$5 billion through special loans to African SMEs in 2011. He encouraged joint projects between state-owned or private Chinese firms and African companies on commercial activities, including agriculture, manufacturing, electricity, transportation, telecommunications, urban infrastructure and in the resource exploration sector on the continent (Hou, December 4, 2012). CDB Chairman Chen Yuan revealed that, by the end of June 30, 2011, CDB had signed special loan contracts worth US$320 million, and committed US$617 million to various regions (see Figure 5.3). This contract follows projects worth over US$1.1 billion covering more than 25 African countries (CDB, 2009).

Beijing's support of the policy bank as an aid vehicle reveals that the central government has a grand ambition to explore the infrastructure construction business and energy industry in Africa. But the low credibility of African borrowers and their poor risk assessment capability have prevented China's domestic capital sources from investing in large projects, as they do not have much motivation or capability for taking political and economic risks in Africa. In contrast, the policy banks have taken Beijing's pledges on FOCAC and expanded their business to African governments and companies. Despite the fact that the central policy banks lack transparency in their overseas business, the analysts believe that these banks have a higher tolerance of bad loans and late payments, which may lead to a larger amount of bad loans and dead debts (Dong, 2012). Fitch's analysis also echoes this argument, by saying that Chinese official loans to African countries are very flexible. They usually provide longer repayment period and concession period; meanwhile, they have fewer restrictions in relation to the borrower's financial status (Brautigam, 2011).However, in terms of implementation, even the leader from these banks, who rarely makes judgement on central policy, has complained of the difficulties in its relationship with Africa. Zhou Xiaochuan, governor of China's central bank, described some China-Africa deals as 'not so good, not so satisfactory' against the background of Beijing's announcement of a US$ 2billion deal with African Development Bank to promote bilateral joint projects (Blas & Rwanda, 2014). The contradictory demands between Beijing's order and the policy

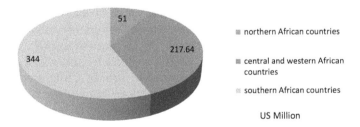

Figure 5.3 CDB loans to Africa by regions.
Source: Author (raw material: China Development Bank).

banks priorities further prove the weakness of the 'fragmented authoritarianism' system: that is, the policy made at central government has not experienced a transparent and comprehensive evaluation, while the implementation agency has little capability or motivation, and sometimes has difficulties in fully following these policies. As a result, instead of rejecting the policy, as many democratic countries did, the agency tends to choose to shrink the policy or continue, but inactively. This inaction has undermined the pledges that Chinese leaders made for African countries.

He Wenping pointed out that ODA donors preferred "soft assistance", such as capability development while Chinese counterparts focused on "hard projects", such as stadiums, conference centres and highways (He, February 27). China avoided the West's experience of spending billions of dollars in Africa with little progress, and by contrast showed quick, efficient and tangible results. However, to what extent the local people could enjoy China's contributions is questionable and dependent on a case-by-case, country-by-country investigation, which will be addressed in the case studies chapters. What's more, Chinese foreign aid projects are usually constructed by Chinese enterprises. Hence, the official assistance is transformed into a kind of corporate social responsibility with joint efforts between Chinese energy companies and construction enterprises. The companies conduct charity or other assistance programs in order to satisfy local communities and further expand their business. It both increases Chinese companies' awareness of giving back to the host country and helps to build a positive corporate image. At the same time, considering the underdeveloped market environment in both China and Africa, it is hard for companies to follow advanced corporate norms, add to this the fact that corporate social responsibility is a new term for many Chinese enterprises, and they tend to categorise charity as corporate social responsibility (CSR) while ignoring the protection of labour and environment, which was reflected in the interviews when subjects were asked about his/her company's responsibility to local people: all of them talked about charity, but none of them mentioned the creation of employment opportunities, nor the protection of labour safety, welfare and environment. Additionally, the dependence on Chinese corporations is unsustainable. The contributions to local communities rely on the companies' profit in the short run. In the long term, infrastructure construction will become less and less attractive to African countries as their economies develop. Take Angola as an example: the country was considered one of the most successful models of "oil for infrastructure" in Africa. Chinese infrastructure helped the country to finish its post-war reconstruction swiftly. But, as more infrastructures were built by Chinese companies, the country was reluctant to receive more infrastructure projects. Instead, it sought other financial support to fuel its economic development.

In addition, compared to the West, Chinese private companies and non-governmental organization (NGOS) were rarely seen in foreign aid area. The analysis suggested that United States Agency for International

Development (USAID) has closely cooperated with 3,500 US companies and 300 NGOS, as well as organisations in the recipient countries (USAID, 2012). US private companies had committed US$2.8 billion for foreign aid in 2000, and its pharmaceutical industry has shared US$0.8 billion, twice that of the World Health Organisation (USAID, 2012). At the same time, its NGOs have contributed more funds than Denmark, Norway and Sweden's ODA (as calculated by the figures provided by the OECD website and the USAID website). By comparison, China's private charity is largely lagging. For a private company in Africa, as a latecomer, the potential benefits of engaging in local charity are not worth investment without government support. Witness 20 said, as far as he knows, the reason for private companies to invest in Africa is mainly out of economic motives, and because the company may be operating on a very small scale, they haven't yet considered making investments to the local society. Meanwhile, China has no mature domestic NGO system, let alone one for foreign assistance. The credibility of Chinese NGOs has been challenged by scandal and non-transparency. China's non-governmental assistance to Africa is still underdeveloped. It should be noted that there does not exist any de facto NGOs in China. This is because, according to China's "Regulations on the Registration and Administration of Social Organisations", an NGO must first find a government or Party sponsor and get their approval to register. After its establishment, the sponsor must continue to play a supervisory role by carrying out annual reviews, approving budgets and staffing plans, and so forth. In this case, the NGOs in China act more like a quasi-governmental organisation, which shares the features of both government and private organisations.

The majority of Chinese NGOs are either government-organised NGOs or quasi-official NGOs, while individually organised NGOs initiated from the bottom-up are relatively small and less influential, sometimes illegal. Those large, national-level organisations receive most of the funding from the government. Meanwhile, their employees were assigned by the government, too. They predominantly play a role in facilitating cooperation with foreign NGOs, providing a channel for civil diplomacy. Although these organisations lack autonomy from government, in practice "the close connection with government is beneficial, allowing these NGOs to operate more effectively within the unique political, economic and social context" (Elizabeth, 1997).

As China enthusiastically pursued a presence in Africa, the NGOs set foot on the continent as well. Government-organised NGOs were pioneers as usual. In 2007, China's largest poverty reduction organisation, the China Foundation for Poverty Alleviation launched a series of assistance projects in Guinea, ranging from small amount credit loans, emergency rescue and health care for puerperal fever and newborn babies. From August 29–30, 2011, the first China-African Civil Forum was held in Nairobi, Kenya, with the joint support of the China NGO Network for International Exchanges and the Kenya NGO Coordination Board. Twenty Chinese NGOs[3] and more than two hundred representatives from African NGOs attended the forum.

However, during the forum, when compared to the African organisations, the Chinese NGOs showed less enthusiasm. The Chinese participants focused on discussing some principles or guidelines in terms of mutual dialogue and understanding, climate change and NGO development, while the African counterparts expected some more tangible results (ifeng, July 10, 2012).

This reflected the current situation of China-Africa NGOs. After some corruption scandals in Chinese national organisations, personal donations have significantly decreased. At the same time, there has been a lot of domestic pressure and doubts as to "why prioritise foreign countries' demands without solving the domestic problem first" (Observation from BBS). In this case, the government-led NGOs in China have been very prudent in their assistance for Africa. Enterprise-sourced NGOs performed more actively than the nationally-funded ones. In 2011, some entrepreneurs launched the China-African Project Hope in five African countries – Rwanda, Burundi, Kenya, Namibia and Tanzania. It promised to expand the famous Project Hope from China to Africa by establishing primary schools for local children. Since enterprises often become involved in assistance projects with the hope of gaining business opportunities, the cost of building a primary school is worth less to them. Therefore, some doubts remain, and there have been some scandals connected to these projects. The space for NGO development in Africa is therefore limited without central government support.

5.2.3 Conclusion

As analysed in the previous section, China has a different aid system to that of OECD countries. Although China's African assistance policy is made and authorised by the three official departments-MOFCOM, MOFA and China Exim Bank-the implementation of China's foreign aid policy relies on Chinese corporations mainly in terms of completed projects. Not only do the three major decision-making departments have their own agendas in mind, but the Chinese companies with their economic-driven nature often deviate from official African policy during the implementation process as well. Despite what outside observers believe, Beijing lacks monolithic control of all Chinese actors in Africa, nor does it have mature and independent NGOs to monitor the assistance projects. Hence, at the implementation level, the win-win situation advocated by Beijing is not always as smooth as pledged/promised. This section has explained the reasons for China not being fully responsible for its own side. The case studies chapters will further explain with the added consideration of Africa's environment.

5.3 Explanation of China's overseas economic system

5.3.1 An ambiguous classification of China's overseas actors

Beijing has maintained a close relationship with African countries and provided a large amount of investment to this continent. However, the people who worked on the "front line", and had a chance to communicate with local communities are far removed from the officials in Beijing, which means, although the central government may have a strategic African policy, it has to be implemented through economic-driven enterprises and local governments who prioritised their own local strategies. The "fragmented authoritarianism" appears more often in China's overseas business than its foreign aid. Regarding China-Africa economic activities, (it is hard to define whether it belonged to aid or to foreign investment), three kinds of actors worked on site within the fragmented system

1   State-owned enterprises mainly undertook the tasks of government-funded projects in infrastructure and public buildings.
2   provincial supported enterprises, often in competition with another province to promote its own exports to Africa.
3   while small-and medium-sized, mostly private firms entered the continent and focused on commodities and trade.

The classification above is ambiguous, as there are problems with identifying the role of SOEs and private firms, government agencies and non-government sectors in practice.

Between 1980 and 1990, China experienced a transition from radical Maoism, which was characterised by privatising state-owned and Township & Village Enterprises. However, it brought forth the issue of how to classify the state-owned enterprises. As Nolan has described it, the "ownership maze" (Nolan, 2005, p. 169). For instance, the old SOEs, namely "owned by all the people" (quanmin suoyou 全民所有) were sold at a very low price to the former enterprises' leaders or those who had connections with local governments during the reforms. In this case, the new owners were often relatives or friends of state officials. Although today the state or local governments hold less than 50% of the equity, which should be categorised as "private" in China, these firms often took advantage of their connections with governments for tender or policy support. Similarly, "many SOEs function as conduits for private gains", which means the people who profit from the enterprises sometimes are not only the owners of the firms but also government officials (Kaplinsky & Morris, 2009).

Due to their ambiguous identities, it is hard to distinguish between official and private ownership, and yet all the activities are credited to "China" as a whole, even if the central government's control over the players in question is limited. Especially for Chinese SOEs that have been involved in official aid projects in key sectors such as infrastructure, refining and telecommunications, it is difficult to separate foreign investment flows from other kinds of capital flows.

5.3.2 Various players in China-Africa economic links

China's investment in Africa has experienced a dramatic increase in this decade. The former vice minister of MOFCOM Sun Guangxiang has revealed that China had invested US$13 billion in Africa by the end of 2010, twenty times the 2003 level. It should be noted that the value has risen from a level of US$1.5 million in 1991 (ERA, October 2009). Chinese Ambassador to South Africa Zhong Jianhua also pointed out the annual return on investment (ROI) in China is around 3%–4%, whilst on the African continent it is 20% and in South Africa 19% (FOCAC, April 17, 2012). Despite these impressive figures, only half of the enterprises have successfully "gone out". A McKinsey Report estimated that 67% of Chinese firms failed in their overseas mergers and acquisitions, due to bankruptcy and unprofitability that is higher than the world average rate 50% (Xiaojuan, January 2, 2012). United Nations Conference on Trade and Development (UNCTAD) suggested that, although the investment was widely distributed across the continent, five countries (Sudan, Algeria, Zambia, Nigeria and South Africa) accounted for approximately half, which increased the vulnerability of their investment (Kaplinsky & Morris, 2009).

China is a latecomer to the continent. In the beginning, large SOEs owned by the State Council were the vanguards entering Africa. They took advantage of loans from policy banks and "operated under formal state-to-state agreements" (Kaplinsky & Morris, 2009). Initially serving the continent as an aid provider, those firms have gradually transformed into international contractors and developers who undertake the responsibility of seeking unexplored reserves and markets. The funds from national banks and preferential policies have facilitated these SOEs to combine investment with aid projects and further to gain access to politically risky markets. Therefore, as Lum and Fischer have argued, China has preferred "projects in countries, areas that developed multinational corporations have avoided", because the Chinese firms have more capability of taking risks with the financial support of the central government and preferred less competition from traditional players (Lum et al., 2009). At the same time, cheap internal labour and friendly relationships with African governments have nurtured Chinese firms' competitiveness in African markets. On the other hand, the Communist Party of China (CPC) Organisation Department is in charge of appointments and removal of senior personnel from the 118 SOEs under supervision by the State-Owned Asset Supervision and Administration Commission (SASAC). Theoretically, the central government and the large SOEs could work together as a team to achieve the central strategy of taking advantage of the underdeveloped African market and shaping those enterprises into internationally competitive multinational corporations.

However, ostensibly the government has called for the "going out" strategy and organised these leading enterprises (longtou qiye 龙 头 企 业) together to establish a national team for its foreign policy. In practice, the central government's policy not only spurred Chinese foreign economic activities but also reflected the enterprises' interests. In other words, Chinese enterprises involving in Africa are driven by various demands besides just following the central government's commands.

First, as mentioned above, the central government controls the careers of senior SOE managers. Additionally, "senior SOE managers can be promoted into government or Party positions, and cadres can be promoted into positions of influence in SOEs" (Fan, Morck, & Yeung, 2012, p. 3). Sometimes, the senior manager of an SOE could be assigned to its competitor by the central government-such as happened on April 8, 2011, when the central government assigned Fu Chengyu, the former chairman of China National Offshore Oil Corporate (CNOOC) to China Petroleum and Chemical Corp (SINOPEC), while replacing Fu with the Wang Yilin, the former manager of China National Petroleum Corp. (CNPC). On the same day, former manager of SINOPEC Su Shulin was promoted to Party Leader of Fujian Province (People's Daily, April 8, 2011). Notwithstanding, what the government can replace is a position, not the interests of these SOEs. Zhao Zhongxiu has argued that evidence shows the SOEs' influence over central decisions and even has an impact on the central government's grand strategy. For instance, the central government had to put an end to its negotiations with the Gulf States over free trade zones due to a conflict of interest with SINOPEC. In light of "mutual benefits", the Gulf States would like to be involved in the refinery industry around the downstream Yangtze River, in exchange for Chinese companies entering their textile and other light industry markets. This "win-win" situation, advocated for by the central government, has been called off as SINOPEC wasn't prepared to share the domestic refinery market with foreign competition (Z. Zhao, November 24, 2011).

Furthermore, the promotion to higher positions within SOE management or into government and party positions is based on meritocracy. Promotions are outcomes of an extremely competitive tournament based substantially on quantitative, if imperfect and pliable, performance metrics (H. Li, Meng, Wang, & Zhou, 2008; Lü, 2000). Therefore, the managers of SOEs tend to prefer economic profits while sacrificing some other, less important elements in the evaluation criteria, such as loyalty to the central policy, efficiency, environmental protection, labour laws, and local community relations. Unfortunately, when it comes to Africa, this economic motivation often doesn't cohere with the original target set by the central government. In practice, the central assignment and "leader saying counts" (yiyantang 一言堂) management style may lead top managers to prioritise personal gains and corporate economic profits rather than political and diplomatic strategy. Even worse, recently many scandals have been revealed regarding SOEs' high-level corruption, improper decision-making, illegal fund raising-such as the China Aviation Oil incident, huge deficits of China National Cotton Reserves Corporation (CNCRC), the former chairman Capital Airports Holding Company Li Yingping's embezzlement, Chen Tonghai, the former chairman of SINOPEC corruption/theft of 190 million RMB, Kang Rixin's economic crime during his leading the China's National Nuclear Corporation. Their personal interest frequently deviated from the central government policy.

Third, although the 118 large SOEs were supervised by SASAC, each corporation has their own subsidiary companies and provincial branches, while their subsidiary companies hold other companies as further sub-sidiary branches as well. Take SINOPEC as an example; it has 16 oilfield companies, 31 refinery factories, 26 distribution companies, eight design and construction firms, nine research institutions, and ten others, includ-ing eight newspapers and magazines, and 12 overseas branches, let alone its 'grandson' subsidiary companies. Different from state-owned, these are joint-stock companies which suggests the central government can hardly control their operations. Witness 23 revealed that those subsidiary compa-nies usually operate independently, and the leaders of these companies lack the ambition to be promoted, because the subsidiary company may offer better pay/compensation.

Alongside the large SOEs owned by the central government and account-able to the State Council, "the provincially owned firms often reflect the initiatives of their decentralized state administrations and often build on regional diaspora" (Kaplinsky & Morris, 2009). Because many of those entrepreneurs rely critically on local connections, their CEOs and boards benefit from the advice of their dedicated enterprise-level Party Secre-taries and Party Committees (Fan et al., 2012). Regarding China-African economic activities where the decision-making is highly centralized, pro-vincial governments and local party leaders remain significant in political, economic relations. Benefiting from local relations, provincial companies came to Africa early through extended connections, such as sister-city and industrial zones. Generally speaking, two bureaus – the provincial Foreign Affairs Office (FAO) and Foreign Trade and Economic Cooperation Com-mission (FTECC) – have the responsibility for implementing the national foreign policy, locally supervised by MOFA and MOFCOM. They collab-orated with provincial Asset Supervision and Administration Commission who took control of local SOEs and branches of national foreign trade com-panies for foreign economic activities. Despite the fact that national SOEs were pioneers in Africa and mostly engaged in resource-rich countries, SOEs of provincial and municipal levels, especially those from south-east provinces, were mainly contributing to exports in the form of manufactured goods ranging from machinery, textiles and garments, to electronics, and accounted for one-quarter of China's outward Foreign Direct Investment (FDI) to Africa. Due to local protectionism and competition, these local SOEs served not only as a project builder or aid provider, but also investor and exporter who, to some extent, have local autonomy (Z. Chen & Jian, 2009). As Witness 3 pointed out, for those central policies that related to national interests, the implementer-local government and agency-may over-implement if they will benefit locally, but if not they may under-implement. For example, the central government has actively responded to African countries' trade deficits, specifically to those least developed countries (LDCs) with rare resource reserves. Since 2004, it has gradually offered zero-tariffs to the LDCs to promote their exports to China through FOCAC. During a June 2006 visit to South Africa, Premier Wen Jiabao announced that China would impose voluntary export restrictions on the export of textiles to South Africa (Program for Environmental and Regional Equity [PERE], 2007). However, Witness 21 says until now the textiles industry is still playing a major role in China's exports to South Africa because it is a large destination of manufacture goods from South-east Province. And the provincial companies have right to cancel or change the restrictions. Given the fact that as ambitious traders and investors, most of the provinces have their own motivations and priorities instead of the central one, which contributes to China's trade surplus with Africa and brings an intense competition with their African counterparts.

The potential contradiction exists not only between provincial economic demands and national objectives but also among the interests of provinces themselves. The Chinese coastal provinces pursued economic growth through export of low-technical manufacturing goods as more high-technical goods could not find an African market; on the other hand, the inland provinces were also seeking low-technical goods markets bringing the two into competition. But Beijing lacks a mechanism for coordinating the fragmented actors from each province. Due to the lateral links, provincial companies formed a better team than the national level. When the pioneering firms settled in Africa, they had to seek sources for parts and equipment. Unfortunately, most of the African countries have a weak supply chain and did not have the necessary infrastructure. Consequently, they have to seek supply from other Chinese companies, especially from their same province with close connections and gradually-formed trade zones. As a result, some coastal provinces, such as Zhejiang, Guangdong, Fujian, Jiangsu and Shandong, have established a more mature clustering of business than others (Z. Chen & Jian, 2009).

The Chinese government has launched a series of measures to support domestic innovative small and medium-sized enterprises, while tightly restricting high-energy-consuming and high-emission industries (two-high industry) at home. In order to upgrade its economic development mode, according to MOF, China spent a total of 26.8 billion yuan (US$ 4.4 billion) to support the innovation by small and medium-sized enterprises from 1999 to 2013 (China Daily, October 26, 2013). During the same period, the state council has issued the Plan for Eliminating Outdated and Excess Capacity in Key Industries to regulate the two-high industries (People's Daily, October 15, 2013). This domestic policy has an indirect impact on Africa. As the analysis indicated, due to the shortage of resource, excess products, labour cost and pollution, many small and medium-sized enterprises in high-energy-consuming and high emission industries have chosen to move into Africa or have dumped their low-quality products into African markets in order to survive (Z. Li, 2007), which has brought some unwelcome private firms to the continent. It should be noted that the private contingent is comprised of a limited number of very large corporations and numerous medium and small companies, which have increasingly become key players in China-Africa economic exchanges. Since we have noted the close connections between large private corporations and the government, the private firms here refer to the medium and small ones who "act autonomously from Chinese government's policy frameworks and existing bilateral arrangements" (Gu, 2009). As Gu revealed in her research, few small and medium companies entered Africa following Beijing's "going out" strategy. Instead, they held a strong entrepreneurial motivation. Some of them have already established mature operations processes in China, while also extending themselves into Africa where there are fewer energy, environmental restrictions. Others started their business on the African continent through pouring Chinese imports, sometimes through illegal ways. For them, business was built on family or community links. These Chinese immigrants become a big threat to African communities, especially in terms of work opportunities.

Compared to SOEs, the central government's control over these groups is even weaker. A manager from a private company in Africa has a typical explanation for the gap between policy and its implementation: "We heard there are some policies, but we do not know what they are about (Gu, 2009)". Witness 2's information echoes the manager, and complained that "they (the Chinese companies) only came for help from the embassy when they got into trouble". It revealed that due to information asymmetry and weak policy implementation capability, the top-down methods had been deviated or neglected by these private companies. For instance, the central government has launched some tangible measures by establishing Small-Medium Enterprises International Market Development Fund to support qualified private companies. According to MOFCOM, 76,000 out of 40 million firms have benefited from this fund with a maximum amount of US$10,000 respectively. But in all the interviews with owners of small and medium companies, and through the observation of the QQ chat groups and BBS, none have confirmed they or their counterparts in Africa have ever taken advantage of these funds. At the same time, none of them have attended any seminar or training session on foreign investment laws, culture and communications. It could infer that Beijing's funds have not been fully taken advantage of by the private companies in Africa or the companies that operated in Africa are not qualified. And the entrepreneurs in Africa have not been well informed about Beijing's policy in Africa. In all these circumstances, it indicates that Beijing has a weak capability to control its agencies and actors in Africa.

As a result, the medium and small enterprises came to Africa mostly on their own volition, which suggests that they often performed more oriented for profit gain. Their employees were considered to work much harder than their counterparts, while the employers were more likely to take the risk of doing business in risky areas or the markets where profits are very low, and supply chains are weak. At the same time, they have to try anything to limit their costs due to the increasingly fierce competition between Chinese firms. It could be said that these types of companies can perform more flexibly in the local conditions and provide affordable localized products and service for ordinary people. However, on the other hand, the low cost and low-quality industries have become a threat to their newly emerging local counterparts. From this perspective, these types of enterprises can hardly meet the expectations of the African countries' demands, in terms of skills transfer, social and environmental development.

Because of the lack of necessary African market knowledge, most private firms tend to use the same management style as they were familiar with in China. They take for granted overtime hours, poor working conditions, disrespect for intellectual property, and the logic of sacrificing the environment for development. For community relations, they prefer to deal with bureaucrats. Even worse, some small firms closed down by the Chinese government due to environmental pollution or poor quality products have relocated to Africa where they enjoy lower scrutiny and less development. (Observed from the QQ chat group) Their poor behaviour has largely violated China's image as a whole. Witness 5 has argued that "There are hundreds of thousands of Chinese people in Africa, but there is no national responsibility awareness among individual people" as a result, for various players in Africa, China's "image is not very good".

The three types of enterprises in Africa have reflected the key players' attitudes towards the continent. Their features of them can be found in Table 5.2.

Table 5.2 Different types of Chinese enterprises in Africa

Ownership	Central state	Province/municipality	Private
Time and motivation of entering Africa	Since the foundation of PRC implemented Chinese aid projects; Mid-1990s resource and market seeking	1980s implemented state to state contracts; 2000 actively involved in economic cooperation zones	2000 African market opportunity and high competitive domestic market
Main sector	Resources and infrastructure	Manufacturing, wholesale	Manufacturing and retail
Fund	Central government; Export–Import Bank (EXIM) Bank	Central development fund; provincial and municipal financial support	Self-financed
Connections	Accountable to State Council	Central government and provincial government	Act Independently of government
Transparency	Relative well-documented; Some has released CSR report	Not always transparent	Only through some interviews

(*Continued*)

Ownership	Central state	Province/municipality	Private
Commitments to Africa	Technological, managerial skills transfers; infrastructure/ Public sector buildings	Supply chains; economic cooperation zones	Employment opportunity; Affordable products
Negative impact on Africa	Connive at the autarchy, bad governance and corruption	Take advantage of local export opportunity, such as African Growth and Opportunity Act (AGOA) and threaten the development of some local industry	Bad products; Bad conditions; Disrespect intellectual property Quality working locally

Source: Author.

5.4 Conclusion

In summary, as Shaun Breslin noted, "some non-China specialists still seem somewhat surprised to discover that China is not a monolithic political structure with all power emanating from Beijing". In fact, many actors with their own agendas have inserted themselves between the policy formulation and policy implementation (Breslin, 2007). In theory, the power of the key actors in Africa was authorized by the central government; however, the key actors' interests have affected policy implementation. In other words, even if the central government may have a broad African policy, it has to be achieved through Chinese enterprises with economic-driven natures and officials with growing autonomy who may not share the central vision (Taylor, 2009). Both assistance teams and enterprises have their own motivations and flexibility, but as for an outsider, their misbehaviour in the continent shaped the image of China as a whole.

Notes

1 Non-profit entities (Shiye danwei 事业单位), is not a governmental executive, but it has a similar function. The administrative ranking of the Bureau of International Economic Cooperation is bureau-level, which is same to the Department of Aid to Foreign Countries.

2 Other official flows are official sector transactions which do not meet the ODA criteria, e.g.: (i) Grants to developing countries for representational or essentially commercial purposes; (ii) Official bilateral transactions intended to promote development but having a grant element of less than 25%; (iii) Official bilateral transactions, whatever their grant element, that are primarily export-facilitating in purpose. This category includes, by definition, export credits extended directly to an aid recipient by an official agency or institution ("official

direct export credits"); (iv) The net acquisition by governments and central monetary institutions of securities issued by multilateral development banks at market terms; (v) Subsidies (grants) to the private sector to soften its credits to developing countries; (vi) Funds in support of private investment.

3 It included some large government-owned NGOs, for instance, All China Women's Federation, the Chinese People's Association for Friendship with Foreign countries, China Association for Science and Technology, China Federation of Literary and Art, Chinese Association for International Understanding, Chinese People's Association for Peace and Disarmament and so forth.

Part 2
Case studies

6 Sudan

Francis et al. argue, "No external power has as much at stake in … [Sudan and South Sudan], nor has any other country been as deeply engaged in the region over the past decade as China" (Francis, Madasamy, Sokkary, & You, 2012, p. 15). Being an important player in this region, China's involvement is critical to the war-torn country. The analysis of China's responsibility in Sudan illustrates not only an assessment of China's impact on African states that suffer from serious civil war and crises but also offers a typical example of the international and host country's influence on China being responsible (or not).

This chapter begins with an introductory background of the conflicts in Darfur and South Sudan, which clarify the fundamental reasons behind the current conflicts and China's growing interests in this area. The second section describes the three most influential factors in shaping China's responsibility policy in Sudan as responses to the three dynamic factors of international responsibility discussed in Chapter 3. It highlights the influence of "international pressure" and "the host country's situation" on China's responsibility in Sudan and argues that, despite international criticism, China's interests do not always collide with the external demands. The third section discusses China's limited role in resolving the crises in Sudan using the cases of Darfur and South Sudan, and argues that, although the China-Sudan relationship is asymmetric in favour of China, Beijing's capability to shoulder responsibility in Sudan and the effect of its Sudan policy is constrained by the environment in Sudan and the oppositions forces in Sudan. Finally, this chapter will employ the cases of Darfur and South Sudan to test hypotheses III – the gap between China's Sudan policy and various players in China-Sudan relations, which is the main reason for China being not fully responsible. The Darfur case reflects China's evolving foreign policy interpretation towards the traditional "non-interference" principle and a transition in diplomatic relations with Sudan. Meanwhile, the case of South Sudan reveals China's pragmatic agenda in protecting its foreign economic interests. But, in terms of implementation, the rebel group in Darfur failed to recognise China's developing Sudan policy, and China was also drawn into the oil impasse between Sudan and South Sudan. Not only was its international reputation damaged by the humanitarian crisis in Darfur, but also it has limited capability to protect its oil supply in the region.

6.1 Background introduction – conflicts in Sudan

Sudan achieved independence relative peacefully in 1955. However, the state inherited many problems after the hasty withdrawal of the British. The Anglo-Egyptian colonists left Sudan with a fragile government ruled by a handful of Arabic elites. The interests of tribal communities, a hardly merged north-south region; marginalised black Africans in the South; and a one-crop economy with weak infrastructure and education have hindered Sudan's peaceful development ever since its independence. Although the north and south signed the Addis Ababa peace agreement in 1972, which ended the first civil war in Sudan, the conflicts – such as for national identity, religion, land and water – are far from resolved. In 1983, President Nimairi instituted Islamic Sharia Law as "the sole guiding force behind the law of the Sudan" (Lesch, 1998, p. 55). Afterward, the government split southern Sudan into three provinces (Equatoria, Bahr al-Ghazal and Upper Nile), which was aimed at weakening the south and prevent it from forming a united sovereignty. Unfortunately, this triggered the second civil war, which lasted about 22 years. Both conflicts "left over two million Sudanese dead and uprooted millions more" (Large & Patey, 2011, p. 1).

With international mediation, Khartoum and the Sudan People's Liberation Movement/Army (SPLM/A) signed a Comprehensive Peace Agreement in 2005 and conducted a referendum after six years. When the southern people voted for independence in 2011, the once-largest, yet also one of the least developed states in Africa was divided into two countries. However, this was not the end of the problems for the two countries, as the demarcation of the border between north and south, the status of the areas of Abyei, the Nuba Mountains and the Southern Blue Nile, and financial arrangements have disrupted the fragile peace from time to time. Tensions in Darfur remain unresolved. Oil-production, revenues and the use of the pipeline to Port Sudan continue to cause unrest. In summary, the conflicts in Sudan are multifaceted, where the marginalised areas and people with different ethnic, religious and tribal backgrounds fight for key resources (oil and water) and freedom.

Against such a background, the traditional players put strict sanctions on Bashir's government. China was initially reluctant to support international military intervention and economic sanctions. After the situation had deteriorated, with increasing violations of human rights, and mounting international pressure, China started to pressure Bashir to cooperate with international political efforts. Different from the traditional donors, China attributed Sudan's crisis as a conflict of interests, which should be resolved through economic development. The following sections will discuss China's impact on Sudan, and its limitations in solving the crisis.

6.2 Shaping China's responsibility in Sudan

6.2.1 *China's motivation*

I Politically

Ali argued there are two main periods in the history of China-Sudan relations: before and after oil (Ali, 2006). He distinguished China's involvement before and after the 1990s, which highlighted the importance of oil in
China-Sudan relations. Oil is an important factor in bilateral relations, but
China's responsibility in Sudan is motivated by its interests in this country,
which has developed from a largely political consideration to a strategic
and multi-faceted engagement, rather than oil thirst. First of all, the two
countries have a close diplomatic relationship. Beijing and Khartoum have
conducted frequent exchanges between senior leaders on party-to-party levels between the Communist Party of China (CPC) and National Congress
Party (NCP). Despite the fact that South Sudan discovered substantial oil
deposits[1] during the late 1970s and early 1980s, China was involved in the
country much earlier than the 1970s. At the same time, China's financial
aid, loans and grants after the discovery of Sudan's oil were invested in the
construction, manufacturing, healthcare and agriculture sectors as well
(Nour, 2010). Furthermore, China's increasing investment in Sudan, along
with the close relationship with Khartoum in the 1990s, was not simply
driven by China's need to secure oil supplies, but by political opportunity.
In the 1990s, the Western governments sanctioned Sudan due to its support
of terrorism.[2] According to the US's Department of State, it imposed economic, trade and financial sanctions on Sudan and banned United States
(US) companies from doing business in Sudan in the 1990s. For example,
the Marathon Oil[3] Corporation – based in Texas – was forced to give up all
activities in Sudan in 1985 due to the outbreak of the civil war (Dralle, 2008).
Another example is Chevron: the well-known company from the United
States started its oil business in Sudan in 1974 and had to quit in 1992 due
to the sanctions imposed by the US government (Rone, 2003, p. 123). Some
other companies left due to Sudan's deteriorating security conditions. For
instance, Talisman Energy, a Canadian oil and gas company, has withdrawn
its oil business from Sudan (Dralle, 2008). The company's annual report revealed that European companies such as Total (a French oil company) and
Lundin (Swedish) suspended their operations in the unstable country. Along
with investment traditional donors' foreign aid has been suspended. Since
1993, the International Monetary Fund (IMF) and World Bank – Sudan's
largest donors in 1970s and 1980s – suspended their assistance to Sudan due
to the accumulation of Sudan's debt and deterioration of the relationship
with the international financial institutions. Large numbers of western companies' absence have created an oil export vacuum for China to exploit, as
well as some other Asian countries – for instance, Malaysia and India. At

the same time, the foreign aid from traditional western donors has largely declined, which forced Khartoum to find alternative sources of financial assistance. China had been isolated by the West because of the Tiananmen Square Crisis, and was in need of international support. China's increasing economic ambition and the calling for "going abroad" by the central government required it to explore new markets. An Agreement on Economic and Technical Cooperation was signed with Sudan in 1990, and another agreement on Economic, Trade and Technical Cooperation followed in 1992. But the pioneering China National Petroleum Corporate (CNPC) did not enter the Sudanese oil industry until 1995. As a result, one could say that political interests and economic strategy put the two states together, rather than pure energy thirst.

II Economically

Sudan met about 5% of China's oil supply [needs] and ranked the sixth largest supplier to China before the secession of South Sudan. Oil investment also brought a series of Chinese businesses to Sudan, which positioned it as China's third largest trading partner in Africa. Yun described Khartoum as "a friendly, resource rich state" to China, and "a long-term overseas oil supply base and an arena to support the global development of Chinese corporations" (Large, 2009). Driven by political, energy and economic motivations, China's agenda in Sudan is to protect its citizens and facilitate its overseas investment.

III Diplomatically

Further to political and economic interests, along with deteriorating crises in Darfur and South Sudan, China has an increasing awareness of its international reputation in Sudan. Despite the fact that Sudan supplied 5% of China's oil, and received large amounts of Chinese investment in its infrastructure, when compared to China's foreign strategy as whole, especially at a time when international society was strongly criticising Beijing for its position on Darfur, and Khartoum's non-cooperation and inability to control its territory, China did not intend to sacrifice its international reputation in support of the Bashir government.

Three explanations illustrate the combined interests of China in Sudan. The first is to protect its citizens and economic investment in Sudan. The second is to play a more helpful part in engaging with a solution of conflicts. Both of these offer a self-interest-based reason for China to promote stability and peace in Sudan. Considering China's traditional support for Bashir, and its large amounts of investment in northern Sudan, Beijing tends to believe in the proper and legitimate role of the Bashir regime in maintaining stability and avoiding the fragmentation of the state. Therefore, Beijing is very cautious about external intervention in the country and is concerned that international sanctions may catalyse "regime change" without any improvement. But, on the other hand, international society's and Bashir's failure to attain any improvement on the crisis pressured China to rethink its relationship with Khartoum.

6.2.2 Sudan and South Sudan's demands

The government of Sudan receives half of its revenues from oil, while the government of South Sudan receives 98% from oil. In this case, Francis et al. argue that Sudan and South Sudan may need China more than China needs them, as China is the largest consumer of the region's oil (Francis et al., 2012). Sudan, after its limited Gross Domestic Product (GDP) growth in the 1990s has made slight progress with "a corresponding average annual growth rate in per capita income of 4.0%" (Maglad, 2008). It is worth noting that the growth during this period largely relied on agriculture. By the end of the 1990s, it accounted for about 50% of total GDP. Agriculture and related industries employed about 80% of the labour force. As a result, the agriculture industry was key to the country's economic well-being and the maintenance of the living standards for a large proportion of the population. When its agricultural industry suffered from stagnancy and drawback, the government had to seek another other supportive industry. After Sudanese President Omar al-Bashir visited China in 1995, China's national oil company CNPC launched cooperation in the oil industry between the two countries, which fulfilled Sudan's longstanding ambition to become an oil exporter. After Bashir's trip, CNPC signed an agreement with the Sudanese government to develop Block 6 in the Muglad Basin. The next year, CNPC quickly won the contract to develop Block 1/2/4 in the region and formed a joint operating company – the Greater Nile Petroleum Operating Company (GNPOC) the year after (CNPC, 2010). In return, China built a 1,506 km oil pipeline from the oil fields to the Port of Sudan, which enabled Sudan's transformation from an oil importer to an oil exporter. In 2000, construction of the Khartoum Refinery, with an annual crude processing capacity of 2.5 million tons, was completed. The operation of this refinery brought an end to Sudan's long history of dependence on imported oil products (CNPC, 2010). Production of oil has brought changes to Sudan's external trade and trading structure. With the boom of oil production, oil exports earned US$276 million and accounted for 35% of total exports in 1999. It rose to US$1.3 billion in 2000, representing 75% of exports, and resulted in a trade surplus of US$254 million after decades of trade deficits (Maglad, 2008).

Apart from oil, Sudan ranked as one of the largest Chinese Foreign Direct Investment (FDI) recipients in Africa, with a 46% share of China's net non-financial direct investment in Africa as a whole in 2004, and 22% of accumulated net overseas direct investment in Africa by the end of 2005 (Large, 2008). According to the statistics of the Bank of Sudan, China's share of Sudan's overall imports has increased from 8% in 2002 and 1% in

2004 to 20.8% in 2006, mainly focusing on the manufacturing industry, such as machinery, transport equipment, textiles and chemicals. The manufacturing investment in Sudan has stimulated the relevant industrial chain, such as material, service industry and equipment. Additionally, there has been a strong Chinese involvement in Sudan's infrastructure and construction sectors, as in other African countries. The China Exim Bank, together with a number of Middle Eastern investors, has underwritten the construction of the approximately $1.5billion Merowe Dam (Schiere, Ndikumana, & Walkenhorst, 2011). The Harbin Power Plant Engineering Company completed the second of the planned four phases of the El Gaili Power Plant in 2007. Transport is another important sector, and China has been involved in the construction of highways, bridges and railways. In 2007, the China Railway Engineering Corporation and its subsidiary Trans-Tech Engineering won a US$1billion contract to build a 700 km-long railway in Sudan, between Khartoum and Port Sudan (Foster et al., 2009). Sudan also served as a major recipient of China's foreign assistance. According to the statistics provided by the Sudan Ministry of National Cooperation Report 2008, the aid and development assistance to Sudan amounted to US$3427.2 million between 1997 and 2008 (Nour, 2010).

Despite the asymmetric economic relations between China and Sudan/ South Sudan, the two governments have been far from passive recipients of China's political and economic largesse. Instead, they attempted to incorporate China into their own foreign strategies. Initially, Khartoum needed Beijing's support for its defensive diplomatic tactics among international players. For example, it requested China not to allow international intervention and sanction. Nafi Ali Nafi, assistant and adviser to the president and deputy president for political affairs of the NCP, openly criticised China when he asked, "Why is China waiting to use the right of veto in the face of unfair resolutions that target its friends?" (Ahmed, 2010, p. 8) After the secession of South Sudan, Khartoum used political and economic pressures and expected China to continue supporting the NCP and hinder South Sudan's interests in new oil-related infrastructure that might by-pass the existing route through the North. On the other hand, Juba didn't trust Beijing due to its historical stance with the North, but it wanted China to pressure Khartoum for a reasonable deal in the oil revenue distribution and foreign assistance to this newly established country. In April 2012, South Sudanese President Kiir visited Beijing requesting development funds and proposed plans to build a new pipeline to export oil from the newly independent state (Waal, February 7, 2013).

Besides the contradicting demands from Sudan and South Sudan, there are other voices within Sudanese society. The central government in Khartoum struggled over control of its territory and resources, suggesting that there was a huge gap between the central governments' interests and that of local communities. The diverse local interests should not be neglected. The attacks targeting Chinese oil operations and Chinese workers revealed opposition groups' dissatisfaction with China's close relations with Khartoum, after being marginalised in Sudan's political discourse and economic distribution. They held that China was liable for the NCP's violent battle against insurgency in Darfur.

6.2.3 International expectation

On the Darfur issue, international society has placed significant pressure on China. European Union (EU) ministers of foreign affairs called for China's more active involvement in solving the conflicts during the 8th Asia–Europe Meeting in Germany, in May 2007 (NetEase, May 28, 2007). At the same time, more than a hundred members of the United Kingdom (UK) Parliament sent a message to Chinese President Hu Jintao, on October 29, 2007, appealing to China to review its policy towards Sudan and to try to convince the Sudanese government to stop attacks against civilians, disarm its militias, co-operate with the International Criminal Court (ICC), and facilitate relief operations (Ahmed, 2010, p. 18). Western celebrities and politicians added their voices to calls for a boycott of the Beijing 2008 Olympics to push China into using its leverage on Khartoum (Sudan Tribune, April 1, 2007). Later, the European parliament sanctioned Chinese oil company CNPC over its unwillingness to pressure Sudan to halt violence in Darfur (Sudan Tribune, March 18, 2008). Under this international pressure, Beijing responded with a more cooperative and effective approach, because Chinese decision-makers had been aware that its policy towards the Khartoum government would affect the wider interests of China as a responsible stakeholder in the international community. EU Special Representative for Sudan and South Sudan Dame Rosalind Marsden clearly listed the EU's core concerns in Sudan and South Sudan, which included peace, security, stability, democratisation, good governance, human rights, and humanitarian and development assistance (European Union Committee, June 14, 2011). As for China's role in this process, Doug Bandow, a senior fellow at Washington's Cato Institute, said, "If they (the Chinese) see a practical reason to try to solve the Sudan problem, well the U.S. and the Europeans also want to solve that. We can work together as opposed to being at odds." (Stearns, May 10, 2012).

6.2.4 Discussions on shaping China's responsibility in Sudan (South Sudan)

Among the three major influential factors on China's responsibility in Sudan, two external issues have pushed Beijing to reconsider its traditional "non-interference" policy that it has followed when dealing with most African countries and also its close relationship with the Bashir regime. The first significant episode was international pressure, notably a campaign named "the Genocide Olympics" to boycott the 2008 Beijing Olympic Games, due to China's resistance to a United Nations (UN) Security Council resolution condemning the Bashir Government over Darfur crisis. The second was Darfurian the attack on Chinese oil operations in Defra, Kordofan in October 2007, by the rebel Justice and Equality Movement, which also issued an ultimatum to Beijing to withdraw from Sudan within one week. It made China aware of the gap between its approach to Sudan with the politics of "non-interference", the provision of aid with "no-strings" (economics), and its role as a responsible stakeholder in Sudan. In response to the international expectations and the appeals from Sudan's opposition forces, China showed a willingness to develop its Sudan policy with a flexible interpretation of its long-term "non-interference" foreign strategy. It became more active in trying to persuade the Khartoum regime to cooperate with the international community. President Hu Jintao pressured Sudanese President Bashir on the humanitarian crisis in Darfur, and urged Sudan's cooperation with the UN on his visit to Khartoum in 2007. Beijing also appointed a full-time envoy, Liu Guijin, tasked with assisting in the resolution of the Darfur crisis (Abramowitz & Kolieb, June 5, 2007). It revealed China's strategy in Africa as not simply driven by national economic interests; instead, it is a combined calculation of various factors, including oil security, economic benefits, and also a responsible image and political influence. It would not blindly grab energy or economic profits at the cost of its international reputation. The Chinese government has shown some willingness to change its approach when faced with international pressure or local dissatisfaction. Therefore, even if it is not realistic to expect China to change fundamentally its foreign policy, there is still space to encourage and push China to cooperate with the traditional actors on Sudan for the mediation of conflicts and humanitarian assistance. Large concluded that the broadly social constructivist explanation for China in Sudan as "external advocacy catalys[ing] a normative evolution in Beijing towards a more constructive engagement on Sudan" (Large, 2009, p. 612).

6.3 China's capability and limitations in Sudan

All the motivation above may account for the dynamics of China's engagement at the policy level. It would also be useful to look at how the motivations work/appear on the ground in Sudan. To assess China's responsibility in Africa, it is necessary to look at the situation in the host country. As for Sudan, the central government is unable to exert effective control over all of its territory. The interests and demands within Sudanese society are diverse, which increases the complexity of China's role. This section will discuss China's constraints in seeking a responsible role in Sudan, including Darfur and Sudan-South Sudan issues

6.3.1 Darfur

As mentioned in the previous section, China, with significant political and economic ties to Khartoum, has been seriously criticised by international actors and local Sudanese opposition forces. They have accused Beijing of unconditionally supporting the Bashir regime, which undermined international resolutions on Darfur conflicts. However, far from benefiting from the close ties with Khartoum, China was in an uncomfortable position and paid a considerable price for Darfur issues.

I China's influence on Khartoum is limited

Since the outbreak of the Darfur crisis in 2003, China has defended the stance for the Sudanese government by arguing that the conflicts were Sudan's internal affairs and external intervention would lead the conflicts to become internationalized. However, international pressure calling for China to adopt a "responsible stakeholder" role in international affairs pushed Beijing to change its position on Darfur, and become more cooperative with other major powers. After that, China began a serious of diplomatic efforts to urge the Bashir government to improve the humanitarian situation in the Darfur region by assigning special envoys and abstaining from the UN's resolution of international intervention in Darfur. At the same time, Beijing tried to persuade Khartoum to "stop the killing and make a real effort to solve the crisis, and not to confront the international community through a hard-line approach or publicity only" (Ahmed, 2010, p. 7). But Khartoum ignored the pressures from Beijing and continued to conduct aggressive policies to arm [the] Janjaweed in Darfur while using oil as a bargaining chip to lobby Beijing for further support. Despite the opposition and rejection from Khartoum, China put forward stronger pressures. In November 2006, Wang Guangya, Chinese ambassador to the UN, made important behind-the-scenes interventions to secure the Sudanese government's agreement to the "Annan Plan", which called for an expanded UN peacekeeping role in Darfur (ICG, April 17, 2009). The Chinese government made further efforts on the Darfur issue during President Hu Jintao's visit to Khartoum in February 2007. He encouraged Sudan President Bashir to show flexibility and allow the deployment of the AU/UN hybrid force. Chinese public statements about the need for a "comprehensive ceasefire" and an acceleration of "the political negotiation process" involving rebel non-signatories to the Abuja Accord, plus the need for humanitarian assistance, were revealing. President Hu Jintao is reported to have told President Bashir that "Darfur is a part of Sudan and you have to resolve this problem" (McDoom, February 2, 2007). Later, Beijing appointed Assistant Foreign Minister Zhai Jun as a special envoy – and later, in May, appointed Ambassador Liu Guijin as a special representative for Darfur, upgrading China's diplomatic role over Darfur.

Sudanese officials responded in anger: Nafi Ali Nafi, assistant and adviser to the president and deputy president for political affairs of the NCP, refused to accept the international resolution and China's advocacy of international peacekeeping and openly criticised China when he asked, "Why is China waiting to use the right of veto in the face of unfair resolutions that target its friends?" (Ahmed, 2010, p. 8) The official spokesman of the Sudanese MFA, Ali al-Sadig, also expressed his anxiety over China's close cooperation with the US. Al-Sadig said: "China is a strategic ally of the Sudan. It should work with the Sudan, through the systematic diplomatic dialogue between us, and any American move towards Beijing is fruitless." (Ahmed, 2010, p. 9) Moreover, the Sudanese government escalated its military actions and bombarded the Jebel Moon area in western Sudan, which resulted in more killings and further displacement of the region's population (BBC, May 15, 2010). The statement from the Sudanese government revealed that, although China is an important ally to Khartoum, its pressures on Bashir regime were limited. China's mediation role between the international community and Sudanese government failed to persuade the Bashir regime to conduct a more contributive approach to control the situation in Darfur. In contrast, Khartoum felt angry about Beijing's changing policy and refused to cooperate with Beijing and facilitate an international intervention.

II The criticism of oppositions in Darfur to China's stance

Even though China made considerable progress in urging Khartoum to improve the humanitarian situation in Darfur, the crisis deteriorated. Therefore, most of the rebellions failed to acknowledge China's commitment; instead, they saw China as being in line with the NCP and served as an obstacle to the resolution to the conflict. Minni Minnawi, the senior presidential assistant of the Sudanese president (who is also the leader of the SLA and a signatory of the May 2006 Abuja Peace Agreement) declared that the NCP ignored the needs of the people of Darfur and, if the "NCP continues to ignore these needs, a return to war would likely be an option. The DPA is implemented only 5%" (Abdelrahman, December 30, 2009). They complained that China ignored their leadership and representatives in this region. Furthermore, Hu Jintao's visit to Sudan in 2007 to pressure Khartoum was interpreted as to evidence that China "supports the Khartoum regime without caring about the war crimes committed by it in Darfur, and that [China] continues to provide the international political cover for Sudan to continue its massacres" (Ahmed, 2010, p. 16). China's proposal to send a peacekeeping force as part of a joint UN and African Union mission to Darfur was rejected by the rebels. The key Justice and Equality Movement (JEM) rebel group accused China of being complicit in the Darfur conflict. Following the arrival of the engineers, JEM leader Khalil Ibrahim advocated for the removal of the 135 Chinese peacekeepers from the Sudanese region, and said that they would not allow the Chinese into areas controlled by their forces, because oil sold to the Chinese was being used to fund the government's operations in Darfur (BBC, November 24, 2007).

The criticism from rebel groups in Darfur grew from condemnation of China's policies to the threat of attack against Chinese economic interests in Sudan. In October 2007, JEM, led by Khalil Ibrahim, attacked the Defra oil field in the Kordofan area, a site managed by the Greater Nile Petroleum Operating Company, with which the Chinese National Petroleum Corporation is affiliated. The group abducted two foreign oil workers and released a statement claiming that "the attack on the Defra field is a message to China which arms the Khartoum Government". Moreover, Ahmed Togo, the senior JEM negotiator, indicated in a statement to Reuters that, "the arms which we captured from the government soldiers during the attack were Chinese made" (BBC, December 11, 2007).

On the one hand, the opposition in Darfur failed to recognise China's role in the resolution of the crisis, despite the fact that Beijing made many efforts to apply pressure on Khartoum, and provided considerable humanitarian assistance to the unstable state. They responded to China's increasing commitment to resolving the conflicts with criticism and attacks. What made it more complicated was those attitudes towards China and Chinese companies among each rebel group was different. Minni Minnawi's SLP, the Darfur rebel group who signed a peace deal and ended its conflict with the Khartoum government, have claimed to help free kidnapped Chinese engineers (Global Times, September 20, 2010). On the other hand, Witness 8 holds that the hard line of rebel groups in Darfur increased China's difficulty in facilitating the negotiations between Khartoum and their opposition. The hostile attitude towards China's involvement and the attacks on Chinese companies forced Beijing to seek cooperation with the Sudanese government in order to protect its overseas citizens and interests.

6.3.2 South Sudan

After South Sudan's independence, issues including oil payments, the status of each country's citizens resident in the other, disputed border areas and the contested Abyei region still unsettled the peace of the two countries from time to time. China has long been seen as an important supporter of Khartoum. Even if it has gradually built up a diplomatic presence in Juba since the implementation of CPA, it is still difficult for China to gain trust from South Sudan. After the establishment of South Sudan in 2011, Beijing was put in a dilemma position between the two governments.

Before the secession of South Sudan, the Sudanese government relied on oil income to fuel its economy and facilitate its war against the south. China, as the largest consumer of Sudan's oil, is considered as acting as a shield for Khartoum against the UN Security Council, protecting it from punishment for its humanitarian violations during the civil war, and issuance of an arrest warrant for Sudanese President Bashir for crimes against humanity and war crimes by the International Criminal Court. Since China has a long friendship with Khartoum and considerable economic investment in Sudan, it is unlikely that Beijing will abandon Khartoum in the short term. However, after South Sudanese independence, China was faced with an oil impasse: roughly three-quarters of the remaining oil now belongs to the South, but the infrastructure to exploit it – pipelines, refineries and export terminals built by the Chinese – is located in the north (ICG, April 4, 2012, p. 26). Therefore, Beijing has pursued a difficult strategy, working on a balanced relationship between Sudan and South Sudan, that is, its traditional support for Khartoum with its new engagement in Juba.

China's historic support to Khartoum and resultant the distrust from South Sudan, have affected China's efforts in playing a balanced role. The South Sudanese people see China's support for the government of Sudan as the root of much of their suffering during the civil war (Francis et al., 2012, p. 14). Juba was unhappy about China's "non-interference" stance regarding its civil conflicts. A senior minister from Juba noted that "as things stand now, the relationship is not between us and China". If China were reluctant to demonstrate its commitment to the relationship with the South, then Juba would seek to leverage Beijing's increasingly uncomfortable position (ICG, April 4, 2012, p. 28). Additionally, because China has benefited from the oil flow from the South to the North, its position on problem solving is questioned by South Sudan. The South Sudanese are deeply suspicious of China's motivations and its role as a fair negotiator, despite the considerable assistance it has given to the newly established country.

6.4 The gap between China's policy in Sudan and its implementation

Initially, China's engagement in Sudan was similar to its approach to other African countries. During the early stages of the Darfur crisis and Sudan's civil war, Beijing defended Khartoum by arguing that the conflicts were an internal affair that should be left to the Sudanese central government to solve. At the same time, China has gradually become a major donor to Khartoum, as its involvement in Sudan increased. Between 1970 and 2008, according to the criteria of the OECD, China's aid and development assistance to Sudan was equivalent to US$2,488.6 million. It estimated that total loans and grants provided by China during the period 2002–2006 amounted to US$1.1 billion, which represented about 37% of the US$2.8 billion of total loans and grants received by Sudan from other sources during that period. In 2005, Chinese loans accounted for three-quarters (75.9%) of the total loans received by Sudan in that year (Maglad, 2008, p. 5). As the situation in Sudan deterioration, the Chinese government's support and assistance turned out to be an obstacle to international sanctions against Khartoum, and a financial source for funding the cost of the war. Later, China shifted its policy on Sudan and became more cooperative with the international society. But its efforts had little effect on the crisis and instead drew China into a difficult situation between Sudan and the new South Sudan. This section will compare China's original strategy to Sudan and its actual implementation within the country, and analyse why and where China's policy has deviated from its targets. Then it will test hypothesis III – if China's (ir)responsible activities mostly were constrained by various factors and players.

6.4.1 Features of China's policy in Sudan

The crisis in Sudan was caused by a variety of factors, including history, tribal tensions and religion conflicts and poverty. In terms of the resolution, China held a different approach and logic to that of the traditional actors in the region. The US and other Western countries, as well as the international financial institutions, preferred sanctions in order to pressure Khartoum into democratic reforms and better governance. For them, the root of the north-south conflict was the political system and poor governance. At the same time, China, who prioritised the economy, and attributed the unstable society, poverty and frequent civil wars to lack of development, a weak economy, and conflicts of interest. For China, Witness 24 said,

> We have emphasised the right to development and the right to survival. We shared similar poverty experience with African countries while the Westerners didn't. People, who put political system establishment in front of poverty reduction have not been to Africa themselves. You will be shocked by what is happening in the continent. Currently, the only solution of the Sudan conflicts lies in economic development.

They believed that the people's dissatisfaction with Khartoum was mainly due to its poor economic performance and unfair wealth distribution. Without resolving the poverty in Sudan, any government would likely be unsustainable. In this case, China's Sudan policy can be summarised threefold.

First, even Beijing has specific economic and resource interests in Sudan, and the overall relationship serves China's political, economic and diplomatic strategy as a whole. The future of China's relations with Khartoum is yet to be determined according to Sudan's situation. As Witness 8 said, China's support for Khartoum was not only a quid pro quo for oil, but it also served China's interests by allowing the Sudanese government to provide security; because China's oil, infrastructure, and other interests depended on stability and security in the country. It implied that China's support for Khartoum was driven by the conditions for a stable environment rather than courting Khartoum. Evidence for this can be seen in China's attitude towards Darfur issues. Beijing would support Khartoum as long as the government could control the situation, but it would not challenge the international society when the Darfur crisis deteriorated, nor to conspire with the Bashir government at the cost of its international "responsible role".

Second, as long as the ruling government showed signs of controlling the situation, and compared to sanctions, China preferred to solve the problem through diplomatic means. The permanent representative of China to the UN, Li Baodong, pointed out that China would always be very cautious about the use or threat of sanctions. He point out that "China has always maintained that the international community should take an objective, impartial and balanced position on Sudan and South Sudan, and avoid taking sides or imposing unbalanced pressure on the parties, and refrain from interfering with the mediation efforts of the African Union and other regional organisations and countries" (Xinhua News, May 3, 2012). Witness 9 further explained the reasons for not supporting external sanctions against Khartoum. As it was not a solution to the conflicts, they may actually have made the situation more complicated: because, if the sanctions failed to solve the crisis in a short period, Sudan could be drawn into a back and forth battle. In this case, the international sanctions would have weakened the Sudanese government's capacity to end the crisis. In a country, desperately in need of financial and material assistance, what Sudan demanded was not sanctions but international support and mediation.

Third, China tended to attribute the crisis in Sudan to economic problems. Hence, instead of an emphasis on good governance, it preferred to provide tangible commitments to the country. Taking the Darfur issue as an example, evidence shows that more people could have died from tribal clashes than from Janjaweed or government forces (Abramowitz & Kolieb, June 5, 2007). Also, the independent South Sudan still fell into a civil war. One could say that the inner power struggles of the rebellion and the number of displaced people are also serious obstacles to peace. In this case, Witness 2 believed that, since the advantage of a better government takes time to be seen, African (Sudanese) people are more eager to see some tangible improvements and benefits. The "four-point plan"[4] proposed to Sudan by President Hu Jintao highlighted the importance of improving "local people's living standard[s]", which reflected China's concentration on economic improvements for the Sudanese people.

6.4.2 The implementation of China's Sudan policy

China's approach to solving Sudan's crisis was different from that of the traditional players. To what extend this approach worked, lay with the Sudanese government's capability and effectiveness in controlling the country. Only if the central government could execute effective measures to deal with the crisis, could China's assistance have the tangible effects that Beijing advocated. In terms of Sudan, where the situation was complicated, there are gaps between China's original Sudan policy goals and the actual effects.

I Darfur

Since the Darfur conflict's outbreak in 2003, China expressed support for Khartoum in the UN Security Council on the basis of its "non-interference" principle. When it realised the seriousness of the situation, the extent of the violations of human rights and Khartoum's incompetence in dealing with the crisis, China started to reinterpret the scope of "interference". On July 30, 2004, China opened the door for Western countries to pressure Khartoum by abstaining from the vote for Security Council Resolution 1556, which required the Sudanese government to fulfil its commitments to disarm the Janjaweed militias and bring those leaders who had carried out human rights violations in Darfur to justice (Ahmed, 2010). In November 2006, Chinese ambassador to the UN, Wang Guangya, made important behind-the-scenes moves to secure the Sudanese government's agreement to the 'Annan Plan', which called for an expanded UN peacekeeping role in Darfur (ICG, April 17, 2009). In 2007, China took a further step to support the hybrid UN-African Union peacekeeping force and exerted pressure on Khartoum to accept an international peacekeeping force by voting in favour of UN Resolution 1769 – this despite the Sudanese government suggestion that only an AU force be allowed to enter Darfur.

The western political elites encouraged China's efforts. US Deputy Assistant Secretary of African Affairs James Swan praised Wang for playing "a vital and constructive role" (Swan, May 3, 2007). US Secretary of State Condoleezza Rice affirmed that "the United States appreciates Chinese efforts in resolving issues such as Darfur, and hopes China will continue to play a positive role." (Qin & Li, February 27, 2008) The US special envoy to Sudan, Andrew Natsios, echoed Rice's statement by saying that Beijing's role in Darfur was "very crucial" and "very helpful" (China Daily, April 12, 2007). At the regional level, the Arab League praised China's contributions to international stability and peace, especially its role on the Darfur question and its efforts to find a comprehensive solution to the crisis (Ahmed, 2010, p. 18).

However, neither the international community nor the rebel groups in Darfur recognised China's flexibility. Notably, the launch of the "Genocide Olympics" campaign, which criticised China's stance, served to obstruct many UN resolutions aimed at improving conditions in the region for the protection of the local population, and forcing the Sudanese government to suspend its support for the violence in Darfur. The rebels in Darfur also viewed China as a supporter of Khartoum and connected the violence to China. In February 2007, former President Hu Jintao visited Khartoum. The Chinese national media reported that Hu's meeting with President Bashir was to emphasise the need for a "comprehensive ceasefire" and an acceleration of "the political negotiation process" involving rebel non-signatories to the Abuja Accord, plus the need for humanitarian assistance (Xinhua News, February 2, 2007). President Hu is reported to have told President Bashir that "Darfur is a part of Sudan and you have to resolve this problem" (McDoom, February 2, 2007). Economic assistance came alongside Hu's visit and the two governments signed contracts for building new schools, a new presidential palace, reduced import tariffs on certain Sudanese goods, a loan of 600 million Yuan (US$77.4 million; €59.5 million) for infrastructure, and gave a grant of a US$40 million (€30.7 million). China also canceled debts of 470 million Yuan (US$60.7 million; €46.6 million) and US$19 million (€14.6 million) (Mail&Guardian February 3, 2007).

Hu Jintao's visit triggered some international criticism. More than a hundred members of the UK Parliament sent a message to the President Hu Jintao, on October 29, 2007, appealing to China to review its policy towards Sudan and to try to convince the Sudanese government to stop its attacks against civilians, disarm its militias, and co-operate with the ICC and facilitate relief operations. One public statement by the National Salvation Front (one of the armed groups in Darfur) claimed during President Jintao's visit that "China's record in the Darfur case was shameful and depressing", and also added that China "supports the Khartoum regime without caring about the war crimes committed by it in Darfur, and that [China] continues to provide the international political cover for Sudan to continue its massacres" (Holslag, August 15, 2007). Chinese political elites called upon their counterparts in the West to influence the rebel groups to engage in dialogue and facilitate the mediation between rebels and the Khartoum government (Zeng, 2012). However, it failed in the mediation role, because the rebels were suspicious of China's intention to bring about a fair and peaceful solution to the conflict. Instead, the Darfur rebels took the opportunity of Hu Jintao's trip to launch a violent campaign against the Chinese stance on the crisis.

Additionally, what made China unreliable for the opposition in Darfur was its arms trade with Khartoum. Since the 1990s, China has been one of the major global suppliers of military equipment and arms to Sudan. Documented reports note the sale of fifty Chinese-manufactured Z-6 helicopters to the Sudanese government, as well as the provision of technical repair services by Harbin Dongan Engine, a Chinese company (Kotecki, 2008). According to UN Comtrade, Chinese weapons manufacturers Changhe Aircraft Industries and Dongfeng Aeolus exported small arms – including rifles, shotguns, and handguns – to Sudan. A report by the UN Panel of Experts established under Resolution 1591 (2005) found that "shell casings collected from various sites in Darfur suggest that most ammunition currently used by parties to the conflict in Darfur is manufactured either in the Sudan or in China" (Kleine-Ahlbrandt & Small, 2008). It furthermore found that 222 military vehicles were procured from Dongfeng Automobile Import and Export Limited in China. In addition, a number of further high-level meetings took place in Beijing and Khartoum during the 2000s. Participants included the highest-ranking members of the SAF, China's Central Military Commission, and the People's Liberation Army (PLA). Some criticism tends to connect arms trade with oil. However, despite China's oil interests in Sudan, there is no particular or preferential military aid to Khartoum when compared with other countries who have similar relationships with Beijing. Furthermore, some African scholars assumed that the arms trade "stemmed from Beijing's apparent expectation that Khartoum would achieve an early military resolution to the conflict in Darfur." Evidence can be found showing that high-level military cooperation was mainly held in 2002 when Khartoum was attempting to crush the Darfur uprising while simultaneously negotiating with the Sudan Peoples' Liberation Movement/Army (SPLM/A) to end the long-standing war with the south (Large, 2008). As time went by, and Beijing realized the deterioration in Darfur, it changed its strategy in Sudan. Additionally, special envoy Ambassador Liu Guijin argued that China was not the only arms supplier to Sudan. A small arms survey reported that the Chinese ammunition that could be found in Sudan changed from heavy weapons to small arms, and was in the hands of both government troops and rebels (Gramizzi & Tubiana, 2012, p. 46). Hence, it would be over-simplified to criticize that Chinese arms supplies to Sudan were only to support Khartoum in return for access to its oil interests. Chances are, the arms trade was not always provided by the Chinese central government to support its oil friend in Khartoum. Granted, Beijing clearly regarded the arms industry as critical to China's national security, and while privatized, was kept under much tighter supervision than other reformed SOEs. However, the supervision of arms exports is another matter entirely (Taylor, 2009). The small arms found in Darfur often made their way there through intermediaries on the global arms market. Nevertheless, a negative image was created by China supporting Khartoum with weaponry and aircraft used in Darfur in order to gain control of the wealth of the region.

Throughout the Darfur crisis, it could see that Beijing made great efforts to maintain the stability in Sudan. It attempted to assure Khartoum that only a diplomatic solution would bring an end to the conflicts. At the same time, it called on Western countries to bring the rebels back to the negotiation table. However, in reality, both the international community and opposition in Darfur didn't acknowledge Beijing's efforts, and China was unable to convince other that it took a balanced role, due to its friendly attitude towards Khartoum. Western activists and media continued to criticise China over its perceived unconditional ties with the government in Khartoum. The rebels even launched attacks against Chinese oil fields and Chinese workers.

II South Sudan

Since the independence of South Sudan in 2011, Khartoum was left with the majority of the former nation's oil reserves. However, South Sudan lacked the infrastructure to refine or transport the oil, and it has to export the oil through pipelines in the north. Both countries heavily rely on oil income for its revenue: roughly 50% for Sudan and 98% for South Sudan. The two sides have had a long dispute over transit fees which South Sudan pays for the use of pipelines in the north. Additionally, their long history of conflict complicates any resolution of the oil transportation issue. South Sudan has accused Sudan of stealing the oil and threatened to shut down oil production (BBC News, January 27, 2012), while Khartoum has blamed Juba's continued support for the Sudan Revolutionary Front (SRF) rebels fighting Khartoum on multiple fronts and declared that it would block the pipeline carrying South Sudan's crude all the way to the Red Sea coastal city of Port Sudan (Sudan Tribune, June 10, 2013). China, who has considerable oil interests in Sudan, has invested more than US$20 billion in these two countries (Lum et al., 2009). It has the motivation and weight to help mediate the dispute. Even if much criticism of Beijing has focused on its relationship with the Bashir regime, it is more of a symbolic rather than actual political tie. Indeed, if China was not a neutral actor between Sudan and South Sudan, this was less because of its own choices in supporting Khartoum but in response to limitations within the existing situation beyond its control.

In April 2012, South Sudanese President Kiir visited Beijing and asked for China's political and financial support in its oil difficulties. During this trip, President Kiir sought the investment of Chinese oil companies to take part in the development of an alternative pipeline (of Sudan) construction project in his meeting with the President of CNPC Jiang Jiemin (Kenneth, April 26, 2012). The oil dilemma for Beijing is a political issue between Khartoum and Juba, but for CNPC it is more of a business issue. CNPC entered Sudan's oil industry in the 1990s when the Western oil companies withdrew from the country. Since then, CNPC and the Sudanese government have signed a series of oil contracts for the exploration of Block 6 (in 1995), Block 1/2/4 (1997), Block 3/7 (2000), Block 15 (2005) and Block 12 (2007) (CNPC, 2010). At the same time, it has been estimated that CNPC has invested more than US$7 billion in the region (X. Chen, January 3, 2014) and constructed most of the oil infrastructure in Sudan, which includes the only oil pipeline from South Sudan (Heglig) to the Port of Sudan via Khartoum, and the Suakim oil terminal at Port Sudan on the Red Sea. However, these business investments have been criticised as a financial source for Khartoum during the civil war. After the construction of this infrastructure, "the Sudanese government openly boasted that oil would fund the civil war: 'Sudan will be capable of producing all the weapons it needs thanks to the growing oil industry', stated General Mohamed Yassin shortly after oil began flowing out of the new pipeline into supertankers at the Red Sea port" (Taylor, 2006a, p. 26). Witness 17 from CNPC argued, "CNPC's overseas investment was more out of business consideration with no preference to support any kind of government". Witness 4 admitted that Chinese oil companies have long been marginalised in the international market, and as a result, they have no other choice but to do business with questionable governments. Actually, CNPC's investment in Sudan was conducted with a similar approach of "oil for infrastructure" as in any other oil-rich African state. The problems arose out of the Sudan government's inability to maintain security and properly arrange distribution of oil income, rather than Chinese oil companies' involvement.

On the other hand, CNPC was drawn into a difficult situation as well. In January 2012, South Sudan shut down all its oil production due to both sides failing to agree on pipeline fees. CNPC's oil exploration and production company, PetroDar Operating Company Ltd. (PDOC),[5] which was responsible for the operations in Block 3/7, with more than 600 oil wells in South Sudan, was one of the largest oil investors in this region (CNPC, 2010). Not only would turning off wells lead to a loss of 250 thousand barrels per day within ten days for CNPC, but also, according to CNPC's chief engineer in Sudan Chen Shudong, southern officials pushed the oil firms to close the wells so quickly that there was a risk of the heavy, sticky crude oil from the eastern fields congealing, which would damage the pipelines (Dziadosz, November 14, 2012). However, officials from South Sudan thought PDOC intentionally delayed the government's decision. Since they use the shutdown of oil production as a bargaining chip at the negotiation table with Khartoum, South Sudan officials considered PDOC's slowness as CNPC's tacit support for Khartoum. Chen complained that officials from South Sudan were not professional in the oil industry, "they were bursting to shut down all the wells in one day", and refused PDOC's proposal of turning off the wells gradually according to the safety standard operating procedure. Additionally, as the two countries could not reach an agreement on the transition fees, Khartoum then decided it could no longer wait for an agreement and started to seize part of Juba's oil pumped through the pipelines as payment in kind. South Sudan accused the oil companies (mainly CNPC) of collaborating with Khartoum in "stealing" and marketing the crude it confiscated (Sudan Tribune, February 23, 2012c). As a result, it expelled the head of Petrodar Liu Yingcai on the grounds of "non-cooperation". The next day, South Sudan said it had started reviewing all oil contracts signed by the government of neighbouring Sudan before the region's independence. South Sudan's oil minister Stephen Dhieu pointed out that "they cannot have it both ways. Cooperate with Khartoum in stealing oil and at the same time pretend to be partners with us. It does not work like that" (Sudan Tribune, February 22, 2012b). Chen explained the limitation of CNPC and said, "In fact, the ports [are] locate[d] in Sudan, it would not have been an effective response to confront the Sudanese government" (ifeng, May 16, 2012). Soon, the Chinese government weighed in, calling for joint efforts to resolve the dispute. Chinese Foreign Ministry spokesman Hong Lei said in his daily news briefing, "We hope that relevant sides step up communication and consultations and put an end to misunderstandings to benefit long-term cooperation" (Sudan Tribune, February 24, 2012d). In response, Pagan Amum, South Sudan's top negotiator for talks with Sudan over oil payments, said: "relations with China were good but added there were difficulties with some oil companies" (Reuters, February 23, 2012), which brought CNPC into an uncomfortable position. CNPC's officials said South Sudan government was supposed to dismiss Liu Yingcai according to the companies' procedures (as proposed at a stockholders' meeting), rather than make the decision unilaterally. Furthermore, even if Liu was dismissed due to his "non-cooperation", as an employee of PetroDar Operating Company Ltd.

(PDOC) who hadn't done anything illegal, he should not have been expelled by the South Sudan government (ifeng, May 16, 2012). Witness 18 revealed that Chinese national companies were not always satisfied with Ministry of Foreign Affairs (MOFA's) attitude towards African countries, especially when the host countries' regulations conflicted with the Chinese companies' interests because the MOFA did little to protect them. The informant held that MOFA should mediate when there existed unfair governmental regulations. Witness 17 said, "From CNPC's perspective, they expected the Chinese government would use diplomatic measures to intervene when Chinese people's safety and economic interests were violated in African countries".

In fact, since the secession of South Sudan, Beijing has continued to send special envoys to Sudan; first Liu Guijin, later Zhong Jianhua, both of whom are diplomatic veterans in African affairs, and tried to mediate the conflicts between north and south and protect its oil companies' interests. However, Beijing's desire to maintain balanced relations was constrained by the situation in Sudan, and hence not fully acknowledged by South Sudan or international actors. On the one hand, South Sudan was unhappy about Chinese companies' involvement in the oil sector and threatened to expel Chinese companies operating in its territories if they were proven to be complicit with Khartoum in what Juba terms the stealing of South Sudan's oil. Meanwhile, it also tried to replace Chinese oil companies with Western companies (Sudan Tribune, February 22, 2012a). On the other hand, it sought China's political and financial support for an alternative oil pipeline in order to pump oil through neighbouring countries but not Sudan. Its demands brought CNPC, the largest purchaser of South Sudan's oil, into a deadlock. In 2012, advisor of CNPC International Tong Xiaoguang suggested CNPC produced 495 thousand barrels of oil per day in Sudan in 2009. The figure was considerably reduced in 2010 and 2011. Currently, as South Sudan has shut down its oil production, only Block 6 in the north has operated and produced less than one-tenth the amount of oil, compared to the 2011 figure. At the same time, Sudan and South Sudan border conflicts over the oil rich Heglig region have seriously damaged oil facilities constructed by CNPC. It estimates that it will require more than two years to repair (Tong, September 6, 2012). The earliest CNPC contracts in Heglig will expire in 2016, while the latest will expire in 2026. At such a time, even without consideration for Khartoum, CNPC will still need to approach President Kiir's proposal for an alternative oil pipeline for South Sudan cautiously. What's more, Chen revealed that his company has already covered its costs and investment through oil imports from Sudan, it even has made some profits from the Sudan market. Therefore, it is not economical to abandon the established pipelines in Sudan and construct a new one. He added, "Constructing an alternative pipeline is a systemic project that requires a lot of work and research en route, geology, feasibility and bid. CNPC cannot make a decision without meeting with other stockholders." (ifeng, May 16, 2012).

In the case of South Sudan, the Chinese government failed to mediate the conflicts between Sudan and South Sudan and facilitated oil cooperation for Chinese companies. At the policy level, it tried to have a balanced role between each side and protect its oil interests in these two countries. But, in practice, the Khartoum and Juba governments used oil as bargaining chips to gain economic support from China, while both sides lacked a willingness to cooperate with the other and the capability to maintain its internal stability. The crisis in South Sudan drew Beijing into an uncomfortable position that resulted in losses for Chinese oil companies.

6.5 Conclusion

Beijing has had a relationship with Khartoum for more than two decades, and initially, its engagement in Sudan had no major difference with Beijing's engagement with other African countries. But the extreme crisis in Darfur and South Sudan challenged China's role and impact in Sudan. In response to the changing politics and different issues within the country, Beijing's Sudan policy developed towards a more pragmatic and complex approach. China's role in the ongoing conflicts in Darfur and attitude towards the newly established South Sudan showed that China has interests beyond access to resources and purely business-related considerations in Africa. The Sudan case tested the limits of China's traditional "non-interference" principle and its "oil for infrastructure" approach. In the face of international pressure and the negative impact on Beijing's reputation, China has pursued a more comprehensive approach to Sudan, with more cooperation on international intervention and resolutions. It is worth noting that Beijing's priority does not intrinsically contradict that of the international community. Its concern with investment protection requires political stability and peace in Sudan. The extent to which the Chinese government is inclined to support Khartoum is not driven by its oil demands, nor arms trade profits, but is rather because of the perceived capability of the Bashir regime to control the situation and maintain peace in the region.

However, playing a constructive and balanced role in an unstable environment is no easy task for Beijing, especially when it has to protect its investments. China's Sudan responsibility was shaped by finding a compromise between the divergent interests of Beijing, Khartoum, Juba, rebels and international society. Constrained by its limited influence in Khartoum and the mistrust of South Sudan and the Darfur opposition, Beijing's Sudan policy has deviated from its original intent. The incapability to manage the situation in Sudan also brought Chinese oil companies into a vulnerable situation and had often exposed them as targets of armed groups working against Khartoum. Witness 10 suggested,

> In order to have an effective African policy, the Chinese government should cooperate and coordinate with Europe and the US in mediating

the crisis and make its measures more transparent to its Western counterparts. Even if there are criticisms towards Beijing in the first place, China still needs to insist on doing that.

Notes

1 The Bentiu district (a border area between the north and the south) in 1978, southern Kordofan, and Upper Blue Nile in 1979, Unity oilfields in 1980, Adar oil fields in 1981 and Heglig in 1982.
2 Northern Sudan's new hard-line Islamist government promoted a domestic project of Islamist social transformation and renewed its war on Southern Sudan against the Sudan People's Liberation Army (SPLA). Islamist support for Iraq and Saddam Hussein during the 1991 Gulf War, notably by Hassan Turabi, caused problems for Khartoum with America and Europe. The NIF was associated with support for terrorism, including the attempted assassination of the Egyptian president in June 1995, which deepened Sudan's regional isolation in the Middle East.
3 Marathon eventually sold its interests in Sudan in March 2008.
4 The plan: (1) respecting Sudan's sovereignty and territorial integrity as the principles for settling 'the Darfur issue'; (2) persisting in dialogues and consultations for the settlement of the issue on an equal footing and through peaceful means; (3) encouraging the AU, the UN, and pertinent parties to play a constructive role in the peace-keeping issue in Darfur; (4) and facilitating the stability of the regional situation and the improvement of the local people's living conditions.
5 The PetroDar Operating Company Ltd is a consortium of oil exploration and production companies operating in Sudan with its headquarters in Khartoum. The consortium was incorporated in the Virgin Islands on October 31, 2001. PetroDar is composed of the China National Petroleum Corporation (CNPC) (41% share).

7 Nigeria

No bilateral China-Africa relationship is evolving faster, nor impacts a greater number of people than the one between China and Nigeria (Egbula & Zheng, November 2011). Compared to other states in West Africa, Nigeria's democracy and economic growth perform relatively better. This African giant is now China's third-largest trading partner in Africa and the top destination for Chinese exports on the continent. In 2012, trade value between the two countries reached US$10.57 billion, and by the end of 2012, China's non-financial direct investment in Nigeria amounted to US$8.7 billion. The figure is so notable because in 1998 it was $384 million, and US$ 1 billion in 2001 and therefore increased ten times in the next decade, which is doubly notable considering this growth was achieved against the background of the global recession (Taylor, 2007).

China-Nigeria relations are a featured case in assessing China's engagement in Africa because Nigeria is the rare African state with large energy reserves and a relatively democratic government system. These two key Nigerian characteristics can be used to test China's attitude towards an oil-rich state and relatively democratic regime, which are two of the most controversial elements of China's activities in Africa. In addition, by assessing China's impact on Nigeria's oil industry and democratic development, this chapter will analyse China's contribution to and the deficiencies of its "oil for infrastructure" approach in Nigeria.

This chapter starts with a brief background on China-Nigeria relations. Then, it discusses three influential factors in shaping China's responsibility in Nigeria – China's national interests, Nigeria's demands, and international expectations – to explore whether these two countries can be complementary at the policy level. Some scholars have indicated that China could treat African countries like colonies, yet if their national interests are complementary, it would be more like a demand-give situation. In its second part, this chapter discusses which factors could limit China's commitment to Nigeria, and also China's capability to be responsible in Nigeria. Then, in the final part, this chapter discusses the actors and context that can affect China's role in Nigeria, from both the Nigerian and Chinese sides.

7.1 A brief background

It was not until February 1971, that Nigeria established diplomatic relations with the People's Republic of China (PRC), the same year that Beijing officially replaced the Republic of China (ROC) (Taiwan) in the United Nations (UN) and on the Security Council. Apart from Nigeria's acceptance of the "One China Policy" and Hong Kong's return to China, there were few connections between these two countries. Former Premier Li Peng's official visit to Abuja in 1997 was the highest-level visit in more than two decades. During the early period of this relationship, pioneering Chinese investors from Hong Kong and Taiwan concentrated on the manufacturing and textile industries, where traditional Western investors were not interested, because of Nigeria's poor supply chain, inadequate infrastructure, and Nigeria's oil fields have been operated mainly by several Western companies. From the late 1990s, China started to establish a closer relationship with Nigeria and pursued the oil-for-infrastructure approach. However, Nigeria's domestic situation had an impact on the successful implementation of China's policy. The unstable relationship by electoral politics in Nigeria and its poor governance has affected China's capability to play a fully responsible role in Nigeria.

7.2 Shaping China's responsibility in Nigeria

The existing literature argues that China's needs in Africa are resources, markets for its exports, and political support on its territory and human rights abuses. As for Nigeria, the African country has vast energy reserves and a large domestic market with more than 170 million inhabitants, both of which certainly meets China's basic needs. Apart from these demands, Nigeria, as the most populous African country has political and economic interests beyond oil, markets and international support. Vice Versa, Nigeria needs Chinese investment, technology and assistance to fuel its economic growth. Hence, bilateral relations have developed on the basis of mutual demands.

7.2.1 China's motivation

I Politically

Regarding China's political motivation in Nigeria, One-China policy is the prerequisite for establishing a bilateral relationship. In the Joint Press Communiqué in 2008, the president of Nigeria explicitly voiced Nigeria's support for the One-China (Xinhua News, February 28, 2008). Nigeria has also spoken out to refuse Taiwan entry into the UN in 2002.

Furthermore, Nigeria has greater significance to China than other African states. As the most populous country in the continent, Nigeria has played a leading role in West Africa. In 2010, United States (US) President Obama stated that "Nigeria is critical to the rest of the continent and if Nigeria does not get it right, Africa will really not make more progress," during his talk with the then-acting President Jonathan (allAfrica, April 13, 2010). On the one hand, it indicated that Nigeria's domestic peace and stability had influenced regional security and development as a whole. On the other hand, as a big emerging nation in West Africa, Nigeria has a responsibility to maintain the regional peace and stability. The Nigerian government has recognised its critical role in the region and expressed its ambition to become an African leader. Not only has it actively participated in regional peacekeeping operations in Chad, Liberia, Sierra Leone, the Democratic Republic of Congo, Angola, Cote d'Ivoire, Somalia and Darfur in Sudan, but it has also made efforts to form an African voice in the international arena. In 2013, during his visit to Cote d'Ivoire, President Jonathan called on all leaders from the Economic Community of West African States (ECOWAS) to work together and create a peaceful and stable political environment in order for economic development (Thisdaylive, March 1, 2013). Nigeria's desire to become a leading African voice and its influence in western Africa provided China with the motivation to establish deeper political ties with this country. The two sides have expressed a willingness to cooperate in solving Africa's various conflicts. In a joint press communiqué in 2008, the parties highlighted that "the Chinese side hailed Nigeria's long-standing role in the cause of peace in Africa", and in return the "Nigerian side applauded the contribution made by China in support of the efforts of the African Union in the peaceful resolution of conflict situations in Africa." (Xinhua News, February 28, 2008).

II Economically

As the former section has indicated, the massive oil reserves and an emerging market with 170 million potential customers, located in the strategic Gulf of Guinea region, has not only provided China with a diverse oil supply, but also an exports and investment destination for its construction, communication, manufacturing and retail industries.

One cannot deny the fact that, apart from the political aspect, energy security is a key driving force for China's interactions with and actions in Nigeria for the following reasons: First, China's domestic political economy is heavily reliant on an energy-intensive industry. In order to achieve its national economic objectives, it has to secure foreign supplies of oil and refined oil products for domestic use. Second, attempting to lower the influence of the international commodity market on oil supply and price, Beijing has sought reliable markets with less competition from traditional developed countries. Nigeria has ranked as the largest oil producer in Africa and the 11th largest worldwide. It produces approximately 2.28 million barrels per day and has a proven oil reserve of 37.2 billion barrels. It is estimated that, at current rates, this could be 45 years of supply even if no new oil fields were found. In addition, Nigeria's fragile democracy and domestic violence have made its energy market too risky for traditional oil importers to access, which provided Chinese oil companies with chances to move in without (much) competition. The successful engagement in the Nigerian oil industry could diversify China's sources of oil and reduce its dependence on the highly competitive markets in the Middle East. As Witness 22 said,

> Lots of people have talked about China choosing to invest in the high risk energy areas, it sounds as if we have a choice. The safe oil fields with good quality energy reserves have long been controlled by the western companies. As a latecomer, China has to start from these marginalised areas.

In short, China is an energy-import-oriented country and will need plenty of oil due to its economic growth and domestic growth. With its abundant oil reserves, China needs access to Nigerian oil fields.

Furthermore, Nigeria is also considered to have great potential for rapid economic growth. Economist Jim O'Neill has introduced Nigeria as a "Mint" country,[1] to indicate its potential to become an emerging economic giant (British Broadcast Company [BBC], January 5, 2014). Nigeria's annual gross domestic product (GDP) in 2012 was estimated at US$268 billion, the second highest in Africa after South Africa. As a large potential market with the largest population in Africa, Nigeria had an import volume of US$4.18 billion in 2012. The imports mainly included: industrial supplies (32% of total), transport equipment and parts (23%), capital goods (24%), food and beverage (11%), and consumer goods (Ministry of Commerce [MOFCOM] & China's Embassy in Nigeria, 2013). The diversity and potential of the Nigerian market have attracted Chinese labour-intensive industries, mainly textiles, industrial machinery, telecom equipment, electrical equipment, vehicles, and other manufacturers. It provides a good export destination for China's expanding industry that has limited customer bases in either its domestic or other developed markets. Nigerian customers' demands for low-price products helped Chinese enterprises to transfer their uncompetitive industries to this country. Consequently, Chinese consortiums have established free trade zones in Lagos and container areas at the Lagos port. Chinese Foreign Direct Investment (FDI) reached US$7.24 billion in 2009 (MOFCOM & China's Embassy in Nigeria, 2013). At the same time, China has become Nigeria's largest import partner and accounted for 17% of Nigeria's total volume. Between 2005 and 2012, Nigeria had the largest share of Chinese investment in Africa – roughly US$15.6 billion out of US$97.8 billion (Odeh, 2013).

Meanwhile, according to a report by Citigroup, Nigeria will experience the highest average GDP growth worldwide between 2010 and 2050, (Vanguard, September 23, 2011) which places it as one of only two countries from Africa among the 11 Global Growth Generators countries. The dramatic growth has brought a substantial appetite for new infrastructure along with increasing consumer demands, which have attracted lots of Chinese enterprises.

In summary, Alaba Ogunsanwo, the distinguished Nigerian academic and former diplomat, has described "third World countries" like numerous "ants" standing behind China, "the elephant" (Mthembu-Salter, 2009). Even if China had the power of an elephant, Nigeria, with its location, resources, size and political influence, can hardly be compared to an ant. Considering its political ambitions and considerable oil reserves, China has plenty of motivation to get involved with this country. To assess China's responsibility in Nigeria, one should explore to what extend China's national interests meet the demands of Nigeria and international society.

7.2.2 *Nigeria's demands*

As mentioned in the preceding section, Nigeria, with its abundant energy reserves, potential economic growth, and human resources, could be considered an influential power in this region. Its active contributions to peacekeeping operations and its critical role in promoting the end of the slave trade and colonialism in Southern Africa has gained it support and improved its reputation with other African countries. Acknowledging its regional influence, Nigeria has ambitions to represent the continent on the global platform. In 2005, the Nigerian Foreign Minister Oluyemi Adeniji expressed Abuja's quest to represent the African voice in an expanded permanent membership on the UN Security Council. In 2013, Nigeria was elected as a non-permanent member of the UN, the fourth time the country undertook this role. The African Union (AU) has also endorsed Nigeria as the only candidate from the continent in the coming election for the UN non-permanent seat (Vanguard, October 26, 2013) to pursue the interests of the continent and maintain international peace and security. Also, Nigeria became the largest economy in Africa in 2013 (Xinhua News, April 7, 2014). These facts all indicate that Nigeria could be the leading representative for Africa.

However, due to its weak democracy, unstable political environment, economic problems and corruption, Nigeria has shown its weaknesses. Militant insurgents from the northeast have launched a series of attacks aimed at destabilising the country. Largely relying on energy exports has hindered the diversity of its economy, especially the development of its agricultural industry. Lacking refinery facilities, the state remains an oil importer despite its abundant energy reserves. According to an investigation by the local newspaper Punch at the end of 2012, "over N5tn (US$32.3 billion) in government funds have been stolen through fraud, embezzlement and theft since President Jonathan assumed office in May 2010" (Ogunseye, Okpi, & Baiyewu, November 25, 2012).

Combining the two faces of Nigeria, the state needs to compete with the other two African giants, South Africa and Egypt, for the two seats that the continent has pursued at the UN Security Council. At this point, it has to seek support from the AU and big powers from other continents. China traditionally considers itself a representative of developing countries and the developing member states of the UN Security Council. Therefore, it became a key political supporter of Nigeria's request. In 2005, then-Chinese Foreign Minister Li Zhaoxing exchanged such views with Nigerian Foreign Minister Oluyemi Adeniji on UN reform (People's Daily, June 5, 2005). At the same time, China's chief spokesman Liu Jianchao said that China supports Africa, the continent with the largest number of developing countries, playing a greater role in the UN, including participation on the Security Council (Ministry of Foreign Affairs [MOFA], March 29, 2005). Nigeria's political needs can motivate it to stand with China for political considerations.

Economically, Nigeria needs China for its economic reform: funds for structural transformation, economic aid, and local production to prevent over-reliance on oil exports. Despite large amounts of energy reserves, Nigeria has not fully taken advantage of its oil income to generate national wealth. The oil industry has played a dominant role in Nigeria's national income. However, the rural sector has been neglected. When the global oil price declined during the 1980s, the country's development stagnated, which led to the deterioration of Nigeria's economic and social conditions. Simultaneously, the structural adjustment introduced by World Bank and International Monetary Fund (IMF) has been challenged by domestic pressure. "Towards the end of 1990, the Government began to retreat from the reforms" – meaning, the loans provided by the funding sources were suspended (Moser, Rogers, Van Til, Kibuka, & Lukonga, April 4, 1997). During the same period, the Chinese enterprises had entered Nigeria market, and bilateral trade began to develop. Beijing, with its large amount of funds, provided the country with an alternative opportunity, especially after assistance from the Western world dropped significantly from 2008, as a result of the global recession. China appears to be filling this gap. As an emerging economic power, China is able to provide investment, loans and other kinds of financial assistance for which Nigeria is thirsty.

Compared to most other African countries that are in need of funds, Nigeria has a more ambitious demand. The state experienced a period of yearning for economic transformation, from being dependent on imports to boosting local production. Nigeria's representative to United Nations Industrial Development Organization (UNIDO), Dr. Patrick Kormawa said that "the only way Nigeria can attain the goal of an industrialised nation is when the country gets out of the habit of a consumption-based economy to one driven by production and value addition" (Thisdaylive, July 2, 2013). As a country exporting crude oil but relying on petrol imports, Nigeria had to develop an industrial sector as a tool for job creation, food security, poverty reduction, and sustainable growth. Similarly, having the largest population on the continent, the country is able to provide cheap labour force. In this case, China's successful economic transformation and industrial development have provided Nigeria with a good example of how to become a "world factory" that produces the goods not only consumed by domestic costumers but also exports to the rest of the world. Furthermore, Beijing has enough funds to invest in Nigeria's industrialisation by providing infrastructure and establishing factories for manufacturers. It offers Nigeria an economic opportunity to achieve its transformation agenda if political elites can properly take advantage of Beijing's pledges.

7.2.3 International expectation

During his visit to Nigeria in 2006, former British foreign secretary Jack Straw remarked that what China was doing in Africa now was much the same as what Britain had done 150 years earlier (Akidi, May 22, 2012). Like Straw, many Western scholars and politicians are concerned that China may become a new colonial power in this oil-rich country, scrambling for Nigeria's natural resources and harming its quest for democracy and improved human rights. On a trip to Zambia, former US Secretary of State Hillary Clinton directly accused China of pursuing a "new colonialism", and warned that "Africans should be wary of friends who only deal with elites". "When people come to Africa to make investments, we want them to do well but also want them to do good," she said. "We don't want them to undermine good governance in Africa." (Lusaka, June 11, 2011).

In short, regarding international expectations, in the case of Nigeria international society has less concern for China in Nigeria than in Sudan, not only because China is not a major player in this state, but also because Nigeria's government is less controversial than the Bashir regime. As a result, China's responsibility in Nigeria lies more in a dual consideration of China's national interests and Nigeria's demands.

7.2.4 Discussions for shaping China's responsibility in Nigeria

As mentioned in a previous section, international society is less concerned with the China-Nigeria link than with China's relationship with Sudan. The problem causing the most concern is China's 'oil for infrastructure' approach, which is criticised as 'new-colonialism'. However, some Nigerian leaders refute this criticism at the policy level and have welcomed the 'cooperation' between China and Nigeria. Bolaji Akinyemi, Nigeria's former foreign minister, and a scholar of Africa's international relations has said,

> China is an emerging world power with a booming economy. She needs oil. Nigeria needs as much investment as possible and to diversify the sources of its investment. In the Middle East, the US regards China's incursion with alarm, but Nigeria is more virgin territory for suitors and Washington should not be too worried. It insulates Nigeria from influence by one power.
>
> (Nigeria2Day, 2006)

In this case, China-Nigeria relations mostly arise from mutual demands. Regarding responsibility policy, China's motivation and Nigeria's demands have more weight than international comments on shaping China's policy. As discussed in former sections, China has political, economic (energy and exports) interests in Nigeria, while Nigeria has a thirst for financial resources and international support. The two sides have a common interest to bond their relationship at the policy level. The following section will discuss to what extent the 'mutual demands' work in the implementation process.

7.3 China's capability and limitation in Nigeria

In the preceding section, this book argued that China and Nigeria share similar goals. However, this situation does not mean a "win-win" situation can be reached simply because of mutual interests. Nigeria's political situation and ambitious plan for local industrialisation limit both sides' effective cooperation.

Obviously, China has conducted its "oil for infrastructure" approach in Nigeria. The two countries have a supply-side and a demand-side logic to follow this measure. Because Nigeria, like many African countries, wanted to develop its infrastructure in order to fuel the growth of its economy, a solid infrastructure facilitated resource extraction in return. But compared to China's most successful "oil for infrastructure" partner in Africa, Angola, Nigeria's oil market is more competitive for Chinese oil companies. At the same time, the Nigerian government is more ambitious when it comes to diversifying its economic structure. President Jonathan emphasised in his national address, "growth in agriculture and other non-oil sectors are crucial, to help diversify the economy and to generate much needed jobs". Chinese Ambassador Deng Boqing's interview concurred with President Jonathan's speech, and he promised that the Chinese "shall continue to encourage more import of non-oil items from Nigeria, especially agriculture products". But considering the unstable situations in Nigeria, this goal is too ambitious for them to realize.

Nigeria is a deficient democratic state. The electoral politics have brought instability and inconsistency to its foreign policy, and that policy can change with the election of a different president. The Nigerian government needs China's funds for infrastructure to show its political achievements, but could also discard China when faced with domestic or foreign problems. Witnesses 3 and 20 both admitted that the Nigerian people were very ambitious about their national strength, and believed Nigeria to be an important power, despite the country's underdeveloped infrastructure, unbalanced economic structure, and security problems. Meanwhile, when spurred by the Western media, the Nigeria government could find a scapegoat for these problems and transfer people's attention away from the Nigeria government and on to China. Witness 2 argued that China is an easy scapegoat for Africa's developmental problems. China's approach of "oil for infrastructure" became an easy target for African economic problem. It could reflect the changes in President Yar'Adua administration. In his administration, the Nigerian government suspended or canceled many of the "oil for infrastructure" contracts signed during Obasanjo's tenure, because Yar'Adua's government thought the oil could command a better price on the international market than that provided by Chinese infrastructure construction. When Jonathan took office, the "oil for infrastructure" policy was re-launched. In July 2013, President Jonathan had a four-day visit to Beijing. During his trip, he signed contracts for US$1.1 billion in loans that included US$0.5 billion for the construction of four international airport terminals located in Lagos, Abuja, Kano, and Port Harcourt (BBC, July 11, 2013), and a 700-MW hydropower station (Reuters, September 29, 2013). However, one must note that these established contracts face another round of change since Nigeria will have its new election in the coming year. Given Nigeria's power transition between North and South, it is questionable whether President Jonathan could serve another term.

In summary, although Nigeria demonstrates its desire to seek a sustainable and balanced developmental path and its ambition to become a big power, the incoherence of the Nigerian government's policy towards China's "oil for infrastructure" approach limits China's capabilities in Nigeria. Furthermore, despite the fact that Abuja may not be satisfied with Beijing's "oil for infrastructure" deals, they have not established an alternative approach. The changing agenda of the Nigerian government lacks a long-term plan and has brought little benefit to the economic development of the state, even less to local communities and the Nigerian people. At the same time, due to inconsistent policy and the social unrest, London-based think tank Chatham House has proven that China and other Asian oil companies haven't benefited from their investments (Vines et al., August 2009). Superficially, Nigeria, as an oil rich state that lacks industrial products, seemed to complement China's thirst for energy and manufactured goods; while China's huge idle funds and experience in infrastructure construction would benefit Nigeria's economic development. However, as Witness 3 pointed out, Nigeria's corruption, mismanagement, incoherent policy, and "oil violence" have constrained the commitment of foreign investment, thus making its oil reserves an illusion to its people and Chinese investors.

7.4 The gap between China's policy in Nigeria and its implementation

In the preceding sections, this book has indicated that China's and Nigeria's national interests can be compatible. Beijing has advocated for creating a "win-win" situation to explore Nigeria's oil fields. Even if we assume that Beijing has a policy for fully supporting the needs of Nigeria, it has to fit into Nigeria's domestic situation, and political changes in Nigeria might create limitations for both sides. Furthermore, Larry Diamond indicates that "political corruption, fraud, and violence" have existed in this country since the First Republic of Nigeria (Diamond, 2008, p. 70). Combined with Nigeria's unstable policy changes and political changes, and the problems with its democracy, there are various issues plaguing China's capability to take responsibility in this country. This section will use "oil for infrastructure" as a start to deeply discuss the problems on the policy implementation especially the impacts of political change, mismanagement, and violence. After the oil case, the problems surrounding China's business involvement in Nigeria's market will be discussed. These two parts are designed to respond to the third hypothesis, that China has a complex role in international responsibility in Nigeria because of these varied issues.

7.4.1 Oil for infrastructure

As mentioned in the previous section, at the policy level, the Chinese government expected to use the provision of infrastructure in exchange for access for the exploitation of Nigeria's oil. As Witness 1 said,

> Our [China-Africa] cooperation is mutually beneficial. We are not neo-colonialists, we are not robbers, the colonialists came to Africa to plunder resources, and the African people hate them; but we helped Africans to build lots of infrastructure and helped them to explore and refine crude oil with Chinese development finance. African people should not suffer from poverty with rich natural resources.

Witness 24 said,

> Despite the fact that China has imported oil and other natural resources from Africa, China has financed African countries for infrastructure construction in return, for which the interest rate is much lower than most European loans. At the same time, these projects were supported by the Chinese government and constructed by Chinese companies that lower the chances of corruption.

Nigeria has the second largest oil reserves in Africa, and the state's economy largely relies on the income it derives from these energy resources. However, the funds raised from the oil industry have not been successfully transferred into diversified economic development. Instead, the money is consumed by political spending and corruption. This mismanagement of oil income has created a vicious circle. Nigeria failed to develop its agricultural and manufacture industries, which led to an unbalanced economic structure, which weakens its economy and makes it heavily reliant on international markets and funds. At the same time, the backward infrastructure, unreliable power supply, rural agricultural industry and civil unrest have restricted Nigeria's economic development and foreign investment.

According to a survey by the World Bank in the African region, "infrastructure has made a net contribution of around one percentage point to Nigeria's improved per capita growth performance in recent years, in spite of the fact that an unreliable power supply held growth back". The same survey suggested that infrastructure constraints are responsible for about 40% of the productivity handicap faced by African firms" (Foster and Pushak, 2011). In contrast, lack of investment and funds meant that the country couldn't meet its demands for power, roads, water, railways, and other industries. Considering the situation in Nigeria, it will require sustained expenditure of almost US$14.2 billion per year over the next decade, which would account for about 12% of GDP; when currently only US$5.9 billion has been spent on infrastructure construction, which is the equivalent to about 5% of GDP, let alone the needs of daily operations and maintenance (UNECA, August 2007). In this case, not only could improving the country's infrastructure contribute to a boost to its economy, but its economy requires greater investment in infrastructure construction. Additionally, the countries' underdeveloped banking system, management and infrastructure, power and water supplies, and transportation make the manufacturing industry very difficult to operate in Nigeria. Witness 19 revealed that most large companies have to rely on imports to maintain their operations because Nigeria doesn't have a sufficient supply chain and infrastructure to support their projects. The medium and small companies can hardly survive, because of the high benchmark interest rate,[2] poor infrastructure, and instability.

Furthermore, Nigeria, as a developing country with huge oil income but corruption, economic mismanagement and lack of accountability and transparency, has suffered from the "resource curse" (Diamond, 2008, pp. 74–75, called it oil curse, and he indicates this phenomenon can be found in most oil countries). With large amounts of oil wealth, the Nigerian government does not need to rely on taxpayers for its income. Therefore, even if Nigeria has a defective democratic political system, the political leaders do not have to answer to the people for voting, but rather for control of the oil industry. In this case, the oil revenues go to the government of which 80% is disbursed to individual governors and their cronies, while just 1% goes to the Nigerian people (Dailymail, August 9, 2013). Not matter how large Nigeria's oil reserves are, little of the income could be invested in infrastructure and local society. Thus, there is no doubt that, without fundamental solutions to its governance problems, the Nigerian people will continue to suffer from rampant corruption and poor economic performance. However, as mentioned, China's responsibility in Nigeria is a combination of national interests and Nigeria's demands. It is unrealistic to expect that the state could change overnight. Infrastructure construction at least provides the country and the people with some tangible contributions and avoids the abuse and corruption of oil revenues by political leaders.

The "oil for infrastructure" approach was initially put forward by Beijing to expand its oil industry alongside favourable infrastructure contracts.

But, in practice, this infrastructure-for-resources deal hasn't worked well in Nigeria because Chinese companies lack experiences in responding to the changing political environment in Nigeria. Political elites in this country have differing interests regarding the "oil for infrastructure" deals. Some favour infrastructure as an achievement for their electoral politics, while others felt that implementing these deals would cut them off from the profits derived from crude oil deals on the international market. In addition, mismanagement and violence have undermined the Nigerian people's ability to enjoy the benefits from the Chinese-built infrastructure and Chinese companies' profits.

I Weak democracy and Incoherent policy

As the book mentioned in the previous section, the Nigerian government established a democratic regime in 1999, when President Obasanjo returned to power. Since then, the state has successfully conducted national elections three times – in 2003, 2007 and 2011. State power has transferred from Obasanjo to Yar'Adua, and then Jonathan. However, the positive steps on the political front haven't brought this country stability and development because of its weak democratic institutions and authoritarian distribution of resources. After two democratic transitions, the political system and elections remain as "access to the state as an avenue for wealth accumulation and conferment of status" (Center for Democracy and Development [CDD], 2003).

Larry Diamond has even called Nigeria's democracy a money democracy because, in this country, the oil curse has caused the political elites to fight against each other for the benefits from oil. The 1999 election was plagued by cheating, corruption and vote buying, and one-third of the state may suffer from serious election fraud. Even in the 2003 elections, these problems with electoral cheating had only slightly been resolved (Diamond, 2008, pp. 70–71, 73–74). Therefore, elections in Nigeria can only be argued to appear to have the form of elections, rather than actually being elections. Winning an election will determine whether someone is able to have access to the resource distribution process. The perception that elections are zero-sum grasps of wealth leads to unsustainable policy decisions that are easily changed in future presidential administrations.

Obasanjo is a Yoruba from Nigeria's Christian south, who represented the interests of his background; while Yar'Adua is a Fulani Hausa and a Muslim from the north. It seemed, therefore, that "Yar'Adua's northern supporters ... will not let Obasanjo's deals proceed unless they are included in them" (Mthembu-Salter, 2009), which explained the fact that, after Yar'Adua took office in 2007, he swiftly reviewed the agreements signed during Obasanjo's administration. It led to a large number of "oil for infrastructure" deals signed between Nigeria and other Asian companies to either be suspended or cancelled. Meanwhile, "no coherent ... policy has replaced Obasanjo's discarded one", the government was ambiguous about what they wanted: cash or infrastructure (Wong, 2009).

When President Jonathan took office in 2010, the bilateral economic relationship between Beijing and Abuja had rebounded. Nigerian Minister of Foreign Affairs Olugbenga Ashiru pointed out in an interview that President Jonathan's "Transformation Agenda with its strong emphasis on infrastructural development: roads, power, railways, etc. make a relationship with China very crucial and imperative" (Nigerian Guardian, July 19, 2013). Evidence can also be found for an increasing number Chinese state-owned enterprises (SOEs) contracts in Nigeria. In July 2012, the China Machinery Engineering Corporation (CMEC) worked with the Delta government to build a vehicle assembly plant at Issele-Uku, in the Aniocha North Local Government Area of the state (Point Blank News, July 8, 2012). Soon after, the Nigeria government endorsed a locomotive contract that cost about US$28 million, for Chinese carriages and railway. This purchase brought Chinese companies an opportunity to enter Nigeria and other African emerging markets. It estimated that Chinese companies had already built roads across Nigeria in contracts worth $1.7 billion (Aljazeera, 2013). In return, China's demand for crude oil produced in Nigeria is expected to rise tenfold to 200,000 barrels a day by 2015, Nigerian officials said, and Agence France-Presse (AFP) reports (Aljazeera, 2013). It is worth noting that Chinese shares of oil exploration in the Niger Delta area was mainly gained through acquisitions from the traditional multinational oil companies, rather than directly from the Nigerian government during Jonathan's administration. In 2009, Sinopec bought Addax petroleum – a company based in Switzerland and listed in the UK and Canada, for US$7.2 billion. This purchase ensured China's engagement in Nigeria and other West Africa oil producers, like Gabon and Cameroon (the Guardian, June 24, 2009). At the end of 2012, Sinopec paid US$2.5 billion for a stake in Oil Mining Lease (OML) 138 from the French oil company Total, which accounted for 20% of its offshore oil fields in Nigeria (SCMP, November 20, 2012) (Table 7.1).

Table 7.1 Nigeria's elected presidents

Years of rule	Name	Type of government	Ethnicity	Religion	Place of birth	Departure from government
1999–2007	Olusegun Obasanjo	Civilian	Yoruba	Christian	South-West (Ogun)	Election
2007–2010	Umaru Yar'Adua	Civilian	Hausa-Fulani	Muslims	North (Katsina)	Election
2010–2015	Goodluck Jonathan	Civilian	Lijaw	Christian	South (Ogbia)	Succeed/Election
2015 until now	Muhammadu Buhari	Civilian	jingoism	Muslims	Fulani	Election

Source: Author.

Politically, the electoral cycle has made the deals between Chinese companies and the Nigerian government unstable, sometimes even the "legal" contracts may be suspended or canceled because of the election of one political leader over another – especially when the regime changes hands from a northern Muslim to a southern Christian. Since the new presidential election will come in 2019 and considering Nigeria's electoral alternative between north and south, the future of China's contracts is doubt. As a Western diplomat described: "When it comes to 'oil for infrastructure', I think the Angolans understood the point that you either get the infrastructure or the money. The Nigerians thought you got both … But it turns out that, forced to choose…" (Mthembu-Salter, 2009). Lacking a clear message on Nigeria's demands made it hard for China to make a judgment on how to "be responsible" in the country. In addition, the incoherent policy left the country with lots of unfinished projects; a waste of both Chinese investment and Nigeria's development funds.

Theoretically, Chinese construction companies have the advantages of China's high-level political dialogue and financial support from China's national banks. The infrastructure construction projects were introduced as a complement to their oil deals, but in reality, the projects did not go through smoothly. Take railway construction as an example: in 2002, a project for the modernisation of Nigeria's railway system was proposed, which China offered to finance with a US$1 billion soft loan from the China Exim Bank. On October 30, 2006, the China Civil Engineering Construction (CCECC) and the Nigerian Ministry of Transport signed a contract worth US$8.3 billion for the Lagos-Kano Railway Modernisation Project (China.org.cn, December 2, 2014), which was linked with the 2006 China-Nigeria "Oil for infrastructure agreement". However, it was suspended in 2008, due to the Yar'Adua government's austerity measures and financial difficulties. The Nigerian government has presented a sharply contrasting attitude towards the project from high-profile support under President Obasanjo to a suspension order contained in a letter.

CCECC was frustrated by the changing policy because this company had lobbied for the US$1 billion loan from the Chinese government in order to facilitate the project in the first place. On the other side, Nigeria complained about CCECC's sluggish performance by claiming that, "in spite of the $250 million released to the contractor for the take-off of the project, Nigerians were yet to see any improvement in the rail sector" (oyibosonline, 2008). CCECC held a different perspective: Shi Hongbing said that even though Nigeria just paid the company $250 million, which only accounted for 3% of the entire project, the company had made progress on the 1,315 km Lagos-Kano double track standard gauge rehabilitation, which is the first phase of the 25-year-long project. Witness 7 revealed that construction projects in Africa were difficult, due to financial difficulties, mismanagement and corruption, which meant that some African government-led projects often delayed payment and lacked credibility. On the other hand, since most African countries don't have a sustainable supply chain to maintain such a big project, lots of materials and equipment for the projects had to be imported. It often happened that, when some big projects were undertaken in the same period, the projects were easily delayed by the shortage of some key materials. What's worse, the shortages created an unbalanced supply-demand of these materials in local markets, which led to an increase in their cost and made the completion of the projects even harder.

CCECC's project re-launched in 2009. The price of the project was reduced to US$8 billion, and China agreed to help finance the project with a US$2.5 billion loan, comprised of export credit for US$2 billion at a competitive commercial rate, and a preferential export credit of US$500 million. In order to relieve Nigeria's financial difficulty, the project was to be implemented in phases. The first phase of the project included modernising the 186.5 km Abuja-to-Kaduna section of the 1,313 km railway from Lagos to Kano. The cost of the first phase was projected to be US$849,750,903 and would be constructed over 36 months. The second phase of the project was the Lagos-Ibadan section of the railway, a double-track line with a total length of 156.8 km and a projected speed of 150 km per hour, for both passengers and freight transportation. This portion is worth approximately US$1.487 billion, with a construction period of 36 months. In July 2013, the Minister of Transportation confirmed that 68% of the work on the Abuja-Kaduna line had been completed, while the contract for the Lagos-Ibadan double track had been signed but was pending the completion of an agreement with the China Exim Bank (Aid Data). The stop-and-go Chinese projects in Nigeria reflect Nigeria's changing political priority and fragile contacts impact on both Chinese enterprises and Nigerian development. As this is an area abandoned by most of the western countries, China's 'oil-for-infrastructure' approach cannot provide effective commitments to local development.

II Mismanagement

The previous paragraph indicated that the elections in Nigeria are characterised by corruption and vote buying and that this leads to mismanagement in this country. Despite President Obasanjo attempts to form a financial crime section to combat corruption and the financial problems in the oil sector, which prevented some governors and political leaders from appropriating oil revenues for private use benefit, he still tried to buy parliament members to give himself the third term as president (Diamond, 2008, pp. 72–73). Oil companies in Nigeria are the core problem that leads to mismanagement. Currently, foreign companies that operate in Nigeria have worked on joint ventures with Nigeria's national oil companies. In May 2002, the Nigerian government commercialised the Nigerian National Petroleum Corporation (NNPC) and increased its independence. In this case, foreign companies could increase their shares and involvement of Nigeria's oil industry.

However, Witness 3 explained that this measure did not prevent bureau-
cratisation and corruption; instead, it turned out to be a transference of
oil interests from the government to bureaucrats, plutocrats, and individuals. For example, South Atlantic Petroleum, which sold OML 130 to China
National Offshore Oil Corporate (CNOOC), was owned by the ex-Nigerian
Defence Minister Danjuma. Witness 20 complained that Chinese companies were confused about the Nigerian governments' role in its oil industry.
After a series of oil reforms, exploration and operation were still controlled
by a few political elites, and sometimes Nigerian oil ministers handed out
licenses at their own discretion. Although not illegal, it did not follow the
practice of using open bids. In addition, the serious corruption and bureaucracy meant the Chinese/foreign companies have to pay extra "public relations" fees in order to win the bidding. As a result, the situation left Chinese
investors with not many choices, except maintaining relationships with a
few Nigerian political elites. Sometimes, as Witness 20 said, "you have no
other methods than bribing the local governors". Similar experiences were
had by Western multinational oil companies as well. In 2000, the Nigerian
government announced that it would issue oil licenses through open bidding
in order to prevent corruption. Two years later, there was a scandal that US
oil company Ocean Energy paid an extra US$245 million to the government
in order to win the bid for Oil Prospecting License (OPL) 256. As Diamond
indicates, political leaders in this oil country all scrambled for oil revenues
(Diamond, 2008, p. 77), and because these political leaders cooperate with
business leaders, the wealth of the states cannot be fully deployed to serve
the people; most of the wealth from oil just serves the elite The corruption
and mismanagement cannot be effectively stopped in these countries. This
situation cannot be ascribed to China's being irresponsible to the host country, and this issue exists widely in most oil countries.

III Violence

The energy industry is a highly sensitive sector in Nigeria. Improper involvement and operation have not only the danger of economic loss but
also of high risks. The Movement for the Emancipation of the Niger Delta
(MEND), a group that has allegedly been involved in numerous armed
attacks in the region – as a response to what they regard as the exploitation
and oppression of the people and the degradation of the natural environment in the Niger Delta (Hazen, 2007) – has complained about the record of
Chinese companies in other African countries.

  They believed "entry into the oil industry in Nigeria will be a disaster
for the oil-bearing communities", as a result, they have warned Chinese
companies to "stay well clear of the oil producing Niger delta or risk facing
attack". From local people's perspective, oil companies bring few benefits,
but they do contribute to the ecological and environmental deterioration
and water pollution. Plus, the unbalanced distribution system, with "limited

economic opportunities and numerous social and political grievances", has bred lots of armed groups and increasing violence and also kidnappings (Hazen, 2007). Witness 3 has explained,

> As people may say, the Chinese has paid back African countries by the construction of infrastructure. The newly built facilities often are not located in or near oil fields. People from oil field communities cannot enjoy the commitments by China.

On the other hand, Chinese oil companies make significant losses from oil-related violence and also oil theft. Witness 22 said, for the overseas companies, what concerns them the most is the safety of their employees. But, in the case of Nigeria, both employee safety and economic safety are at risk. According to a report by Nuhu Ribadu, the former anti-corruption chief, Nigeria has "lost out on tens of billions of dollars in oil and gas revenues over the last decade from cut-price deals struck between multinational oil companies and government officials" (Reuters, October 24, 2012). The destruction of pipelines and oil theft that cost oil companies significant losses have also contributed to the drop in Nigeria's oil exports in 2013.

Generally, China's "oil for infrastructure" policy has brought Nigeria loans, technology, and facilities to improve the Nigerian people's living conditions and ensure the distribution of Nigeria's oil income on public services, while effectively preventing corruption. But, due to the political struggles within the Nigerian government, its policy is unpredictable to Chinese investors, which has led some to suspend and cancel projects, which is a waste of time and resources for both sides. In addition, the interest gap between political elites and the majority of people living in oil-rich areas has drawn Chinese companies into a hard position: on the one hand, they have to satisfy the officials to gain the contracts; while on the other hand, they have the responsibility to meet the demands of local communities. As a new comer to the country where is left by the western experiences' investors, Beijing's policy is incapable of protecting its assets and citizens in Nigeria. The "oil for infrastructure" fails to benefit the majority of Nigeria people.

7.4.2 Chinese business

Nigeria experts suggested that they 'appreciated that Chinese investment gave African new leverage' and urged 'China to relocate some of its industries to Africa' (Amosu, 2007). Meanwhile, Nigerian officials have voiced concern about Chinese products. The Supervising Minister of National Planning, Bashir Yuguda, has said to the Chinese Ambassador to Nigeria, Gu Xiaojie:

> On our own part, we have been striving to ensure that Nigerian businessmen do not go to China to demand substandard products. We also

try to discourage them by ensuring that as much as possible such products do not cross our borders. We want China to also be able to control things from their end, because we believe that there should be a minimum standard for all countries. There is no doubt that fake products have a potential of hurting both economies.

(Osayande, 2014)

This section argues that, although the Chinese government may not need to take responsibility for the policy level, Chinese businesses may still be the actors that prevent China from being a fully responsible player in Nigeria. There are two major problems related to Chinese businesses in Nigeria: The dumping and quality issues of Chinese goods, and the cultural differences between Chinese and Nigerian labourers. The Chinese government is trying to solve this but has not offered an effective and comprehensive solution to Nigeria's complaints.

For the first issue, as Director General of Nigerian Textile Garment and Tailoring Employers' Association JP Olarewaju has complained since the Nigerian government eliminated the import ban on textiles in 1997, Chinese products swarmed into the Nigerian market, and some of them entered Nigeria through smuggling (Fibre2Fashion interview). These products have a negative impact on the local textile manufacturing industry, As Olarewaju said, in 1994 when he had just taken the position of Director General of Nigerian Textile Garment and Tailoring Employers' Association, they had 124 members. But, in 2013, there were only 30 left. The number of employees in the textile industry has reduced from 170,000 to 25,000 (BBC, January 8, 2013). By contrast, a veteran Chinese entrepreneur in Nigeria Sun Guoping responded to the criticism, saying that Chinese entrepreneur can only survive in Nigeria because the Nigerian people accepted the products. Most of the Chinese came as investors rather than the labourers. Therefore, instead of stealing jobs from the Nigeria people, many of them have created employment opportunities (BBC, January 23, 2013). Their argument revealed that China's involvement has a dual impact on Nigeria's manufacturing industry. Chinese manufacturing operations contribute to the country's employment, but also bring tough competition for local producers. Comparing the claims from both sides, Nigeria's manufacturing industry has welcomed the Chinese in terms of investment, rather than Chinese products.

Nigeria's manufacturing industry is underperforming for China, which is reflected in the fact that bilateral trade is unbalanced. According to China Customs, the bilateral trade value between China and Nigeria in the first half year of 2013 reached US$6.02 billion, up by 18.8%. During this year, China's exports to Nigeria were valued at US$5.43 billion, up by 28%; while China's imports from Nigeria were US$590 million, down by 28.3%. China had a surplus of US$4.84 billion. There are mixed reasons for this large trade deficit, and the manufacturing industry offers a look at the whole picture. Even the Director General of Nigerian Textile Garment and Tailoring

Employers' Association JP Olarewaju admitted that the reason for Nigerian products being uncompetitive lies with the poor infrastructure. He argued that,

> we are unable to compete with the Chinese, because the power supply here is insufficient. Our factories need to generate the electricity by themselves. They need a generator. The generators need gas or diesel. The production of textiles also needs energy. Additionally, the transportation in Nigeria is very poor in which the railway could not operate smoothly while the road is unreliable as well. The logistics are very expensive due to the high insurance. As a result, the cost of our products is much higher than China's.
>
> (BBC, January 8, 2013)

Nigeria's domestic textile industry is not able to cope with cheap imports and increased smuggling from China.

Another complaint from Nigerians is the quality of Chinese goods. Inferior and fake Chinese products are considered to swarm into Nigeria's market. Some of them have even violated Nigeria's intellectual property. They take advantage of the tariff concessions but copy Nigeria's designs, which harms the development of local industries. In response to this criticism, Witness 1 said,

> As a Chinese saying goes, 'in a big forest there is every kind of bird.' Among the huge volume of Chinese products, and besides the ones manufactured for the high end markets, there also exists fair quality products targeted for the medium and low end markets, as well as disqualified ones manufactured by a small number of lawless businessmen.

Witness 23 argued,

> Even if the quality of Chinese products does not enjoy good reputation, as a 'world factory', the Chinese manufacturing industry has developed enough to become a production line of the famous brands of high quality. That proves Chinese manufacturing has the capability to meet the high quality requirements. Constrained by African countries' limited purchasing capability and consumption level, Africa became the most vulnerable destination for the low quality products.

Due to a limited consumption level and capability, economic products are welcome in Nigeria's market.

Witness 20 offered another reason,

> We have no other choice, the African middleman offered low prices, which leaves little profit to the Chinese manufacturers. Thus, the

producers lowered the quality. And due to the mismanagement, smuggling is rampant in Nigeria. You cannot imagine how serious corruption is in Africa. Money can do anything.

Actually, the flood of inferior Chinese products affected not only Nigerian companies, but local Chinese investment as well. Many of the textile factories that have been forced to shut down were Chinese-owned plants that had been operating in Kaduna since the 1970s (Egbula and Zheng, 2011). Those low-quality products labeled "Made in China" have affected African people's confidence in Chinese products. It has required both governments from Beijing and Abujia to levy stricter regulations. Witness 3 said that:

> Beijing has launched various ways to control the spread of inferior products. The government has set up monitoring and complaint platforms, conducted special controlling programmes, urged enterprises to assume responsibility for the quality and safety of their products, enriched the quality and safety standard system, and worked to speed up the perfection of the quality inspection and supervision system.

Additionally, it has attached particular importance to the quality of products for export and taken steps to conduct a comprehensive quality inspection of those goods, in order to prevent an outflow of substandard products (Tribune, December 15, 2013). On the other hand, these measures need the cooperation of the Nigeria government as well. In March 2011, the Chinese embassy in Nigeria, together with the National Association of Nigerian Traders, co-hosted a seminar on China-Nigeria Trade Promotion to exchange ideas on how to raise the quality of Chinese products in Nigeria, and to push forward the sustained development of bilateral trade relations (Ng-embassy, December 13, 2012). But due to the fragmented authoritarianism problem discussed in Chapter 5, these measures have not been well informed and implemented by local Chinese business.

Furthermore, labour unions also complain about working conditions in Chinese companies, where "they say Nigerian workers are poorly paid and rarely rise to management level. Chinese companies have been accused of flouting labour laws and discouraging unions" (Egbula and Zheng, 2011). Recently, there have been protests over poor labour practices in Lagos. The Nigerian workers of CCECC protested the abuse from and anti-labour treatment by the management in February 2013. What made them unsatisfied was their welfare. Complaints included "no medical facility for workers", "poor salaries", "working in other areas with no additional wage", "work on public holidays and weekends", and "lack of labour union". After the protest, Deputy Manager, Materials and Equipment Department, CCECC, Wang Chunjing promised that the company was planning to increase the workers' salaries. Concerning the other allegations, however, he offered no specific solutions. The complaints by Nigerian workers reflected cultural differences between the Chinese labour force and Nigerian. A carpenter, Mr. Henry Okoye, complained that "I was hired as a carpenter, but I am forced to work as a gardener and bricklayer on the same pay." Meanwhile, the deputy manager Mr. Wang explained, "that if a carpenter or mason's job was finished, the company could use the person in the section or area that had tasks so as not to lay them off... You cannot deploy a bricklayer to be a personal manager. The manual job is where he can function well. I do not see what is wrong with a carpenter being asked to be a gardener." (allAfrica) The Chinese working environment is flexible; it may need an employee to serve multiple roles with one title, at the same time, and it is normal to work over time. This difference led the Chinese management to consider the Nigerian workers as not work as hard working as Chinese workers, while the Nigerians feel mistreated. What's more, although CCECC is a state-owned company, their employees are categorised in different levels. According to its website, CCECC, handling several construction contracts across the country, has about 50 regular staff and more than 200 casual workers who are paid by their supervisors, and engages more casual workers if there are more jobs to be done. Although these casual workers worked for the Chinese project of CCECC, the company does not manage their payment and welfare. As a result, a large number of workers actually work for their supervisors, a management more like a private company, in the name of CCECC. The management of these supervisors differs and is random. Witness 16 also mentioned this phenomenon by saying,

> It is admitted that the working condition in Chinese companies is not as good as western companies. But African labour force is not as good as Chinese worker as well. We have to hire local supervisor to monitor them ... Sometimes, in order to finish the on-going construction on time, we may require the workers to work on weekends or public holidays and pay them extra money. Despite the workers can refuse to work extra hours, yet as a casual worker, they may easily be replaced by other people in the excuse of laziness or disobedience.

The criticisms of Chinese business in Nigeria exist in the majority of African countries, including the quality of products, poor working conditions, and lack of labour force protection. During the interviews, nearly all witnesses recognised Chinese companies' deficiencies and admitted the distance between Chinese companies and Western multinationals. Witness 22 suggested that,

> In response to these criticisms, there are only two ways: the first one is to expel all Chinese business, and the second one is to improve. Whether expelling all China's presence in Africa is good to the continent?

Witness 22 admitted that the problem of China's business in Nigeria is caused by Chinese enterprises. But currently he holds that the companies operate independently in the host country, and the central government lacks the ability to control them.

> I've done fieldwork in lots of African countries. None of them have ever thought about China's image. What they cared about was very practical, such as, when the Chinese government could help to simplify the visa application process in African countries.

Therefore, the witnesses also agreed that, even as the government and academia have recognised Chinese companies and businessmen's irresponsible behaviour in Nigeria, which may violate China's international reputation as a whole, there are no tangible methods to solve the problems from the top on down in the short run.

In summary, this book indicates that Chinese businesses in Nigeria may need to be responsible for complaints from Nigerians, or even Western countries. The Chinese government cannot avoid these issues without a sound supervision on its overseas business, but Chinese businesses also face difficulties in Nigeria, such as a lack of electricity or diligent labourers. As witnesses indicated, the Chinese government does not offer any feasible solutions to help Chinese businesses, and eventually Chinese businesses only care about their revenue, rather than China's image.

7.4.3 Summary

To summarise, China's state development economy and a large amount of investment are attractive to the Nigerian government and people. The two countries have a broader chance of cooperation on economic development. Theoretically, the 'oil for infrastructure' approach meets both demands. At the implementation level, because of the constrictions in Nigeria and the weakness of Beijing, China was not a fully responsible actor in the country. For the Nigerian side, a weak democracy, incoherent policies, mismanagement, corruption, and violence all create serious problems that hinder Nigeria's demands, which were mentioned in the previous sections. Weak democracy and incoherent policies lead to an unstable attitude towards the oil-for-infrastructure policy; mismanagement and corruption directly weaken the ability of Nigeria to use its oil revenue to improve infrastructure for industries and transform their economic structure. Political elites are only seeking a share of the oil revenues to benefit themselves, rather than the people or the state. Violence can exacerbate the problems within Nigeria, rather than solve them. As for China's side, although Beijing has launched some measures to solve the problems arising by Chinese business, such as, the quality of Chinese products and the protection of local labourers, it is not very effective, because the Chinese companies lack the motivation to follow the policy and measures. As a result, both governments need to focus on their own problems and present feasible policy solutions.

7.5 Conclusion

China-Nigeria relations grew closer on the basis of diplomatic and economic motivations. In the bilateral meetings and visits between high-level officials, both countries have confirmed their willingness to broaden cooperation. Beijing's "oil for infrastructure" approach does not have many significant challenges that must be solved if both are to realise their economic demands. And, according to the Pew Research Centre, the Nigerian people generally hold a positive attitude towards China. Thus, the discussions in the first section of the chapter indicate that at the policy level, China and Nigeria could cooperate with each other because both countries have complementary motivations and demands.

However, a clear limitation that could affect China's capability of taking responsibility in Nigeria has also been suggested in the middle of this chapter. Nigerian political elites do not continuously follow the same energy-for-resources deal and are also ambitious to develop their own industries rather than getting infrastructure projects from China. Beijing, on the other hand, was been slow to respond to Nigeria's changing policy. Its efforts on infrastructure construction are undermined by Nigeria's high cost of governance. And, due to the ruling People's Democratic Party's (PDP) political upheavals and domestic crises, the Nigeria government has been unable to provide sustainable and long-term economic stability for foreign investors. These situations all directly limit China's capability for responsibility in Nigeria. Since there will be a general election in 2015, the Nigerian government is estimated to concentrate on politics and struggles between the two major parties, PDP and All Progressives Congress (APC); which means they may be slow in dealing with certain economic problems, such as oil theft and the Nigeria's Petroleum Industry Bill (PIB).[3] It will likely increase Chinese investors' concerns for the environment in the Nigerian oil industry.

The main factors in Nigeria that affect the country's development and cause problems for China are Nigeria's weak democracy, incoherent governmental policies, mismanagement, corruption, and a political elite that fights with itself for control over oil revenues, and violent groups. Chinese companies have also become problems for Nigeria, hindering its ambitions and worsening its domestic situation. Chinese goods are not welcome in this country for many reasons. Meanwhile, those Chinese employers who are willing to do business in Nigeria often neglect the accepted working standards on employment, environment, security, and the local community in order to boost profits, which exacerbated the dissatisfaction of the Nigerian people.

In short, it can be concluded that China's presence in Nigeria has partly met the country's policy level demands, especially with regards to financial support and "infrastructure for oil", for its economic development. However, its effectiveness is constrained by Nigeria's political elites, weak democracy, mismanagement, violent groups, and Chinese businesses' lack of awareness of corporate social responsibility. These actors and contexts hinder the capability of China to be responsible in Nigeria.

Notes

1 The term was coined by economist Jim O'Neill, who has now identified the "Mint" countries – Mexico, Indonesia, Nigeria, and Turkey – as emerging economic giants.
2 Nigeria's benchmark interest rate was 12% in 2013, while most economies' benchmark interest rate is below 10% – for example, China's is about 6%.
3 PIB is a controversial bill, which aims at oil reform. It is believed to have a huge impact to oil mutilations in Nigeria if passed.

8   South Africa

The relationship between China and South Africa represents many features of emerging states and newly industrialised countries (NICs), such as resource conflicts, South-South cooperation, and regionalism. South Africa, as the single "superpower" on the continent, is included among the association of five major emerging national economies: Brazil, Russia, India, China and South Africa (BRICS), with expectations to serve as a bridge between fragile states and developed states politically, economically, and diplomatically, and serve as a representative for sub-Saharan and south African countries. At the same time, it has yet to become a competitor to emerging powers in this region, due to its political and economic interests. This chapter will discuss South Africa's role in China-Africa links and the impact of China's engagement with the state.

China-South Africa relations are a featured case for assessing the impact of Chinese business on Africa, because South Africa is the most developed country on the continent, its economic structure is the most similar to that of China's, by which it means South Africa's industry is most likely to be able to compete with Chinese business involvement, and also be impacted by its Chinese counterparts. Hence, this chapter will analyse China's contributions and deficiencies in its engagement with South Africa. The chapter starts with a brief background on China-South Africa relations. Then it discusses three influential factors in shaping China's responsibility in the country-China's national interests, South Africa's demands, and international expectations – to explore to what extent China's policy can help South Africa. In the second section, the chapter will discuss China's capability to be responsible in South Africa. In the final part, this chapter will explore the actors and contexts which could affect China's role in South Africa, from both South Africa's and China's perspectives.

8.1 A brief background introduction

China became South Africa's largest export and import partner in 2009, and South Africa is also China's largest trading partner in Africa, with bilateral trading volume reaching US$60 billion in 2012. However, bilateral official relations were not established until 1998. Before that, South Africa had official relations with Taiwan. Since January 1998, Pretoria, under the government of Mandela, switched its official recognition from the Republic of China (ROC) to the People's Republic of China (PRC) due to strategic and economic considerations. Bilateral political and economic communication developed quickly after recognition, with frequent high-level visits and a forty-fold increase in trading volume.

In 2000, during Chinese President Jiang Zemin's visit to South Africa, the two countries signed the Pretoria Declaration on Partnership Relations. In the same year, they established a Bi-National Commission, under which five sector committees were established: diplomatic affairs, trade, education, science and technology, and defence. Soon after, in 2004, during then-Chinese Vice President Zeng Qinghong's visit to South Africa, the two countries further defined their relationship as a strategic partnership of equality, mutual benefit and common development. In 2006, China and South Africa signed 13 agreements on cooperation for a wide range of fields, such as politics, economics, trade, national defence, agriculture, technology and sciences, as well as an agreement to deepen the strategic partnership between the two states during then-Premier Wen Jiabao's trip to South Africa. One year later, when then-President Hu Jintao conducted his eight-nation African tour, he highlighted the agreements reached during the Beijing summit in 2006, including eight measures to benefit African countries, which pushed the China-South Africa strategic partnership to a new height. Bilateral mechanisms for strategic dialogue were established in 2008, and four rounds of meetings were held over the next four years. In 2010, when President Jacob Zuma first visited China, he signed the Beijing Declaration with Chinese President Hu Jintao, establishing the comprehensive strategic partnership. The Parliamentary Regular Exchange Mechanism of the two countries was set up in 2011 and has already conducted two rounds of talks (Embassy of PRC in South Africa).

Economically, South Africa became China's largest trading partner in Sub-Saharan Africa in 1993. Despite the trade value in that year was only US$660 million, it accounted for a quarter of Beijing's trade with the continent. At the time when official bilateral relations were established, this figure grew to US$1.5 billion. It rose 40 times in 15 years, and almost reached US$60 billion in 2012. According to the statistics from Ministry of Commerce (Mofcom), the growth rate of China-South Africa trade was larger than China-US and China—ASEAN (Association of Southeast Asian Nations) in the first half of 2013. In 2012, China-South Africa imports and exports volume was US$24.7 billion – of which, South Africa exported US$10.1 billion and imported US$14.6 billion from China, with a deficit of US$ 447 million. Compared to other African states, South Africa's deficit with China is relatively small, but the products exported from South Africa are low value-added, such as raw materials, while it imported high value-added products from China, including mechanical and electrical products, textiles, and telecommunications. This unbalanced economic relationship prevails in other African countries as well and is a widely-held concern of African political elites.

8.2 Shaping China's responsibility in the South Africa

The motivation for China's engagement in South Africa is clearer than with other states since the country is a regional leader with the strongest economy on the continent. However, in terms of responsibility, as the national strengths of these two countries are much closer than in China's relations with other African states, China's assistance in South Africa has produced less concern in both the country and international community than with other African states. This section will explore China's political and economic interests, and to what extent they complement South Africa's agenda and international expectations.

8.2.1 China's motivation

South Africa, as a regional power accounting for approximately a third of Sub-Saharan African gross domestic product (GDP), is no doubt of great significance to China. Not only is South Africa a major player on the continent, but it is also a mediator of China's strategic expansion in the region.

I Politically

1   Friendly governments
    The Chinese government has attached great importance to its relationship with South Africa., which s evidenced by the fact that South Africa is the first developing country with which China established a "comprehensive strategic partnership", and the two governments have maintained frequent high-level visits. Since the establishment of bilateral relations 15 years ago, almost every senior Chinese politician, provincial governor and municipal mayor have traveled to South Africa. South African government delegations are also frequent visitors to Beijing. Leaders of both countries have met at all kinds of international conferences. In 2012, then-President Hu Jintao met with President Zuma four times. The new Chinese President Xi Jinping chose South Africa as his first overseas trip. Such frequent high-level exchanges have brought the two countries closer together. During Xi Jinping's trip to South Africa, both countries agreed to make the relationship the "strategic pivot and priority" of each other's foreign policy, highlighting the strategic significance of the relationship (Tian, June 28, 2013). Additionally, they have set up various exchange mechanisms for closer diplomatic relations. Apart from the Bi-National Committee at the vice-presidential level mentioned earlier, the two countries have also established regular

exchanges between the two parliaments, the strategic dialogue, and the joint working group. South Africa is now the African host of the Forum on China-Africa Cooperation and a rotating chair of association of five major emerging national economies: Brazil, Russia, India, China and South Africa (BRICS) (MOFA, July 2, 2013). It can be said that through various communication platforms and channels, the two governments have been in a "honeymoon" period during their 15 years of official ties.

2   Diplomatic support

Internationally, Witness 11 argued that all developing countries shared the same or similar views on international affairs: that is, calling for a fair and balanced new global political and economic order, as opposed to the North-dominant system in place. Africa, as the continent long-ignored by international society, has a quieter voice and receives few benefits from the current international system. South Africa, as one important member of the continent, is fated to play a constructive role in promoting the reform of global governance, and safeguarding the interests of developing countries. Witness 11's argument reveals that Beijing considers South Africa to be a significant ally on "south-south cooperation" and multilateral cooperation among developing countries. In a Bilateral Joint Communiqué, "the two sides appealed to countries all over the world to establish a more equal and balanced global partnership for development, and address global challenges through unity and cooperation for mutual benefit". Emphasising their shared identity as developing countries allowed China to gain greater understanding and support from South Africa. Although the two states have different domestic political systems, they still can stand on the same side on international events; as evidenced by two countries' cooperation on climate change negotiations, within the BRICS framework. During President Xi Jinping's trip to Pretoria, the two countries "called for upholding the legitimate rights and interests of developing countries and making the international order and system fairer and more equitable" (China Daily, March 27, 2013).

Regionally, South Africa's domestic achievements, international reputation, and position in Africa place the country in the role of a regional leader. It is commonly agreed that the peace, security and development of Africa require joint efforts from continental leaders and external commitments. South Africa offers not only a successful model of transformation from apartheid to democratic government but also plays an instrumental role in fostering engagement with external actors on conflict resolution in the continent. Considering Africa's constraints, South Africa is expected to deliver the African agenda for the region's "hot spots" to a broader platform in order for gain support and resolutions. It is worth noting that, despite Pretoria's different political system to that in Beijing and more effective cooperation with the North than China, the state exhibits more similar stances with Beijing on some hot issues – notably, the attitude towards military intervention in Libya and Syria. South Africa was reluctant to agree to the use of force in resolving African countries' domestic crises, especially in the absence of host government approval. It revealed that Pretoria's awareness and greater concern for its status as a developing African country than for the collective policies of the North. Given its role as mediator in Africa's regional conflicts and in finding international peaceful resolutions, as well as its position in the African Union (AU) and other regional organisations, South Africa's attitude reflected the regional collective security concerns. Along with its support, Beijing could strengthen its influence and increase its identity as a developing country within this area. As a result, Chinese President Xi Jinping "pledged cooperation with South Africa on African affairs, and vowed to play a constructive role in matters concerning African peace and security" during his state visit to South Africa (China Daily, March 27, 2013). At the same time, both sides "called on the international community to pay more attention to and offer greater support for Africa, respect African countries' efforts to solve regional issues on their own, and help them enhance capability for self-generated growth" (April & Shelton, 2014, pp. 29).

3   Domestic agenda support

Before the establishment of diplomatic relations between China and South Africa, the recognition problem was a major barrier to bilateral official communication. Due to South Africa's diplomatic and economic requirements, it switched its official ties from Taipei to Beijing, in 1998. After that, nearly all South African presidents have recognised Beijing as the representative of China in many circumstances. In his speech at the University of Pretoria, in 2011, President Zuma reconfirmed South Africa's support for the "One China Policy" by saying, "the People's Republic of China is the only representative of the Chinese people" (Daily Maverick, Oct. 14 2011). Even if South African officials have claimed their support for the "One China policy", it could be realistic to admit that "most Africans do not care much who the real China is or with whom official diplomatic ties should be established" (Taylor, 2009). Pretoria itself has put forward a "Two China's" situation in order to "maximize South Africa's manoeuvrability and overseas investment from the two rival countries" (Byrnes, 1996).

The issue of the Dalai Lama's visa application in 2009 and 2011 also presents a similar situation. In 2009, the South African government refused to grant a visa to the Dalai Lama, who was to attend a peace conference in Johannesburg; it was "a matter of relations between states", explained South Africa's finance minister Trevor Manuel (Mail and Guardian, March 27, 2009). Beijing considered the Dalai Lama's trip a political statement about the secession of Tibet. Meanwhile, South Africa's Nobel Peace Prize winners, Archbishop Desmond Tutu and FW de Klerk, berated Pretoria, saying it was "disgraceful to ban the Dalai Lama from attending following Chinese pressure" (McGreal, March 23, 2009). In 2011, the Dalai Lama had been invited to South Africa to receive the Mahatma Gandhi International Award for Peace and Reconciliation and to speak at a number of events, including a lecture in honour of Tutu's 80th birthday. However, he withdrew his visa application after South Africa's delay (Cable News Network [CNN], October 4, 2011), which caused much debate in South Africa, where some accused South Africa's home affairs department of "unlawful" practices, and being "not entitl[ed] to deliberately procrastinate", while some others were concerned with the pressure from Beijing, as China is South Africa's largest trading partner.

Both cases revealed that anti-secession is a core interest of Beijing's, and that there are pre-conditions in China's political and economic relationships with African countries. China tends to use its muscle and influence to get recognition and political support on issues related to Taiwan and Tibet. African countries, on the other hand, are affected by Beijing's commercial and diplomatic clout and have to express their support for China's positions in many circumstances. The acknowledgment is a calculation of national interest. The next section will explain the close China-South Africa relationship from South Africa's perspective.

II Economically

South Africa has the largest and most sophisticated economy on the continent – its GDP of US$384.3 billion was ten times larger than the average sub-Saharan economy in 2012. Its GDP represents 24% of the total African economy and constitutes 18% of sub-Saharan Africa's economy. With one of the best investment environments in Africa, South Africa has a stable and democratic government, a sound legal system, a relatively well-developed social environment, and better infrastructure for foreign investors. At the same time, South Africa, compared to other African countries, has much more experience with foreign investment and international standards, which makes its market easier to access. Furthermore, as a member of the World Trade Organization (WTO) and the most developed country in Africa which enjoyed the Cotonou Agreement, African Growth and Opportunity Act (AGOA), gained the state advantages in accessing occidental markets. Consequently, according to China Customs, bilateral trade value reached US$59.9 billion in 2012, and the data from China Ministry of Commerce (MOFCOM) showed that Chinese enterprises have undertaken projects worth US$700 million and assigned 3,000 workers to South Africa in 2012. What's more, China's direct non-financial investment into the country approved or registered by Chinese Ministry of Commerce (MOC) has accounted for US$170 million. In return, South Africa has invested 206 projects worth US$145.78 million (MOFCOM, 2013b).

Another attractive feature of South Africa is its rich mineral resources. South Africa has large amounts of mineral reserves. It is the world's largest producer of chrome, manganese, platinum, and vermiculite, and the second largest producer of limonite, palladium, rutile, and zirconium. Also, the state has a large reserve of coal and iron ore. Since 1994, the government has released a series of reforms to develop its mining industry and make it an economic pillar sector. In contrast, China has a strong demand for these minerals and imports US$100 billion worth of base metals every year. In 2012, South Africa overtook India to become the world's third biggest iron ore supplier to China, who is the world's largest consumer of iron ore. As the Mineral Resources Minister Susan Shabangu described, "there is a lot of interest from China. They are interested in manganese, platinum, uranium and I would say almost every commodity" (Macharia, March 10, 2013). Meanwhile Chinese analysts also speak highly of South Africa's mining industry and technology, which are equipped to meet China's increasing demand for resources (Y. Wang, 2012). Currently, leading Chinese mining companies have become actively involved in the state; Sinosteel, Zijin, Minmetals and Jiaquan Iron and Steel have made investments in the past decade.

Additionally, South Africa gained advantages because of its strategic role in facilitating China's access to the African continent. Currently, South Africa's GDP is US$384.3 billion, with a market similar to southern and northern Africa. Its membership in Southern African Development Community (SADC) and the negotiation of expansion of COMESA-EAC-SADC (Common Market for Eastern and Southern Africa-The East African Community-Southern African Development Community) provided South Africa with an opportunity for foreign investors to access a free trade zone of 560 million consumers, with a total GDP of US$1,000 billion from 27 countries. Along with South Africa's inclusion into BRICS, it facilitates developing states' possible future entry into Africa. As for China, all five major Chinese banks have established a presence in South Africa to support trade and investment between China, South Africa, and the rest of Africa, including providing services to existing (Chinese) clients, which can be understood as the market-sustaining investment (Gelb, 2010). According to the data from an institute in Johannesburg, the majority of Chinese firms with a long-term strategy appear to have entered South Africa for market-seeking purposes, selling into the domestic South African market as well as the regional Southern African market. Meanwhile, the China-Africa Development Fund (CADFund) showed the same feature of South Africa as an important place for Chinese companies' expansion into the region, evidenced by the fact that among the 60 projects in over 30 countries in Africa, eight are in South Africa, which is the largest number in any country. The total investment CADFund has made in South Africa exceeds US$400 million, which is also the largest total CADFund investment in any African countries.

In short, South Africa, as the regional leader, has great significance to China in terms of political, economic, and diplomatic strategy. Not only do its domestic resource reserves and markets attract Chinese investors, but its government also is a supporter of China on both international events and China's stance in the international arena.

8.2.2 South Africa's demands

I Politically

Present Zuma, who is friendlier to Beijing than his predecessor, identified China as a "key strategic partner for South Africa" during his trip to the Sino-South African Business Forum in Beijing. Dr. Mills, former National Director of the South African Institute of International Affairs, also commented on the frequent high-level visits between these two governments, and stressed that "South Africa should take advantage of its strong governance institutions to form a robust relationship with China" (KPMG, October 19, 2011), because China plays an important role in bringing the African agenda to the world stage, which enlarges the significance of South Africa.

In December 2010, when China was the rotating chair of BRIC, President Hu Jintao issued an invitation letter to South African President Jacob Zuma, inviting him to attend the third BRIC leaders' meeting to be held in Beijing (Xinhua News, December 24, 2010). Since then, BRIC enlarged to become BRICS, in which South Africa is expected to represent Africa as an emerging power, despite its small population and economy. With this invitation, South Africa could expand its trade with the BRIC countries.

South Africa made efforts to join the BRICS, as its minister of Trade and Industry, Dr. Rob Davies said at the fifth BRICS summit: "the Importance of BRICS can never be over emphasized". As for South Africa, its trade and economic relations with the BRICS countries has increased since its participation began, Total trade between South Africa and other BRICS countries has grown from 11.6% to 27% in the next year. In 2013, 31 projects by 25 companies from BRICS countries were constructing in South Africa, accounting for R12.6 billion, (the Daily Times, 2013). Additionally, South Africa's partnership within BRICS could benefit the continent as a whole. It has increased the weight of the long-marginalised region and brought more industrialisation and integration to the area. Take the recent fifth BRICS summit as an example: the five countries jointly establish a business council in the hope of strengthening trade and investment among members. South Africa is expected to become a mediator between the emerging markets and Africa, and to help BRIC countries understand the continent while negotiating bilateral agreements.

Additionally, China and South Africa appear to share similar stances on some recent issues, ranging from the conflicts on the continent to climate conferences. Along with Beijing's high profile emphasis on the continent, South Africa also took this opportunity to gain support on the world stage. During the latest election for the African Union commission, South Africa's candidate, Nkosazana Dlamini-Zuma, sought support from China based on South Africa's friendly attitude towards Beijing and expressed willingness to strengthen cooperation between the African Union and China. In 2012, Dlamini-Zuma defeated Jean Ping, whose father is a Chinese trader, from Gabon, and was elected as chairperson (Bathembu, July 16, 2012).

II Economically

Along with the increasing significance of its political influence, South Africa showed a willingness to transfer the political significance and economic relations into regional and domestic social and economic benefits, which means that the Zuma administration's strategy is to connect its diplomatic achievements with the key issues in this region – notably, infrastructure, employment opportunities and poverty reduction. In 2010, Zuma was elected as the president of the Programme for Infrastructure Development in Africa (PIDA), a project dedicated "to promote socio-economic development and poverty reduction in Africa through improved access to integrated regional and continental infrastructure networks and services" (New Partnership for Africa's Development [NEPAD], 2010). Pretoria "particularly championed the cause for infrastructure investment in the region as a precursor to regional integration" in the BRICS summit in Durban (BRICS, March 27, 2013). At the first BRICS Business Council meeting, South Africa's Trade and Industry Minister Rob Davies declared that "We need to promote a much more value-added economy. We need to do this by integrating our continent [Africa]. We need to consolidate this by a massive infrastructure development program on the continent". (South Africa [SA] News, August 19, 2013) The BRICS members expressed support and interest in infrastructure construction on the continent, which is particularly significant as a result of the economic crises experienced by the developed economies. China, as the largest economy among BRICS, with large amounts of funds and interest in this region, became an alternative resource to support the growth and modernisation of the continent's infrastructure. The economic ties between China and other southern African countries could provide South Africa with stronger and more reliable economic growth opportunities and drivers.

Considering the domestic priorities, South Africa is seeking value-added trade with China and also to change its current economic status as a source of raw material, while pursuing a wish/dream to become a key player in the global economy. At the fifth Forum on China-Africa Cooperation in 2012, President Zuma described the unbalanced economic relationship with China as "unsustainable" in the long term, and expressed a willingness to export value-added products from South Africa to China. Especially, after South Africa suffered from widespread strikes, export deficits, and the depreciation of the Rand, the country relied on changing its trade deficit and the unbalanced situation in order to encourage future economic growth. South Africa would like to diversify its exports by exporting more industrial products. Meanwhile, it requires China to increase its investment and create employment opportunities.

In addition, like many other developing economies, South Africa has shown an interest in the development model of Asian countries as well. The Zuma administration launched the "New Growth Path" in 2010 for employment creation and economic growth. The centre of this plan is to use "massive investment in infrastructure as a critical driver of jobs across the economy", and to establish "smarter coordination between government and private sector" (gov.za, 2010). The focus on infrastructure and the greater role of government is similar to China's development path. The new approach is in contrast with former President Mbeki's more free-market approach. In this case, the state played an active role in the economy. As the head of the ANC's Economic Transformation Committee put it, "The Chinese model of building infrastructure and growing jobs will be a key focus of the ANC's economic policy". To be specific, the China model here, interpreted as state capitalism, requires a greater role of government in the markets. Despite the fact that the China model itself is very controversial, Beijing still invited African leaders to train. South Africa's Minister of Public Enterprises Malusi Gigaba and Economic Development Minister Ebrahim Patel have visited China to study how the Chinese use their parastatals to control strategic assets and grow the economy. Gigaba, specifically, was assigned the task of learning how the Chinese consolidated their parastatals under one umbrella (Naidoo, Molele, & Letsoalo, February 3, 2012).

8.2.3 Discussions for shaping China's responsibility in South Africa

China has a strong motivation to engage with South Africa, not only is the state a regional leader that has a significant influence on the continent, but also its friendly relations with Beijing have provided China with political support for its "One-China" policy and on Tibet issues. In addition, South Africa's resources and relatively mature market are attractive to Chinese investors who wish to expand both South Africa's market and to establish a gateway for access to the rest of the continent. On the other side, South Africa relies on China to expand its international and regional influence and expects Chinese investment to fuel its value-added exports and learn about/from Chinese economic development.

Comparing China's interests with that of South Africa, one can see that the two countries find it relatively easy to reach agreements on political issues and support each other in the international arena. China, in line with international expectations and South Africa's political ambitions, helps South Africa to represent the continental voice on the world stage. Furthermore, both countries consider themselves as leaders of developing countries, they have similar stances on international events, calling on the interests of developing countries. But, at the economic level, what the Chinese government provides to South Africa and other African countries is mostly infrastructure, which does not always meet with South Africa's demands. The country has placed value-added industry at the centre of its economic growth strategy, which has led to an economic relation between China and South Africa more akin to competitors. The following section will discuss China's impact on and limitations in South Africa.

8.3 China's capability and limitations in South Africa

As has been mentioned in the previous part, the significance of South Africa largely relies on its connection to the continent. In return, the state has benefited from the representation of the region. Indeed, South Africa has the most political power political and economic strength on the continent, with Africa's strongest voice in the international arena, even more so than Nigeria. However, there are still plenty of doubts about its leadership and representation of Africa. Many agree that the country is still a junior player in the global field. As one African analyst said, "It wanted to be too much too soon whereas it was not ready for this international role" (Marthoz, 2012). Not only are its scale and strength unable to compete with other emerging powers, but also its acceptance on the continent as a leader is limited. As Daniel Flemes notes, "the acceptance of Pretoria's leadership seems to be limited to the global level. The acceptance of its regional leadership is constrained by the historical legacy of apartheid" (Sidiropoulos, 2007, p. 2). During the AU's chairperson elections between Ms. Dlamini-Zuma from South Africa and Mr. Ping from Gabon, voting had been broadly split. It revealed that South Africa's influence in the continent is not as much as one might expect. And the linguistic, religious, and diversified national interests barriers have hardly given the continent one voice. In this case, the role of South Africa as a gateway to the continent hasn't yet worked out for Beijing.

Furthermore, as a relatively small economy compared to the other four powers, South Africa's inclusion in the BRICS is perceived as a gateway to its continent. how effective South Africa could be depends on a lot of factors: such as the coordination between BRICS members, South Africa's influence within BRICS, and to what extend the country could represent Africa's broad interests. First, the BRICS itself: like many other organisations, it has some basic differences between members. China-South Africa within BRICS has the same problems. One is the most successful democratic state in Africa, while the other is autocratic. These two states, with divergent policies, diplomatic strategy and different forms of government, are in some way like competitors, rather than allies. At the same time, the strengths of China and South Africa are different. When the BRICS leaders met in St. Petersburg before the G20 summit in 2013, they agreed to establish a development fund of US$50 billion and a reserve fund of US$100 billion. For the US$100 billion, China would contribute US$41 billion. By contrast, South Africa would only contribute US$5 billion. Even if we cannot prove that larger donors have a louder voice, this can suggest the difference in status of China and South Africa in this club of emerging economies.

Meanwhile, as Jinghao Lu, a China-Africa analyst at the consultancy Frontier Advisory pointed out, South Africa "is far from representing the complexity of African political economy" (the Guardian, March 24, 2013). Currently, China tends to deal with African states bilaterally. As Witness 14 said, it is more common to see Chinese enterprises doing business directly with the countries they want to engage with. With a limited capability to become a bridge between China and the continent, China-South Africa trade, like other African countries, remains as a passive recipient of Chinese goods and an exporter of mineral resources. Additionally, South Africa's economic relationship with the continent is like China and other emerging economies – that is, reliant on its energy imports while exporting manufactured goods. This trade pattern has shaped China more as a competitor to South Africa, in terms of energy resources and markets.

China-South Africa's friendly governmental relations and their stance on the South do not change the fact that South Africa's pillar industries, such as mining, telecoms and banking, are still dominated by the global North. What Chinese enterprises could get are marginalised sectors in the downstream industry chains. China itself operated at the same level in the global value chain with South Africa, and it would be to help South Africa's industrialisation and growth in value-added exports. Inevitably, when scrambling for manufacturing markets in labour-intensive sectors, China has demographic advantages and a cheaper labour force than that of South Africa. According to research by the University of East Anglia, South African exports to other African countries have experienced a loss of market share, from 20% to 15% between 2001 and 2010. Meanwhile, China has increased its share from 5% to 25% during the same decade. It is estimated that, if it were not for Chinese competition, South Africa's exports to these countries would have been almost 10% higher – or, $900 million more (Edwards & Jenkins, 2013). In short, the overwhelming amount of Chinese goods available has had a negative impact on South Africa's domestic industries and its exports in relevant sectors.

On the other hand, in China there are some voices that question whether South Africa should be a recipient of Chinese aid. They have pointed out that South Africa's GDP per capita was ranked 83rd, with US$11,281, while China was ranked 93rd with US$9,005 in 2012. It is seen as unreasonable to provide assistance to a "rich" country while the domestic population remains in poverty. Furthermore, South Africa has a lead in mineral and agricultural technology, plus its economic pattern with the continent is similar to China and other emerging economies. The rival status has brought more doubts and domestic pressures on China's assistance to South Africa's development. Meanwhile, different from other African countries, South Africa's market environment seems less attractive to Chinese investors. South Africa's mining industry, for example, which is believed to be the most appealing sector to China, was ranked 54th by a Global Mining Survey 2012/2013, issued by the Canadian Fraser Institute – this is behind Botswana, Namibia, Mauritania, and Zambia (Prinsloo & Marais, February 10, 2013). Even though it has much more standardised and systematic policy for international deals than other African countries, the major mining resources are controlled by the Northern companies, and the small ones are left to local owners. Especially when it comes to the BEE (Black Economic Empowerment), the Chinese investors have to find local black partners in order to be involved in South Africa's mining industry. However, a local BEE qualified partner often lacks the ability to complete the project. The ambiguous ownership, language, and cultural barrier, as well as unclear contracts, only increases the uncertainty and difficulties of investment. Also, compared to other African countries, Chinese enterprises have received far less preference and fewer favorable offers. As Mr. Li Shenglin, the Executive Director of CADFund pointed out, "in countries where there is not vibrant interest of foreign investment, the government usually approaches Chinese investors quite actively and pledges with a lot of preferential conditions, such as lower tax… We never receive such treatment in South Africa" (Y. Li, 2013).

8.4 The gap between China's policy in South Africa and its implementation

Different to other African countries, South Africa displays two characteristics: one is its identity as an African state with low economic growth, and the other is its democratic political system and relatively sophisticated economy. Driven by these two features, the state has contradictory foreign strategies, falling between international norms and interests. On one hand, based on its history of anti-apartheid struggle, the democratic government supports the liberal internationalists and human rights; while, on the other hand, it emphasises South-South solidarity and tolerates authoritarian regimes. According to University of Johannesburg professor Chris Landsberg, South Africa not only prioritises development issues and issues of poverty and inequality, but also advocates for a "fundamental redistribution of both power and resources at the global level" (Marthoz, 2012). South Africa's attitudes towards "military-humanitarian interventions" reveal its values and identity as an African country and a third-world state, as well as the ANC's wariness of foreign interference. Additionally, the unsatisfied and dual economy requires the government to prioritisep its domestic development, to pay more attention to the social debt of apartheid and needs of the majority black population. This priority was reflected in its foreign policy of emphasising economic development with tangible results. In this case, the countries with sympathy for Africa and who can offer economic benefits tend to become ideal partners for South Africa.

China, who has also experienced growth and development with its status as a developing country, became a key cooperator for Pretoria. Its identification as a member of the Global South and the G-77 (seventy-seven developing countries signatories of the "Joint Declaration of the Seventy-Seven Developing Countries") in the United Nations (UN) is of significance to South Africa because both countries have called for multipolarity and the benefits of the South by being included on the global stage. In recent years, China's high-profile involvement in Africa has brought the continent into the spotlight, which has aligned with South Africa's own foreign strategy that prioritises African peace and security, and its ambitions" to be seen as an African leader. Beijing's concentration on African affairs has provided South Africa with a greater voice in the international organisations. South Africa's inclusion in BRICS is more due to its African identity rather than its economic strengths, as with the other four emerging economies.

8.4.1 Politically

The close relationship with China has brought with it multiple effects for South Africa. First, in order to have a broader representation of the black continent and the majority of black people at home, it tends to side with China and other developing countries on the matters of debt relief, free trade, technical transformation, climate issues, and the reform of international institutions and international rules to make them less favourable to the North. In terms of the frequent African conflicts, although a prioritised African agenda has pushed Pretoria to make more contributions to peacekeeping operations, it has also made the state more cautious about "foreign intervention". South Africa stood in the company of Russia and China on the vote over Libya and Syria, which was considered to be a setback of accepted norms and the "responsibility to protect". Also in the case of Zimbabwe, despite strong pressure from the U.S. and European Union (EU), Pretoria has preferred talks rather than confrontation and the imposition of sanctions. South Africa's standing for the South may undermine Pretoria's strong relationships with the EU and US. Second, Beijing has provided South Africa with an alternative source for not investment and trade, but also for a political system. South Africa's transition from apartheid to democracy has set an example for the rest of the African countries. It successfully avoided large-scale violence and chaos while establishing a stable government and a developed legal system. However, some leading liberal voices feared that the close relationship between the African National Congress (ANC) and CPC might draw the country into copying China's political model of an authoritarian developmental state. The ANC has shown signs of intolerance towards its critics, especially those in the media. The South African Broadcasting Corporation is under tight political control and a law of secrecy. "In the new South Africa, with its freedom hard-won from apartheid", Nobel Prize laureate Nadine Gordimer said in 2012, "we now have the imminent threat of updated versions of the suppression of freedom of expression that gagged us under apartheid" (Gordimer, May 24, 2012). Meanwhile, Pretoria's refusal to end delay in issuing the Dalai Lama with a visa has been criticised by Nobel Peace Prize Laureate Archbishop Desmond Tutu as unlawful. Third, China's involvement drew the world's attention to this continent and thus brought international strength as well as regional accountability to this country. The future development of the long-marginalised continent has been hotly debated at international conferences and in the media. The fifth BRICS Summit in 2013, in Durban, was launched with the theme of "BRICS and Africa: Partnership for Development, Integration and Industrialisation". South Africa as the host had a platform and a strong voice to deliver the African agenda to other emerging countries. Also, Dlamini-Zuma's leadership of the African Union has placed South Africa as a better and more visible diplomatic actor in international affairs.

8.4.2 Economically

I Unbalanced trade pattern

In response to the huge expectations of the majority of black people, the ANC is under considerable domestic pressure to improve the social and economic situation among its poor population. As a result, its foreign policy is expected to make tangible contributions to solving the problems of poverty and unemployment, as well as to reach highly ambitious growth and development goals. During the fourth BRICS Summit in India, President Jacob Zuma said, "Our participation in BRICS is designed to help us achieve inclusive growth, sustainable development and a prosperous South Africa" (dfa.gov.za, August 01, 2014). To evaluate the influence of China's involvement based on South Africa's expectations, one should look at to what extent Chinese investment and trade have had a positive or negative impact on local industry and employment. Beijing provided the state with more opportunities than other African countries, due to its regional influence and economic strength. Witness 9 said Chinese enterprises tend to choose South Africa as their first centre for expanding their business in Africa. The leading Chinese enterprises Sinosteel, China Construction Bank, China Civil Engineering Construction Corporation (CCECC), China Development Bank and China-Africa Development Fund (CADF) all established their headquarters in Johannesburg. Take a province-owned enterprise Jinchuan Corporate as an example: the largest Platinum producer in China has purchased a South African copper-cobalt company, Metorex, with its office in South Africa and its mining resources in Zambia and Congo. As the chief delegate of CADF, Zhengyi Lu said,

> Johannesburg, as the economic and financial centre in Southern Africa, has the branch of nearly all world major banks, including China Construction Bank, Bank of China and China Industrial Bank. 85% financial operations in the continent have achieved through this city.

> (China News and Report, 2013)

The expanding number of centres located in South Africa have brought large amounts of financial support and investment opportunities to this country. According to the statistics from MOCOM, China's non-financial investment into South Africa has reached US$170 million, most of which is aimed at infrastructure and construction projects. Recently, South African Deputy President Kgalema Motlanthe invited Chinese companies and investors to participate in his country's infrastructure construction and to connect South African regions through new railways. Soon after, President Xi Jinping pledged new support for Africa's infrastructure construction, and the funding for such projects has become the Group of 20's priority (Xinhua News, October 30, 2013). The China Development Bank has agreed to provide US$500 million in loans to South Africa's national transport company, Transnet, for its repair and maintenance of the railway (Reuters, 2013). According to data from CGD, Beijing has provided US$230 million in financial aid to South Africa between 2000 and 2011. Meanwhile, it has also gradually emerged as an important source of infrastructure development in this country.

South Africa, like any other African country, exports raw materials and imports consumer products and capital goods from China, which is reflected in the trade balances between the two countries, with South Africa having surpluses in exports of raw materials and primary products, and large deficits in consumer and capital goods. Despite the fact that South African President Jacob Zuma is friendly with Beijing, he has still warned of "the unbalanced nature of Africa's burgeoning trade ties with China is 'unsustainable' in the long term". Deputy Trade and Industry Minister Elizabeth Thabethe also called for a strategy to "foster a more balanced and sustainable trade relationship with China" at the opening of the last in a series of three South African Expos in Beijing (SAnews. gov.za, September 12, 2013). South Africa has shown keen willingness to change the current "raw materials and commodities for manufacturing products" trade pattern. China's ambassador to South Africa Zhong Jianhua has demonstrated how Beijing could conduct various platforms to promote the export of South Africa's value-added goods. In September 2013, South Africa hosted a six-day "South Africa Expos in China" in Beijing, Shanghai, and Xiamen under the supervision of the South Africa Ministry of Trade and Industry and China's Ministry of Commerce, in order to increase the reputation and visibility of its products and technology in China. The promotional event in Beijing concentrated on attracting trade and investment and was sponsored by China's MOCOM. The potential cooperation area in this expo included agri-processing, chemicals, plastics, steel, aluminium, automotive, capital equipment and allied services, electro-technical, mining and refining, renewable energy, infrastructure, oil and gas. At the same time, like all other African states, South Africa showed an interest in cooperative opportunities on infrastructure projects, with which Chinese companies are familiar (China Daily, September 23, 2013). However, the results of these promotional events depended on whether South Africa's industries could provide the value-added products to Chinese markets with both accepted levels of quality and at a reasonable price.

Calculated from the data of UN Comtrade, by 2010 China was ranked as the principal source of imports to South Africa in 27 of 45 manufacturing industries, mainly focused on knitted and crocheted fabrics, clothing, leather and leather products, footwear, household appliances, electrical lamps and furniture. Chinese products accounted for between 48% and 77% of total South African imports of those products. The overwhelming tide of Chinese products in these labour-intensive industries has given rise to concern for South Africa's domestic manufacture industry and its increasing unemployment rate. Comparing Chinese products' share of South Africa's market in 1995 and 2010, the figure had increased from less than half a per cent to around 6% in 2010. The Congress of South African Trade Unions (COSATU), South Africa's leading trade union confederation, identifies China as a threat to South Africa's economic interests.

Some industries face stiff competition from China considering the imbalances in the bilateral trade pattern; although there is a possibility that an increased share of Chinese products may replace imports from other countries rather than South Africa's domestic industry, according to the data from UNComtrade. Take the clothing sector as an example: its loss to Chinese imports accounted for 31.1%, while the local industry declined 7.6% between 2001 and 2011. The same losses could be found in some other manufacturing sectors. It revealed that large amounts of imports from China, especially in the clothing and textile sector and in small goods, have negative impacts on the growth of local industry. Meanwhile, according to research by the Southern Africa Labour and Development Research Unit, South Africa has lost market share to China in its major export markets (Edwards & Jenkins, 2013) in these sectors as well. The decline in such labour-intensive industries as a result of Chinese competition has also led to greater unemployment. Not only the loss of jobs associated with the bankrupt of local companies, but cheap Chinese goods have resulted in lower profits generated by local products. In order to increase the competition and lower the cost, the surviving producers tend to reduce labourers' salaries.

Apart from the unbalanced trade in value added industries, the two countries' trade value is also said to be in favour of China. In 2004, South Africa acknowledged China as a market economy and started free trade agreement (FTA) talks with China on behalf of the Southern African Customs Union. After that, bilateral commercial activities largely increased. According to China's Customs, China-South Africa trade value reached US$59.9 billion, with a growth of 32% in 2011, of which China exported US$15.3 billion and imported US$44.6 billion, with a deficit of US$29.3 billion (MOFCOM, 2013b). But, according to the statistics from South Africa, South Africa's exports to China were just over R81[1] billion in 2012, while it imported from China was R120 billion in the same year, which indicated a deficit of R39 billion to South Africa (South African Government News Agency, December 9, 2013), which revealed that there existed a huge statistical gap between each government. Since all the statistics are released by governmental websites, the figures have already excluded illegally smuggled goods. Therefore, there is a gap generated through different approaches to making the calculations. As for South Africa, the data is based on an annual survey of companies, while in China the figure is collected from the approval and registration of proposals. Additionally, many companies 'route' their investments through third countries in order to obtain favourable tax or regulatory treatment, or to disguise the actual source or destination of goods from their host or home governments (Aykut & Ratha, 2003), which increases the difficulties in data collection; for example, knowing whether the figures included goods transferred from Hong Kong or the gold and diamonds sold to China through the London Metal Exchange. In this case, the prerequisite of reducing the deficit is setting up an equal criterion through negotiation between the two governments. Without mutually-accepted statistics, it is hard to find further solutions.

Lastly, the SOEs that came to South Africa were latecomers compared to the traditional Northern companies. Add to this the fact that South Africa has long been considered to be a relatively developed country; it is hard for Chinese investors to shoulder a grand energy and policy strategy from the beginning in such a state. On one hand, as Witness 16 pointed out, the charity projects appointed by headquarters as a part of the companies' corporate social responsibility performance only benefited a small group of people; but, for a large portion of the African labour force and local communities, they haven't shared in the commitments the companies have made. On the other hand, Witness 15 suggested that people who choose to come to Africa are often young opportunists, most of whom have a strong profit-driven motivation to be in South Africa. They only consider the country as a place to earn money. When they have accumulated enough funds, they do not think about paying back to the local community, but rather to move to other developed countries, or return home. As a result, they would take the risk to smuggling, disrespecting local labour protection laws and competition, and violating the development of local industry.

In summary, as the largest and most developed economy in Africa with a sound constitutional system, South Africa's relationship with China carries more weight than most other African states. Even if its economic strength is smaller than China, it still represents the "S" in the BRICS. China-South Africa interaction hence presents a different picture. Currently, considering the constraints on both sides, China's economic commitment to this state is limited. The ubiquitous Chinese construction projects in many African countries are not commonly seen in South Africa. And Chinese business's competition negatively affects its South African counterparts and local employment opportunities.

II BEE

Constrained by economic structures, China's engagement in South Africa's manufacturing industry has not benefited the state. On the other hand, China as a latecomer to the state has experienced difficulties in its resources market. Large scale Chinese engagement didn't come until the mid-2000s. Initially, Chinese enterprises showed strong interest in and ambitions for the mining industry. However, this didn't go as smoothly as expected. Even the leading mining corporations backed by the central or provincial government have encountered difficulties and experienced losses. It reminded Chinese investors that, although South Africa has more developed infrastructures and administrative processes, the risks and difficulties are no less than in other African states. By contrast, compared to the experienced multinationals, Chinese enterprises are still beginners and have a long way to "going out".

Sinosteel, under the administration of China's State-Owned Assets Supervision and Administration Commission, entered South Africa's mining industry in 1996. In order to gain further expansion, the company established three subsidiaries there: Sinosteel South Africa (PTY) Ltd., ASA Metals (PTY) Ltd., and Tubatse Chrome Minerals (PTY) Ltd. What's more, Sinosteel paid attention to localization in its operations. Among its total employees of 7,000, only 19 came from China (New Century, December 13, 2010b). In ASA Metals, the Chinese were responsible for production, while local managers took charge of operations, community and human resources. In 2008, ASA Metals, in which Sinosteel holds 60% of its shares, made a bold decision to conduct an expansion project named "Xuri" (rising sun). The whole project cost about US$440 million, and included a closed electric furnace with an annual output of 240,000 tons of ferrochrome, a pelletizing plant of 600,000 tons per year, a broken ore factory that is able to deal with 100 tons of ore per hour, two new slopes each with an annual production of 540,000 tons of chrome ore, and a concentrating mill factory that has an annual chrome ore mining capacity of 1.1 million tons (People's Daily, February 22, 2008). The ambitious project was supposed to start operations in May 2009. It is estimated that, with the operation of this new factory and plant, ASA Metals would produce one million tons of chrome ore and 380,000 tons of ferrochrome per year. It would place ASA Metals as the second largest chrome producer, behind only Xstrata.[2]

However, large amounts of investment have also brought another side to the story. Due to the BEE Programme released by South Africa government in 2007, Sinosteel has experienced bitter losses in order to maintain its control of ASA Metals. Currently, the ownership and exclusive selling rights problems are still waiting to be solved. According to the introduction of the ASA Metals biography, the company was set up as a joint venture between East Asia Metals Investment Co., Ltd. (EAMI) and Limpopo Economic Development Enterprise (LimDev, former NPDC) in 1996. Since EAMI is Sinosteel Corporation's wholly-owned subsidiary, Beijing has a 60% stake in ASA Metals, while LimDev from South Africa has only 40%. But Beijing's control of ASA Metals has been challenged by the BEE Programme because its partner LimDev is not a BEE company. In order to meet the requirements, ASA Metals has to sell 25% of its shares and a one-vote veto to BEE share holders (Black share holders). It means EAMI and LimDev should sell 25% of their 60% and 40% shares respectively. In this case, as for Sinosteel, its share would reduce to just 44%, which would lead to Beijing's loss of control of ASA Metals. It has created a dilemma. On the one hand, with such a risky investment in the mining industry, Sinosteel can hardly ensure its interests without the controlling stake. Plus, the company has launched the "Xuri project" for further expansion against a backdrop that global chromium prices were increasing in 2007 and 2008. Without holding shares of the company, the huge investment would be meaningless. On the other hand, holding a controlling stake may violate the BEE Programme.

In order to maintain control of ASA Metals, Beijing has sought help from local political elites. Chinese diplomat Ji Peiding used his personal connections to Moeletsi Mbeki, the younger brother of former President Thabo Mbeki, a critic of BEE. He claimed that "BEE is legalized corruption... that has enriched a small black elite while doing nothing to boost South Africa's economy" (Harrison, June 19, 2009). He also said that "BEE had been all about shuffling ownership of assets" (LEBELO, March 27, 2004). Since the ownership of the Dilokong mine belongs to the Limpopo Province rather than Sinosteel or ASA Metals, Sinosteel tried to argue that BEE companies' shares should come from the province. Under pressure from local political elites and their thirst for China's investment, then-Premier of Limpopo Mr. Moloto agreed that the provincially-owned company LimDev would sell 30% of its shares, with 5% to the Maroga community and 25% to BEE companies. In this case, Sinosteel could maintain its 60% stake, which was not the end of the story, however. The BEE programme was introduced by the South African government as a measure to balance the huge gap between Caucasian elites and black people and to transfer the economy from one dominated by white people to one shared by the majority of the population, in order to create more employment opportunities. However, in the case of ASA Metals, it only benefited a few of the new black elite, rather than the majority of black people. Local newspaper The Sunday Times disclosed that in the ASA deal, the Limpopo government decided to sell BEE shares to five consortiums from 43 bidders. Each of them would get a 12.5% stake from the total 30% of shares. If you kept an on eye on the five consortiums, you would find those who were "involved in the deal include[d] soccer boss Irvin Khoza, Chairman of National Empowerment Fund Ronnie Ntuli and Kgomotso Motlanthe, the son of deputy president Kgalema Motlanthe" (Fin24.com, March 14, 2010). A Chinese newspaper exposed that some of the five consortiums were even owned by the relatives of the Limpopo governors (Deng, July 2, 2011).

Instead of making more people enjoy the benefits of the chrome mine, the deal instead launched infighting and struggles among black political elites at the expense of their impoverished communities. The party, unions and community all struggled to get more of the benefits from the deal. It is reported that the controversial politician, Commander-in-Chief of the

Economic Freedom Fighters political movement, Julius Malema used to be involved in the deal as well, but was forced out due to media exposure. Later, he publicly advocated for the nationalisation of mines. Despite a local newspaper suggesting that "Malema's increasingly strident calls for nationalisation were designed to deflect attention away from the ASA transaction" (Fin24.com, March 14, 2010), his voice represented the majority of black people's widespread anger over inequalities, and their willingness to share the mining income. Therefore, even though the ANC rejected the nationalisation plans, "the supporters of nationalisation" including an impoverished population and the ANC Youth League, "have remained vocal and active" (York, December 20, 2012). Superficially, it is China's aggressive control of the mines that fanned the struggles and conflicts between black elites, but Sinosteel had its sorrows as well.

The reality that many of the new black elites have little or no experience in business, and they have insufficient funds, made the deal more complicated. In the ASA deal, Sinosteel paid not only funds for the expansion plan, the "Xuri" project which was estimated to considerably increase the Dilokong mine's value, but also the responsibility to help BEE consortiums financing. In 2010, after investing US$350 million for the "Xuri" project, Sinosteel and LimDev could not reach an agreement on how to finance the five BEE consortiums and the price of LimDev's 30% shares. LimDev held that, since the five BEE companies were ready, Sinosteel should finance them to get the stakes. Meanwhile, Sinosteel would prefer to help them by finding loans from China or abroad, rather than providing the loans themselves because Sinosteel already had a debt ratio of 90%. Even the funds for the expansion project were borrowed from China's Exim Bank – US$275 million out of the US$350 million needed. Currently, the deal remains suspended, because if LimDev stopped selling its shares, Sinosteel might lose its control of the mines. In contrast, Sinosteel lacks the capability to finance the BEE companies (Deng, July 2, 2011).

Sinosteel's case in South Africa reveals many of the problems facing both China and South Africa. As for South Africa, despite the fact that the state has a sound legal system, implementation is another matter entirely. The interest conflicts between white and black, elites and population, ANC, labor unions and local communities present a harsh, complex and unclear environment for foreign investors. In order to argue for their stances, foreign involvement is the easiest scapegoat for domestic social problems, and therefore their interests are the easiest to be sacrificed. It is worth noting that the foreign interest and national interest are not always contradicted by each other. South Africa's society should be prepared to take advantage of and enjoy high international expectation. As for the case of Sinosteel, ASA's former manager Suwei Zhang revealed that the company had an annual profit of US$77 million before the dilemma; but it has lost US$3 million per month due to the unsettled problem (L. Liu, July 5, 2011). If South Africa had a more sustainable and favourable investment environment for Sinosteel, the chances are that Chinese enterprises may bring in more funds for further expansion, and hence more employment opportunities.

Regarding China, it has strong ambitions to safeguard its national resource security, but in reality, the state-owned enterprises are far from working as a national team. The gap between national strategy and enterprises' operations makes it hard for all the relevant actors involved. Take Sinosteel in South Africa as an example: as a state-owned enterprise, it has shouldered the responsibility for Beijing's "going out" strategy as well as the profit-driven business strategy. In order to explore overseas resources, the central government and national banks provide loans to support the pioneering enterprises. In return, it requires proportional imports of resources back to China. The administrative intervention violates the profit-driven nature of enterprises, and can sometimes even harm the survival of the enterprise. The pressure of national grand strategy contributed to ASA's failure. Before 2008, its main ferrochrome export destinations were Japan, the US and Europe, because chrome prices in the overseas market were 13%–15% higher than domestically (New Century, December 13, 2010a). However, after getting the loans from China Exim Bank for its "Xuri" Expansion plan, ASA had to reserve 20% of its production for the domestic Chinese market. From the central government's perspective, it diversified its mining supply and assured its national resources security. Though, in terms of ASA, due to the long maritime distance from South Africa to China, its products could hardly compete against those imported from Turkey or Kazakhstan. In addition, human resources and costs in China are lower than in South Africa, and it is, therefore, more worthwhile to import chrome ore rather than the products from ASA Metals. The contradiction between Beijing's strategy and ASA's interests make it harder for the company to survive in the highly competitive international market. Suwei Zhang has argued in an interview, that "Developing is the only way to benefit our country. Only when Sinosteel's assets were five times larger, then we have the capability to support national strategy, otherwise, even a small and medium private company has more strength than ours". (Deng, July 2, 2011)

The case of Sinosteel in South Africa is one of failure for the Chinese enterprise, its local partners and the local community. In this case, China didn't show much concern for the local black people, and instead, it was involved in the mining business under-the-counter for the control of stakes. Unluckily, the Chinese company lost its interests as well, which reveals the gap between the central government's grand strategy and the real difficulties at the micro-level. It is unrealistic to expect a profit-driven enterprise to either give up all its profits to the national interests or to sacrifice its interests for international ethics. A corporate ethic exists in the form of its long-term profits.

Although the BEE is designed to protect and benefit the majority black population it actually turned out to be a grab for resources among black elites and made the market harder/riskier for foreign investors. It revealed the fact that, although China is considered to be the stronger country at the national level when facing its African counterparts, it has limits and constraints at the local enterprise level. Chinese enterprises, as newcomers on this continent, are still very weak compared to the traditional, Western multinationals. Without a sustainable operation, it is impossible for a company to talk about paying back to the local community, no matter how powerful its home country. Indeed, Beijing is an easy scapegoat for all Chinese behaviour in Africa, but to what extent it can control its own companies, as well as the host country, is questionable. When the entire continent is rushing to take advantage of available Chinese funds, the key questions lie not in pushing China to invest more, to pay more assistance, or to transfer more technology, but rather it requires the African governments and enterprises to think about how to take advantage of China's engagement, since this trend is inevitable. In terms of taking advantage of China's engagement and the opportunities, the more developed South Africa didn't offer any advantages. By contrast, South Africa is more like a competitor to China on the continent. The more sound political system and economic strength face Pretoria with a dilemma: on the one hand, it criticises the negative impact of Chinese goods and labour force on its local industries, which implies it has equal relations with China. On the other hand, like many other African countries, it calls for China's funds and aids, which indicates its willingness to gain from China. China's approach to and strategy for the various African countries is mostly the same; it is in Africans' hands to turn it into a blessing or a curse.

8.5 Conclusion

Currently, South Africa and China have a close relationship in the political and economic fields. Zuma's administration has shown support for cooperation with China in the international arena – notably by refusing the Dalai Lama's visa and taking the same stance on sanctioning Libya and Syria. China has supported South Africa's leading role in the continent and welcomed the country into BRICS. However, the ANC's opponents, civil activists, and researchers in South Africa have widely questioned South Africa's political and economic alliance with China, and are concerned that it may undermine the hard-won democratic achievements. In fact, there is no evidence that Beijing intentionally affects South Africa's democratic development through diplomatic pressure. As Witnesses 18, 22 and 24 all pointed out, China has a different political system to that of the Western countries. It does not force African countries to follow it. It is the African countries who can choose the development path for themselves. In contrast, the ANC's choice to occupy similar stances to China's much more likely came out of its African identity, representation, and economic considerations. From China's perspective, China's approach to South Africa assistance was also challenged domestically, because the majority of people considered South Africa an ally of the North, rather than as an African state.

Economically, South Africa has sought financial support for improving its infrastructure and value-added industries, while China was interested in its mining industry and market. Due to them occupying a similar economic development level, the two countries have found it hard to gain mutual benefits if both are to pursue their economic interests. On the one hand, South Africa's instability and corruption have limited Chinese investors' desire to upgrade its industry further, but many of them have chosen the country as a springboard for access to the European market. Meanwhile, South Africa has strict limitations on imports from China, and also the BEE to protect local black African people's businesses, which make Chinese companies struggle to gain access and invest.

Notes

1 South African Rand approximately equals to 0.12–0.14 to US dollar in 2011, Since South Africa's currency, fluctuates relatively sharply. The book has used the source calculated in Rand instead of dollar.
2 Xstrata is an Anglo-Swiss multinational mining company headquartered in Zug, Switzerland. It was a major producer of coal (and the world's largest exporter of thermal coal), copper, nickel, primary vanadium and zinc and the world's largest producer of ferrochrome.

9 Ethiopia

Ethiopia, as one of the least developed countries in the world, has always been labelled as poor, landlocked, and lacking in resources. With lots of features that Beijing may be uninterested in, China–Ethiopia relations have expanded and deepened in recent years both politically and economically. High-level visits have been maintained for 43 years, ever since the two countries established bilateral diplomatic relations in 1970. Emperor Haile Selassie, then-President Mengistu Haile Mariam, and then-Prime Minister Meles Zenawi, Prime Minster Hailemariam visited China; while then-Vice Prime Minister Qian Qichen, President Jiang Zemin and Prime Minister Wen Jiabao have visited Ethiopia in return. The new president Mulatu Teshome even got his education in Beijing. Also, Ethiopia is one of the top four African recipients of China's investment in the infrastructure sector. The three other countries are all oil-rich, including Angola, Sudan, and Nigeria (Raine, 2009, p. 43). Calculated from the data from AidData, Beijing has invested more than US$3.5 billion in infrastructure construction in Ethiopia between 2000 and 2011, mainly focused on energy and water supplies, as well as transportation. In 2007, the state was selected as one of the four countries (the others being energy-rich Nigeria, Angola and the Democratic Republic of the Congo [DRC]) to receive soft loans for developing Africa's infrastructure from China's state financial institutions, including the Exim Bank (Thakur, 2009). It is also significant that Ethiopia was chosen to host the second ministerial conference of the Forum on China-Africa Cooperation (FOCAC), in December 2003, and it was the cohost of the China-Africa Summit in Beijing in 2006. Dukem was selected as one of the five areas in Africa that will host one of China's Overseas Special Economic Zones. Additionally, China's bilateral trade with Ethiopia has been growing rapidly, largely due to China's promotional measures. The figure jumped from just US$32 million in 1992, to US$100 million in 2002, and to US$1.83 billion in 2012 (Ministry of Commerce [MOFCOM], 2013a). There were 580 registered Chinese companies in Ethiopia in 2010, with 1,065 investment projects, and operating with an estimated investment capital of US$2.2 billion (Raine, 2009, p. 43). What's more, China funded the African Union (AU) headquarters located in Addis Ababa, which increased Ethiopia's significance on the continent. Meanwhile, a large number of volunteers and medical assistance teams have been sent to Ethiopia, with an estimated number of between 5,000 and 10,000 skilled professionals (Gebre-Egziabher, 2009, p. 169).

All this evidence reveals that Ethiopia is the exception to the general rule, that "the designated countries reflect China's commercial priorities in Africa" (P. Davies, 2007, p. 143). In this case, Beijing seeks to gain political and diplomatic influence in Ethiopia, even if the state lacks political and economic strengthen when compared to other African countries, and sometimes even if in the sacrifice of short-term profits. It reflects that China has interests beyond just making economic profits in this country.

9.1 A brief background introduction

Ethiopia was among the first wave of African countries to establish diplomatic relations with Beijing. Since then, China-Ethiopia relations have passed through three stages: the imperial period, the Dergue period, and the Ethiopian People's Revolutionary Democratic Front (EPRDF) period. The contemporary bilateral diplomatic relations are conducted between Beijing and the EPRDF. Since the TPLF (abbreviation for "Tigrayan Peoples' Liberation Front", which held office between 1991 and 1995) and OPDO ("Oromo Peoples' Democratic Organization", in office between 1995 and 2001, and also from 2013 to the present) were different groups within the EPRDF, the EPRDF period will be divided into further sections.

9.1.1 The imperial period (1923–1974) and the Dergue period (1974–1991)

Modern bilateral communications started after Premier Zhou Enlai's visit to Ethiopia in 1964, and Emperor Haile Selassie's visit to China in 1971. However, for historical and ideological reasons, the two countries' relations remained stagnant. After a short period of initial contacts, a military group toppled Emperor Haile Selassie in 1972, the new Dergue regime established an authoritarian socialist state allied with the Soviet Union, and hence was alienated from Beijing. However, even at a time when the two governments were not close, economic and trade contacts began. China and Ethiopia signed an Agreement for Economic and Technological Cooperation in 1971 and 1976, and trade agreements in 1984, 1986 and 1988. China provided a series of assistance programmes, broadly ranging from building roads, to training and research support. As early as 1974, Beijing sent a science team to conduct pharmaceutical research on and laboratory training in local herbs in Bahir Dar, a city located northwest of Addis Ababa (Bräutigam & Tang, 2012). One year later, China provided a zero-interest loan for the construction of Ethiopian roads that linked three agricultural regions in the north of the country (Wolfgang, 1989, p. 63). Other assistance projects during this time included water supply projects and power stations. The aid projects were limited in scale and value, yet showed many features of Chinese international aid. While bilateral communications were still in an infant stage, the military regime was overthrown in 1991, by the EPRDF. After that, the country was governed by EPRDF and remains so today.

9.1.2 The EPRDF period (1991–present)

In 1991, a transnational government led by Meles Zenawi (Ethiopian president from 1991 to 1995; Prime Minister from 1995 to 2012) was established. At that time, the TPLF group within the EPRDF dominated the government and adopted a constitution in 1994. An election was held the next year. When the Meles Zenawi government came into power, bilateral relations got warmer with high-level ministerial visits. Ethiopia expressed an interest to "learn" from China's practice of market-led socialism and agricultural development (Adem, 2012). In 1995, the Ethiopian prime minister visited China, followed by President Jiang Zemin's visit to Ethiopia the following year, which promoted China–Ethiopian relations to new heights. Since then, the two countries have gradually developed better relations. In 1998, the two countries signed the China-Ethiopia Joint Commission, whose major task was to review and assess the bilateral relationship every two years and recommend measures that would contribute to their further improvement/strengthening. As years passed, diplomatic ties between the two countries grew closer. Chinese Prime Minister Wen Jiabao visited Ethiopia in 2003 and concluded an agreement covering various aspects of the relationship with his Ethiopian counterpart (Ethiopian Herald, 1996, 2003). Ethiopia was selected to host the second and fifth FOCAC in 2002 and 2005 (Kim, 2013).

Ethiopia launched an economic reform programme as part of a structural adjustment in 1992. Its successful implementation led it to qualify for debt relief under the Enhanced Heavily Indebted Poor Countries Initiative of 2001, and in 2005 the International Monetary Fund (IMF) forgave all of Ethiopia's debts (Thakur, 2009). Economic progress brought little political reform, however, and in 2005 the EPRDF managed to form a new government after a poor election performance, and the Parliament reelected Zenawi as prime minister for another five-year term. But the crackdown on the opposition also generated considerable criticism and disapproval, particularly from the West, and resulted in the suspension of the World Bank's new lending programs for Ethiopia (Adem, 2012). It was in this context that Sino-Ethiopian relations entered their next phase.

In November 2006, Zenawi visited China for the second time, and his trip promoted a lot of cooperation and assistance. China became the main trading partner of Ethiopia and bilateral trade rose from US$100 million in 2002 to $860 million in 2007 (MOFCOM, 2013a). The trading pattern was shaped in this period. China imported leather goods, coffee, and some other raw commodities, and exported clothing, machinery, food and electronics to Ethiopia. Similar to China's experiences with other trading partners on this continent, there is a significant trade imbalance between these two countries: China exported US$284 million worth of goods, and imported US$85.7 million in 2005 (MOFCOM, 2013a). In 2007, China and Ethiopia reached an important agreement: the two governments worked together to create a special economic zone, 30 km south of Addis Ababa (Geda & Meskel, 2010).

Ethiopia held another general election in May 2010, and in October 2013. The EPRDF or its affiliated groups won the elections and parliamentary seats. In the process, the EPRDF created, as one researcher described it, a "one-party state" (Tronvoll, 2010). A similar political system and a shared stance on international affairs brought about friendly relations with Beijing. The data provided by China's Ministry of Foreign Affairs (MOFA) reveals that China accomplished 19 complete projects in Ethiopia since 1971; including roads, animal hospitals, power stations and improvements to water supplies. Additionally, in 2012, the bilateral trade value reached US$1.84 billion, of which China exported US$153 million and imported US$30.9 million, which shows that, despite measures put in place by Beijing to encourage a more balanced trade structure, the asymmetry between the two countries remains.

The Chinese government in return provided lots of assistance to Ethiopia, including providing special or preferential treatment (duty-free and quota-free) for 442 commodities, which covers most of Ethiopia's exports. China also assisted Ethiopia with infrastructure construction and low-interest loans. From 1988 to 2013, China has supported 529 Ethiopian students to get an education in China, and also sending large numbers of Chinese agricultural experts and volunteers to Ethiopia.

9.2 Shaping China's responsibility in Ethiopia

9.2.1 China's motivation

Researchers tend to attribute China's motivations in Africa to access to resources and commercial opportunities (Alden, 2007, p. 8; Brautigam, 2010, pp. 64–65; Taylor, 2009, p. 19). Ethiopia, as a resource-poor state, does not produce oil or other significant raw material for China. Its landlocked geographic position makes it hard to act as a gateway for Chinese enterprises into other African markets. China's trade value with this country remains small. Beijing made great efforts to expand its engagement with this state with large amounts of financial, infrastructural and personnel assistance. The motivation behind this is beyond resource or business interests because Ethiopia is attractive to China in the following ways.

Like any other African countries, political and diplomatic support is of significance to China. The leading party EPRDF maintains a close relationship with Beijing and supports China's positions in the international arena. Apart from the support of China in relation to Taiwan and Tibet issues, as a voting member of the United Nations (UN) Commission on Human Rights, Ethiopia, along with a coalition of other African states, has thwarted any attempts to censure China for its human rights record (Thakur, 2009). Compared with China's relations with other African governments, Ethiopian leaders have deeper and friendlier relations with Beijing. Former Prime Minister Meles Zenawi defended China's African policy and China's development path on many occasions. His speech "China is not looting Africa", at FOCAC 2006, argued that,

> There are people who say the flood of Chinese goods will undermine Africa's national industry, but I don't think this is a problem … If you can't compete with the global market, you have to get it from the global market. There is no alternative. That is globalization
>
> (People's Daily, October 17, 2006)

In an interview, Zenawi said that "Chinese transformation disproved the pessimistic attitude that 'if you are poor once, you are likely to be poor forever'… the rise of China has a tremendous moral impact on Africa, and it is a lesson that many African countries can and should learn from China", (People's Daily, December 22, 2008). New Ethiopian President Mulatu Teshome has spent 14 years in China and got his college education in Beijing. He has called China his second home. During an interview, he described China-Ethiopian relations thus:

> we have common aspirations, that are fast growth, prosperity for our nations, for our countries; prosperities for our peoples and peace and stability in our countries and in our regions and to the world at large. So, we have got a lot of common agendas, common aspirations and we have to work hard for that.
>
> (Xinhua News, October 31, 2013)

The presence of a pro-Beijing government in Addis Ababa provides China with a supporter and defender in the international arena. It is representing a voice from Africa, which is opposite to the claim that China is a new coloniser, or that exploitation serves as the motivation behind China's increasing assistance in this country.

Ethiopia is a state that has long been marginalised by international society. After its two-year border war with Eritrea, Ethiopia's political situation has become more stable. The ruling EPRDF party, under the provisions of the current constitution, held an election in 1994 to elect the membership of local governments. After that, general elections have been held in 1995, 2000, 2005, 2010, and 2013. Despite the fact that the elections have been criticised as "unfair" by international society, and incidents of monitoring political activists or torturing and abusing political prisoners have happened recently, the Ethiopian government is not as notorious as some other African regimes, such as Sudan and Zimbabwe. As a result, the close relation with such a government is also not a criticism targeted at those other controversial governments. Plus, due to Ethiopia's underdeveloped status, giving assistance to this state will be less contentious and more internationally acceptable to Beijing. Furthermore, Ethiopia has political clout in Africa, due to its history as a symbol of black freedom and stimulator of pan-Africanism. Ai Ping, the former Chinese ambassador to Ethiopia, said in his memoirs, "Ethiopia plays a very unique role in Africa, UN Economic Commission for Africa and Africa Union both established their headquarters in Addis Ababa, which placed the city as the political capital of Africa" (Ai, 2005). Meanwhile, the location of Ethiopia is key to East Africa. As the source of the Nile, the country controls the lifeline for Egypt; this regional influence and power have been recognised by Beijing. China's foothold in this country will help Beijing expand its influence and reputation from Ethiopia to the rest of Africa. This can be seen in China's provision of finance for the construction of the African Union headquarters in Addis Ababa, at the cost of over US$200 million. As former President Hu Jintao put it, "Ethiopia could play a pivotal role in enabling China to consolidate its cooperation with other African countries" (the Embassy of Ethiopia in China, 2013).

Beijing clearly recognised the fact that Ethiopia was not a major trading partner for China in Africa, and might not become one anytime soon. The deep engagement strategy was more likely born out of political and diplomatic calculations. China as a rising player on the continent, its international image is key to China's future agenda. As growing criticism about China's presence in Africa has grabbed news headlines, Beijing has to change its negative profile within the continent and also worldwide. Ethiopia, with a stable government but a lack of resources, enables China to access the country less controversially. The positive feedback from Ethiopian leaders acknowledges China's contribution to the country, and hence increases the credibility of the Chinese government in Africa. It revealed that China's ambition in Ethiopia was beyond economic expansion and the quest for resources. China's image and its responsibility as a rising power are of great significance to Beijing's strategy, even at the cost of economic gain.

9.2.2 Ethiopia's demands

According to the principles of Ethiopia's foreign policy released by its Ministry of Foreign Affairs, Ethiopia considers economic development, poverty reduction and good governance as its national strategy. As a result, "Ethiopia judges other countries on the basis of their preparedness to engage in a mutually advantageous partnership for economic cooperation, investment, trade and development, as well as for peace and security" (Ministry of Finance and Economic Development [MOFED], 2010). China, like many other countries and organisations, is expected to provide economic opportunities alongside political and diplomatic support.

The Ethiopia economy relies on agriculture, a sector that depends on weather conditions and cultivation practice. The Ethiopian government disclosed that 85% of the population earns a living from agriculture (Diao, 2010). Both food security and economic development require agricultural growth. Therefore, the government encourages labor-intensive agriculture to increase productivity, to "diversify strategies in different ecological zones and [to] strengthen marketing system" (MOFED, 2010). Based on a governmental strategic framework for 2005–2010, named a Plan for Accelerated and Sustained Development to End Poverty (PASDEP), poverty in Ethiopia was primarily found to be a rural phenomenon. Food security remains a fundamental concern, and poverty can be attributed not only to local factors but to the declining terms of trade for Ethiopian agricultural products, such as coffee and tea, in the global economic system. PASDEP also mentioned a series of reasons for the poverty in Ethiopia, such as low income and investment, low levels of education, poor environmental conditions, and also low levels of peace and stability in Ethiopia and the region as a whole. As for the role China could play in this development path, Ethiopia was very realistic to suggest that "the country needs to maintain close relations with China, as a means to promote trade and investment while also securing a market for Ethiopian products in China" (Thakur, 2009). To be specific, it required Chinese aid for infrastructure construction to create a better environment, investment and trade for economic growth, and technical assistance and vocational training to increase the quality of its labor force. Although they recognised China as a newcomer to the market, former Prime Minister Zenawi asserted that the "Chinese entrepreneurs could play a leading role in the construction, infrastructure and natural resources development endeavours of Ethiopia by diverting their capitals and introducing the easily adaptable Chinese technology" (Adem, 2012).

Apart from the common requirements similar to those of other African countries, Ethiopia has an enthusiasm for China's development path. China's success in feeding a fifth of the world's population with only 8% of its arable land is well known. Chinese experiences of modernising its economy in a relatively short period are of interest to Ethiopian leaders, who are struggling to raise their country out of poverty. Furthermore, Ethiopian leaders believe that China and Ethiopia share similar social, economic conditions. China's one-party government has maintained internal stability and dramatic economic growth which aligns with EPRDF's own priorities. These features are attractive to Ethiopian political elites, even if Beijing does not lobby for its development model in the Ethiopian government. During Ethiopian Prime Minister Hailemariam Desalegn's visit to Beijing in June 2013, he said to President Xi Jinping that,

> China's development has brought hope and opportunity for developing countries. Ethiopia is committed to achieving national modernisation, hopes to deepen party-to-party exchanges with the Chinese side, to

learn from China for the successful experience, and to enhance cooperation with China in the fields of infrastructure construction, energy and
resource exploitation, manufacturing and human resources training.

(MOFA, June 14, 2013)

As one of the least developed countries, Ethiopia is keen to get external support to help with its poverty reduction. Challenged by numerous developmental obstacles – such as poor infrastructure, food insecurity, low illiteracy
rates, and communicable diseases – the state needs tangible contributions
and assistance that could change its current status. As a result, China and
its aid appeal to the appetites of the Ethiopian elites.

9.2.3 Discussions for shaping China's responsibility in Ethiopia

Ethiopia has long been marginalised on the international stage. As was
mentioned above, China's foreign aid to this country is more out of diplomatic consideration than political, economic and resource calculations.
China's large amount of foreign aid meets Ethiopia's eager demand for developmental funds. And China's economic development path also provides
the country with an alternative choice. Hence, the case of China-Ethiopia
is less controversial than the other three cases. Not only does the country
draw less international attention to itself, but also the bilateral relationship
is based more on international ethics and benefits for Ethiopia. The following section will discuss the limitation of China as a model for Ethiopia, and
further to analyse China's impact on the country.

9.3 China's capability and limitation in Ethiopia

Relative economic strength and political clout of China and Ethiopia favours China. As a significant player in Africa, China has the motivation and
willingness to find its place on the continent and the world scene. Ethiopia's
unique domestic situation provides China with a less controversial field to
provide development aid and help with poverty reduction, hence the chance
to establish a positive image for itself in Africa. Ethiopia views China as one
of many partners that will help the country achieve its strategic and policy
goals, development and poverty reduction. China's successful economic development path presents Ethiopia's political elites with an alternative choice
because China is more similar to Ethiopia than Western nations. The Chinese
development path emphasises a strong centralised government and one-party
politics while remaining deeply involved in and focused on economic growth.
Even China itself is feeling (cross the river while feeling the stone 摸着石
头过河) its way through this kind of "authoritarian development" path, and
its influence on and adaptability for Ethiopia needs further discussion.

No doubt, the dramatic economic growth in China and other Asian
economies is attractive to Ethiopian leaders, and it at least provides hope

for the continent. Some comments and researchers have argued that the Ethiopian regime is following the model of Beijing's "authoritarian developmental state", in which economic growth trumps all and is pursued at the expense of political development, democratisation, and justice (Adem, 2012; Hackenesch, 2011; The Economist, 2010). Evidence of this is drawn from the fact that the Ethiopian government has adopted five-year plans to give itself targets for economic development, which is similar to China's own economic plans of every five years. Meanwhile, it has set up special economic zones, much as China did at the beginning of its economic reforms. The Eastern Industrial Parks, sponsored by China's Ministry of Commerce and Trade, are set to encourage foreign direct investment and bolster the manufacturing industry, which was one of the ways in which the Chinese government led and fostered its own development. Furthermore, the Ethiopian government supported large-scale infrastructural construction, notably the controversial Gilgel Gibe III Dam, which former Prime Minister Zenawi promised to complete at any cost, while critics pointed out its social and environmental impact on the indigenous people and communities. This project increased the concern that Ethiopia's developmental path would be at the cost of political and environmental interests, as was Beijing's.

Regardless of whether China's development path is unique or not, China itself has experienced a period of transition. It has its own internal problems of human rights, democratisation, corruption and the huge gap between rich and poor. These side effects, along with one-party government, means the state has no right to export its own political system, nor to criticise EPRDF's leadership. Even if Beijing is not instinctively against good governance in Ethiopia, when it has struggled to tackle corruption issues at home, it lacks credibility to call for political reform in Africa. Ethiopia's leaders also were reluctant to admit that their country was following China's political example. In Prime Minister Hailemariam Desalegn's interview with the British Broadcasting Corporation (BBC), he expressed a willingness to learn from China's way of development by saying, "Chinese development has ... some important lessons that we can learn. They have focused on human development; human capacity development and you know accumulation of human capital. And they have also focused on technological development and technological capability accumulation". But, when asked about his political preferences, he has argued that they have actually learned from "the fast growing Asian tiger economies Korea, Taiwan, Singapore, Malaysia..." (Kassa, May 21, 2013). Similarly, one official from the Ministry of Foreign Affairs pointed out that,

> Ethiopia is not necessarily interested in following the Chinese model per se; rather, the model to emulate is that of Taiwan and South Korea, which are 'developmental states' and focus not only on economic growth, but also on uplifting the population economically, politically and socially.
>
> (Thakur, 2009)

Although the so-called "China model" provides a negative example for Ethiopia's democracy, it is better to say Ethiopia's internal one-party leadership was born out of its domestic political needs, rather than the influence of Beijing's African policy of aid with no-strings. Ethiopia is currently going through a very difficult stage in its political development. Despite the fact that the government is claiming to democratize in all its official discourse, the political reforms within the country have a long way to go. The country has experienced 2,000 years of imperial rule, 17 years of military rule, and only about a decade of civil government. Additionally, the current administration has prevented the emergence of powerful independent economic actors that might be able to translate their economic power into political influence, through the strict control of land. With such a political history and status, the country lacks internal forces for democratisation. Furthermore, the opposition parties are not strong enough to compete with the EPRDF. During the 2005 election, the opposition parties united against the EPRDF, forming the Coalition for Unity and Democracy (CUD). After the election, however, personality conflicts and the lack of a shared strategy led to the collapse of the political opposition. The government also made efforts to crush the CUD and other political opposition. After the 2005 election, there were no strong competitors for EPRDF for the elections in 2010 and 2013. The lack of unity among the opposition reinforced the dominance of the EPRDF regime. Even if the government used the rhetoric of democracy promotion, respect for human rights, and poverty reduction, international society and NGOs pointed out that Ethiopia's human right has sharply deteriorated, and many the scandals of unlawful imprisonment and punishment of political activities have been disclosed.

Ethiopia is a de facto one-party state, and it is a centralised regime in which no balanced institutions exist; for example, a judiciary to monitor the current government. Opposition parties are only present in order to legitimise the EPRDF regime and give it the veneer of democracy. China does not intend to, nor does it have the capability to pressure Ethiopia for fundamental change. Indeed, China's assistance on large infrastructure projects can easily be seen as support for an authoritarian regime that only pays lip-service to open political space and good governance. However, the motivation for political space lies inside Ethiopia, with either a well-organised opposition party or inner-party competition, as Ethiopia has at the moment. Without assistance or an aid package beyond Ethiopia's current social capability, it is easier to bring the poor country into chaos rather than real democracy and human rights.

9.4 The gap between China's policy Ethiopia and its implementation

Witness 1 said,

> Currently, there are certainly some Chinese companies or some Chinese people in Africa whose conduct has triggered discontent in local

populations. There are a variety of factors in this. One reason is that although China supports Africa, culturally the communication between China and them [Africans] is very limited, Africa does not understand China very much.

As it is discussed in the previous sections, the motivation of China's diplomacy in Ethiopia is different from their traditional economic and resource considerations. Its engagement in this country tends to be seen as a way to seek positive feedback, rather than short-term profits. China is a large donor to Ethiopia. Since 1995, the Chinese government has allocated US$24 million to the Ethiopian government in the form of grants to help with the construction of low-cost housing; rural school construction; the rehabilitation of roads and bridges; and vocational, agricultural and management training. Also, since 1988, the Chinese government has provided US$82 million in loans for mainly the construction of roads, flyovers and bridges, and machinery acquisition. It should be noted that most of the assistance from the Chinese government comes in the form of conditional aid, as each loan and grant has stipulated that Chinese products must be purchased. In 2006, China cancelled Ethiopia's bilateral debt (Thakur, 2009).

Since Ethiopia's major development challenges include the acceleration of economic growth and poverty reduction, the correlation between these and infrastructure developments and investment, trade, growth and poverty reduction has long been recognised (Higgins & Prowse, 2010). China considered infrastructure an especially important driving force for growth in its own development. As a result, China's approach to accessing Ethiopia's market has mainly been through economic assistance in terms of concessional loans and infrastructure. Indeed, China has its own interests in infrastructure construction. Meanwhile, Ethiopia can still enjoy the benefits of Chinese companies' economic engagement, for instance, the provision of services to the Ethiopian people and the indirect benefits to other sectors and industries, thus to add value and spur growth. However, these original targets are to some extent marred by some side effects.

9.4.1 Infrastructure

The Gilgel Gibe III Dam is currently under construction, together with an associated hydroelectric power plant located on the Omo River, in southern Ethiopia. Since the launch of this project in 2008, it is estimated that the total investment would reach 16 billion Ethiopian Birr (more than US$ 800 million). Once installed (estimated to be complete in seven years time), it would have a capacity of about 1,870 Megawatts (MW), which would be the largest hydroelectric plant in Ethiopia, with a power output that would more than double Ethiopia's total capacity, from its 2007 level of 814 MW (News One, April 17, 2011). It is expected to supply about half of its power to Ethiopia and export the other half to Kenya (500 MW), Sudan (200 MW), and Djibouti (200 MW) (allAfrica, July 21, 2006).

The World Bank, the African Development Bank and the European In-vestment Bank all considered funding for the Gibe III Dam in 2009/10. In the end, none of them got involved in this project due to the possible negative environmental and social impacts (Bosshard, May 22, 2012). In August 2010 Ethiopian Prime Minister Meles Zenawi vowed to complete the dam "at any cost", saying about critics of the dam that, "They don't want to see de-veloped Africa; they want us to remain undeveloped and backward to serve their tourists as a museum" (the Guardian, March 7, 2011). In the same year, the Ethiopian Electric Power Corporation (EEPCo one of the major funders of the project) and Dongfang Electric Machinery Corporation, a Chinese state-owned enterprise (SOE), signed a memorandum of understanding to provide electrical and mechanical equipment for the project. The agreement was backed by a loan from the Industrial and Commercial Bank of China, covering 85% of the US$495 million cost (Xinhua News, November 28, 2011). Three NGOs – International Rivers, Friends of Lake Turkana, and Bank Track – wrote a letter to Industrial and Commercial Bank of China (ICBC) chairman Jiang Jianqing on May 21 and said, "the Gibe III Dam raises se-rious technical, economic and financial questions". The Gibe III Dam is Africa's most destructive power project. It will ravage the fragile ecosystems of the Lower Omo Valley in Ethiopia and Lake Turkana in Kenya, and the 500,000 poor indigenous people who depend on them, said Peter Bosshard, policy director of International Rivers, an international non-governmental organization (NGO) focusing on dams (South China Morning Post, June 2, 2011). Furthermore, the environmental damage could cause social conflicts as well. A study revealed Ethiopia's Gibe III Dam would cause humanitar-ian catastrophe and major cross-border armed conflict in the trans-border Region of Ethiopia, Kenya, and South Sudan (Africa Resources Working Group – ARWG) (Shih, June 2, 2011). In response to this criticism, ICBC's first chief risk officer Wei Guoxiong said that, ICBC, as a global bank, will not support environmentally unfriendly projects, no matter whether at home or abroad, and he further explained that ICBC had employed Equator Principles,[1] or even stricter policy to evaluate its loans (Ifeng, June 30, 2010). Wei's reply didn't clearly answer the wide criticism of ICBC's loans without transparent environmental and social evaluations. And, actually, the bank didn't join the Equator Principles until 2012, but the loans were pledged in 2010. A controversial project without a sound explanation, ICBC's reputa-tion as China's leading bank was violated. Ikal Angelei, chair of Friends of Lake Turkana, an NGO working with local people living around the lake, said: "ICBC is underwriting the destruction of our people. Their funding is a hideous gesture of the destruction Chinese funds can bring to Africa's poorest communities" (Hathaway, September 17, 2010).

In fact, the Chinese Ministry of Environmental Protection released Environmental-Protection Policies in Chinese Foreign Investment to pro-vide rules for Chinese projects of dam construction and oil exploration in Africa, which are frequently criticised by the West. Since 2007, China has also imposed the Green Credit Policy, under which Chinese companies that violate China's environmental laws would be blacklisted and unable to receive future loans because of their pollution record. At the same time, Zhang Hongli, vice president of ICBC, said the bank imposes its Green Credit Policies on 61 sectors, which reduced 70% (about US$7.4 billion) of its loans to environmentally unfriendly industries in 2008 (Xinhua News, July 21, 2013). According to the comments of an American environmentally sustainable financial analyst, currently few governments have the capability or willingness to promote such a policy, but it brought about important progress in regulating economic policy in banking systems. The major deficiency lay with the transparency of the loans and financial trade in China's banking sectors (Matisoff, July 26, 2010). The Chinese Banking Industry Environmental Record 2010, released by nine Chinese NGOs, remarked that the ICBC made improvements to establish a Green Credit System, and offered/included data about its energy consumption and loans to energy inefficient, highly polluting, and environmentally friendly industries (Friends of the Earth, 2010). It also introduced a strict "green" threshold for the management of loans to ensure the "green" allocation of loan resources, while applying "a veto with only one vote" for rejecting any application from enterprises that fail to meet the eco-standards (ICBC, April 18, 2011). However, it didn't disclose details of the implementation of these policies. In the case of Ethiopia's Gibe III Dam, despite the controversial impact on the local community and criticism from international environmental NGOs, ICBC continued to provide loans for the project, which led to damage to its reputation as a socially and environmentally responsible lender, and also to a loss of capital for shareholders. As a leading bank in China, ICBC's failure to follow the international standards and disclose its loan information with the public also violated Beijing's reputation-building strategy in Ethiopia, and thus its soft power efforts on the world stage.

Well-designed infrastructure projects could indeed contribute to poverty reduction and the improvement of living conditions in Ethiopia, as well as provide new opportunities for trade and employment. As a country that went through many years of internal conflict that left it with insufficient and undeveloped infrastructure, Ethiopia is desperately in need of financial support to improve its infrastructure. In addition, the country has long been constrained by the lack of adequate finances, a weak capacity at both the government and corporate levels, ineffective local private sector investment, and a technically unskilled labour force. Chinese companies with better management, technology and financial support from national banks would complement Ethiopia's deficiencies in these aspects. However, in reality, as Witness 12 pointed out, Chinese companies' major advantage is their low costs and, due to high competition in international markets, Chinese investors have to participate in the marginalised, risky or controversial projects abandoned by the traditional multinationals. Additionally, compared to the experienced trans-national corporations, Chinese companies lack overseas experience and awareness of international standards. Environmental protections and local community relations have long been neglected by Chinese companies. During the interviews, many interviewees from Chinese enterprises, no matter whether from SOEs or private companies, tend to emphasize their commitment to economic growth and working opportunities, but neglected environmental protection in its responsibilities to local people. ICBC's example revealed the environmental risk in China's overseas operations. As for the overseas project, the operation process was watched by the whole international society, and even with the approval of the host country, it still needed to consider the widely accepted international standards.

Another criticism of Chinese infrastructure projects included harm caused to local business. With regards to the issue of quality, most Ethiopians perceive Chinese infrastructure as being of poor quality. As one official stated, "if we have the Germans making our roads, it will last for 50 years; if the Chinese build our roads, we will be lucky if it lasts for even 10 years" (Thakur, 2009). What's worse, some Chinese firms are known to submit bids below cost in an effort to secure the contracts, and because of this, many may have to forego quality. Also, the considerable involvement of Chinese companies has the potential of completely alienating domestic firms, which will be detrimental to Ethiopian growth in the medium and long term. Regarding this, Witness 23 said, "the multinationals in the world market have developed systematic corporate social responsibility (CSR) operating procedures, but Chinese companies considered CSR as building bridges and roads. Actually, Chinese entrepreneurs do not realise that a well-established corporate culture is the best CSR to local community". Witness 7 agreed, suggesting that even though the Chinese people always thought of Africa as a less-developed continent, even if the economy of Africa is backward, Africans' awareness of international standards is much more developed than China's because they have inherited them from the colonist period. The distant awareness among Chinese entrepreneurs and Ethiopian people violate China's reputation.

9.4.2 *Agriculture*

With a primarily agricultural economy that accounts for more than 46% of gross domestic product (GDP) and 85% of the labour force, and with its major exports to China composed of agricultural products, the significance of the rural sector in Ethiopia's economy is obvious (Diao, Hazell, Resnick & Thurlow, 2007).

China has been engaged in Ethiopia's agriculture sector since the 1970s when the two countries established official diplomatic relations. Initially, the involvement was limited and one-way, most of the projects were Chinese assistance in infrastructure, researching support and training. In 1996, China joined the Food and Agriculture Organization's (FAOUN's) "South-South Cooperation Program". Under this programme, China has sent more than

700 Chinese agricultural experts and technicians to seven African countries (Li, 2011). Ethiopia was one of the earliest participants in the program (China Daily, January 15, 2014). Along with this engagement, the scope of agricultural cooperation expanded to concessional loans, volunteers, and agricultural technology demonstration centres. The first youth volunteer group was sent to the small Ethiopian village of Asossa, in 2005. Apart from official assistance projects, a growing number of Chinese companies have invested in Ethiopia's rural sectors such as wind farms, leather factories, and sugar plantations. A notable example is a leather company from Henan, which got 45% of its equity from the China-Africa Development Fund (CADfund) and opened a factory complex in Suluta that employed 350 local staff with 20–25 of them directors or group managers, 65% of them are women (Sina, June 11, 2014).

It could be said that China entered Ethiopia's agricultural industry at an early time in the 1970s. However, due to political and economic reasons, many Chinese companies' investment projects are still on a limited scale or in the planning stages; this is revealed by the fact that China sent the first group of Chinese technicians to Ethiopia, under FAO's South-South Cooperation Program in 1998 (China Daily, January 15, 2014). But, as progress was being made, the Ethiopia-Eritrea war broke out, and the construction of two agricultural demonstration centres was suspended, and Chinese experts had to be evacuated. Ultimately, the work restarted in the Amhara Region in 2000, and in Tigray in 2003. The Food and Agriculture Organization (FAO) programmes in Ethiopia are conducted with the joint efforts of a tripartite cooperation: FAO's representative office in Ethiopia, Ethiopia's Agricultural Ministry, and China's Agricultural Ministry. The FAO programme budget was US$2.027 million, with the Ethiopians contributing a further US$195,886. The FAO, China, and the government of Ethiopia shared the cost of the salaries of the Chinese participants. According to the recent report based on joint inspections by FAO representatives in East Africa and Ethiopia, officials from Ethiopia's Agricultural Ministry, and Chinese experts, the demonstration centres in Amhara and Tigray made progress in practical assistance, including growth in rice, vegetable, and commercial crops, which met the demands of local partners. "In Amhara, the rice they introduced was greatly accepted by the community because the Chinese were right down there with them" (Bräutigam & Tang, 2012).

In 2008, China set up a trust fund with the FAO, donating US$30 million to support agricultural improvements in developing countries, which made it the first strategic partner of FAO in financing South-South Cooperation (China Daily, January 15, 2014). A new, US$1.5 million, two-year, South-South Cooperation Program is currently being finalised between China, Ethiopia, and the FAO, and should start early in 2012 (Bräutigam & Tang, 2012). According to the FAO, the new programme will be integrated into and complementary to Ethiopia's Agricultural Growth Program, and focus on the high-productivity areas of Oromia, Amhara, and Tigray. Currently, about

30 Chinese experts have been deployed in these three regions, and the southern region, where the Chinese transfer knowledge, skill, and technology to Ethiopian experts (allAfrica, October 25, 2013). Among those centres, the Oromia demonstration centre has developed more quickly. In this centre, the Chinese experts are divided into four groups: agricultural, animal, machinery, and irrigation. They brought planting methods, prevention and treatment of animal diseases, agricultural production skills, machines and irrigation system designs, and technical support to the local people (Davis et al., 2010). These experts and professionals actively promoted agricultural techniques and assisted Ethiopia in increasing its agricultural productivity. In addition, the agricultural technology demonstration centres in Ethiopia have helped local people to acquire agricultural production and storage skills and provided animal health laboratory equipment and planting machinery. China, with its experience in agricultural development at home, could make significant contributions to the Ethiopian rural sector.

At the moment, China's engagement in Ethiopia's agricultural industry remains in an early stage. According to the report from FAO, the Chinese experts merely developed detailed proposals and designs for a number of irrigation schemes. Other projects, such as agricultural technical and vocational training schools, are limited in number and scope. And the spread of technology needs time to evaluate its influence properly. The agricultural industry, as a slow sector, also needs more time to realise profits and effects. As for China, the official supported projects tend to concentrate on large infrastructure construction like roads, dams or power generation. It lacks more micro-assistance, such as "promoting small-holder subsistence agriculture or agro-based manufacturing industries" (Thakur, 2009). At the same time, although Ethiopian Minister of Agriculture Tefera Deribwe has emphasised that his country "is keen to ... further strengthening cooperation between the two countries in the agriculture sector", it lacks of initiatives to attract foreign private investment, because the Ethiopian government has "prevented the emergence of powerful independent economic actors that might be able to translate their economic power into political influence" through controls for land equality (Lavers, 2011). In this way, foreign investment can hardly access the small agricultural business, nor provide tangible financing. It is estimated that, in 2010, only 4.3% of Chinese companies with projects in Ethiopia were engaged in the rural sector. Chinese assistance in rural sectors has been divided into two parts: national investors on large projects and training, but limited contributions to majority smallholders in remote and rural areas, like agricultural machinery equipment.

9.5 Conclusion

Generally, China's involvement in Ethiopia is less criticised by international society and local people, since the country has neither large energy reserves nor large consumption potential. As the least-developed country, Ethiopia's foreign policy towards China is focused on economic diplomacy: that is, on the one hand, the country wants the experience of rapid economic growth and development witnessed in China; while on the other hand, Ethiopia also hopes for increased trade and investment with China. In this regard, Ethiopia remains positive about China's presence. Additionally, China has pursued a non-intervention approach, which is in contrast to the traditional donors' intervention measures. Ethiopia views China more like one of its development partners that will not hinder or prevent, but rather assist it in achieving its economic and development goals.

Plus, China's active support for Ethiopia's infrastructure development, which not only provides the government with political achievements, but also facilities to Ethiopian people, and necessary conditions for economic growth. Also, China's sharing its own experiences and technical skills will help Ethiopia develop strategies for poverty alleviation and sustainable production, especially in the agricultural industry. In addition, Chinese firms investing in the agricultural industry have helped to transfer technology and machinery. As a result, the Ethiopian government views China as a generous supporter, and ordinary Ethiopians can benefit from visible and symbolic projects such as dams, conference halls, and roads.

At the same time, it should be noted that large Chinese companies' presence in Ethiopia has brought negative impacts on local businesses, the environment and communities. As for the lack of transparency in SOEs' investment, risk management, and lack of corporate social responsibility awareness (the same for small- and medium-sized businesses), their aggressive competition has negatively impacted their vulnerable local counterparts.

Note

1 The Equator Principles are a risk management framework, adopted by financial institutions for determining, assessing, and managing environmental and social risk in projects, and is primarily intended to provide a minimum standard for due diligence to support responsible risk decision-making.

Part 3

Conclusion

Discussion of case studies

In the conceptual chapter, this book tried to indicate that there should be more criteria (from a developing countries' perspective) to consider whether China is a responsible player in Africa or not. It mentioned that traditional players' interpretations of "being responsible" are flawed when one considers China in Africa because the relationship is different from that of the traditional Economic Cooperation and Development (OECD) donors' relations with Africa. Whether China, itself a developing country, is responsible or not is dependent upon its capabilities in the host country. This Part 3 conclusion will include a general discussion of the case studies to answer hypotheses II and III, and then offer a supplementary note for responding to the hypothesis I and evaluation, as discussed in Chapter 3.

In Part 1, it was argued that, although China holds a different political philosophy and approach to dealing with crises and development in Africa from the traditional players (mainly the OECD countries), it does not necessarily mean that China is irresponsible in Africa. Regarding the responsibility of an emerging country like China, there are other factors that could affect China's ability to be a responsible actor in Africa. In Part 1, this book mentioned the gap between the policy and implementation levels for the Chinese government and Chinese enterprises. Even though the central government has a clear strategy for the promotion of African development, the interests of influential players' are diverse, and that has affected the implementation of Beijing's pledges. Thus, this book analysed the first layer: Chinese domestic players, which includes Chinese government branches and offices, as well as Chinese companies. At the government level, the three key actors are Ministry of Commerce (MOFCOM), Ministry of Foreign Affairs (MOFA) and Exim Bank. Each of these has their own priorities and interests: MOFCOM highlights the interests of the national economy and budget, while MOFA has much more consideration for China's reputation in African countries, and Exim bank cares more about the financial credibility of the host African country. With different concerns in mind, the implementation of the central governments' pledges is a compromise between these three actors. Furthermore, the implementers on the ground, Chinese companies operating in Africa, also have their own interests. Private companies focus on profit maximisation and seeking out profitable markets wherever they may be. By contrast, SOEs are subject to a more complex calculation involving the political interests of the central government. To summarise, Part 1, especially Chapters 4 and 5, focused on China's perspective and responses to the first question of Hypothesis II and III.

Part 2 mainly analysed the second layer, the particularities in each African country, in order to test the remaining parts of hypothesis II and III. Four featured case studies were selected to assess China's engagement: Sudan (South Sudan), Nigeria, South Africa, and Ethiopia. The four cases represented different types of government, different levels of development, different attitudes towards Beijing, and different amounts of energy reserves.

The four case study chapters were conducted with the same structure. In the beginning, each case started with a brief introduction of China's relations with the host country, and the situation in that country. Secondly, based on the political, economic, and diplomatic environment in the host country and its ties to Beijing, each chapter then examined the possible motivations relevant for Chinese engagement there. Generally, the motivations could be summarised into three categories: China's national interests, the host country's demands, and international pressures. These three influential factors have shaped China's responsibility in the host country. In some countries, where there is less of an international concern, the main factors come from just China and the host country. This section is designed for hypothesis II, and at the end of each case chapter, there was a discussion of the compatibility of China's interests in the host country with the external demands. The conclusions were that, in most circumstances, China had shared similar expectations with that of the 279-international communities and the host countries.

Then, the second section for each case study discussed China's capability and limitations in the host country. Often neglected in the current literature on China's engagement with Africa is China's own vulnerability. Not only does it remain a developing economy confronting immense challenges, but also although it seems that Africans lack much bargaining power, the Chinese companies that operate in the host country are actually largely constrained by local regulations, environment and communities. Additionally, international society, the host country's government, local communities and NGOs have different expectations from China's presence. Sometimes one may contradict the other, hence it increases the complexity of assessing China's responsibility in the host country. Finally, each chapter highlighted the gap between China's strategy in the host country and its implementation, in order to directly answer hypothesis III regarding whether China's responsibility in the host country was tailored to local political and economic situations.

The influential factors that shaped China's responsibility in Africa

Based on the analysis in the theoretical chapter, China's motivations and responsibility in Africa are shaped by three dynamic factors: a combination of its national interests, the host country's demands, and international expectations and pressures. As for the four case countries, China's responsibility is tailored according to the political and economic environment therein. Table III.1 makes a comparison of these factors. It is worth noting that the three influential factors do not enjoy an equal role in the host countries. Instead, the significance of each factor differs from case to case, based on its situation.

According to the dynamic influence of these three factors, China's responsibility in the four case countries presents the following features: In Sudan, where the Darfur conflicts and war with South Sudan have drawn the world's attention to its human rights violations, the international expectations played a greater role in shaping China's responsibility. Under pressure from international society, China showed flexibility in interpreting the "nonintervention" principle, which was long viewed as an obstacle to international sanctions on the Bashir regime. As in Nigeria, oil interests and market access were key to China's involvement.

Table III.1 The comparison of three influential factors in shaping China's responsibility in four African states

Three influential factors	Sudan	Nigeria	South Africa	Ethiopia
China's national interests	1 To safeguard its economic interests 2 Its international reputation	1 Oil interests 2 Market 3 political support	1 Political support 2 Gateway to the region 3 Economic interests	1 International reputation 2 Chinese business expansion
Host country's demands	1 Khartoum: to help control the crisis and protect Bashir from International Criminal Court (ICC 2 Juba: oil interests 3 Darfur: international intervention	1 Balanced trade 2 Financial support to its development 3 Political support of its leading role in the continent	1 International support as an African leader 2 Value-added trade	1 Economic growth and poverty reduction 2 China model
International expectation	Jointly sanction and intervention	Conditional investment and assistance	Not to violate the democracy and human rights	to respect international standard

Source: Author.

China's approach of "oil for infrastructure", and later the acquisition of shares from multinational corporations, mainly came out of motivation to protect its economic interests in Nigeria. South Africa, as a regional leader, is of great importance to China both politically and economically. The main driving forces of China's involvement in this country is South-South Cooperation and trade. Different from the other three countries, Ethiopia has neither a controversial regime, nor a strong economy, nor resources. China's presence in this country goes beyond economic interests and cares much more for improving China's reputation and diplomatic interests.

From Table III.1 and the discussions of each country, China's main principle is clear: noninterference, yet the methods can be flexible. This characteristic can be found in Elizabeth J. Perry's explanations for China's policy: the principle should be strictly insisted upon, yet approaches should be planned and acted upon according to circumstances (Heilmann & Perry, 2011). China's motivation in the case of each country differs, yet to safeguard its economic interests and international reputation requires China to be more active in shouldering the responsibility for Africa's development. Most African countries are anxious for financial assistance to fuel their economy. China's funds and projects brought the continent sources of finance and tangible commitments, which are in Africa's interests. At the same time, China's approach contradicts international expectations, but its aims are consistent with those of international society and leave the country space to be more cooperative with joint efforts.

The factors which effected China's ability to be fully responsible for African countries

The elements that have affected China's ability to be fully responsible to African countries are mainly from two sides. From China's side, the conflict between the profit-seeking nature of Chinese enterprises and the policy needs of the Chinese central government have become a major problem, which leads to an inability for China to be a responsible player in Africa. As for the African countries, there are various contexts – like unstable domestic political and economic situations; policy flip-flops; conflicts between political or interest groups; and inconsistent attitudes towards China between the government and the people – that affect China's ability to fulfill its responsibility in these African countries.

Although most of the literature argues that China-Africa relations are asymmetric, and African countries without a unified voice find it hard to bargain with China for their own benefit, in reality, Chinese companies operating in Africa are very vulnerable. Their operations are constrained by both the Chinese central government's policy, which often contradicts their profit-driven nature and the regulations of the host country.

Table III.2 illustrates the major limitations that are preventing China from being responsible (or, the negative effects that are not the original intention of China's African policy). In Sudan, China's nonintervention policy is intended to help Khartoum maintain stability and safeguard China's economic interests there. However, as the crisis in Darfur and South Sudan became worse, Beijing realized that the Bashir regime was unable to control the worsening situation, and that its nonintervention stance largely affected its international role of being responsible. Therefore, it changed to support for international peacekeeping in Darfur, but the opposition groups failed to recognise China's evolution; this placed China in an uncomfortable position between Khartoum and its opposition/South Sudan. China would like to establish an approach to oil for infrastructure in Nigeria, like its engagement in most of the oil rich countries. This method is designed to ensure oil interests for China and to provide tangible economic benefits for Nigeria. However, Nigerian political elites were suspicious of the commitment of "oil for infrastructure". Constrained by corruption, mismanagement, and underdeveloped infrastructure, the Nigerian government could not provide a sustainable, alternative substitute for the current approach. In terms of South Africa, the state has the most developed economy, political, and legal system in Africa. China, who actively promoted the inclusion of South Africa in association of five major emerging national economies: Brazil, Russia, India, China and South Africa (BRICS), would like to expand its influence in Africa through close political and economic ties with Pretoria. But not only is South Africa's representation on the continent doubted by both African countries and international society, but also the Chinese government was challenged at home for its economic assistance to South Africa. The criticism of China being irresponsible in Africa focused on China's no-strings-attached approach to doing business in Africa. In Sudan, it has been questioned for supporting unsavoury regimes. In Nigeria, it is blamed for scrambling for oil. In South Africa, an economically powerful state on the continent, there is a concern in international society that China may violate South Africa's democratic development. In Ethiopia, neither viewed as a controversial regime nor as an economic powerhouse, China receives less criticism for its engagement there.

These results demonstrate a clear message: various conditions within African countries – like domestic conflicts and problems, political considerations, instability – all affect China's ability to fulfili its responsibility in Africa. These situations suggest that China's role in fulfilling responsibility in these countries is decided by the conditions in the African countries. In the meantime, for the Chinese, its state led Foreign-Aid decision model also cannot fulfil the needs of the actual implementing agents, Chinese businesses in Africa. These findings also support hypothesis III, that we cannot judge China's responsibility in African without considering these contexts in Africa countries.

Table III.2 The influential factors of China not being fully responsible in the four countries

Country Elements	Sudan	Nigeria	South Africa	Ethiopia
Chinese Domestic	China's large economic interests in Sudan	.	Challenge of South Africa as recipient of Chinese assistance	The deficiency of China model
Host country	1 The close relations with Khartoum 2 The distrust of opposition in Darfur and South Sudan 3 Lack of recognizing China's evolving policy in international society	1 The changing electoral politics 2 The gap between Nigerian's ambitions and its underdeveloped market environment 3 Corruption, mismanagement, oil violent and insufficient infrastructure	1 Incompetent as a representative and a leader of Africa 2 The BEE 3 Corruption	

Source: Author.

Horizontal comparison of the four cases

A state's responsibility is a combined calculation of international expectations, national interests and the host's impact. In order to assess China's responsibility in Africa, this part is targeted against the three main criticisms of "China as a new coloniser", "China's scramble for resources in Africa", and "China violates the human rights and good governance in Africa".

The four case countries represented different levels of energy reserves:

1   Sudan and Nigeria have similar backgrounds: Both Sudan and Nigeria have oil reserves located in the southern region of the country, while the refinery factories are in the north. The governments are mainly controlled by the northern Muslims, which divides them from the Christians in the southern areas. Nigeria, with the second largest oil reserves and largest oil producer on the continent, produces 2.28 million barrels per day. As for Sudan and South Sudan, combined, they produced 486,000 barrels of oil per day in 2011. Following the separation, 75% of its oil reserves are located in South Sudan. China imported about 20,000 barrels per day from Nigeria and 66% of Sudan and South Sudan's oil production went to China in 2011 (Francis et al., 2012). Due to the separation of Sudan and South Sudan, South Sudan shut down the oil fields in July 2013.

2   South Africa: It is the world's largest producer of chrome, manganese, platinum, vanadium and vermiculite. It is the second largest producer of ilmenite, palladium, rutile and zirconium. It is also the world's third largest coal exporter. South Africa is also a huge producer of iron ore. In 2012, it overtook India to become the world's third largest iron ore supplier to China, who is the world's largest consumers of iron ore.

3   Ethiopia: The resource reserves in Ethiopia are very small, and have little significance for China's resource supply.

The four case countries represented different levels of democratic development and governance.

1   South Africa is a parliamentary representative democratic country, which has been dominated by the African National Congress (ANC). The ANC is the ruling party in the national legislature, as well as in eight of the nine provinces. The major challenger is the Democratic Alliance. Other major political parties represented in Parliament include the Inkatha Freedom Party, which mainly represents Zulu voters. Also, South Africa has a sound legal system. The Constitution of South Africa asks for the protection of the people's freedom. It is the most stable democratic country in Africa.

2   Nigeria is not a fully democratic country, but it has developed towards a democratic path. In 1999, it conducted its first election and ended military rule, which marked its start on the path to democracy. Since then, the country has held four general elections, in 1999, 2003, 2007, and 2011. Despite the fact that the elections were condemned as unfair, Nigeria has shown marked improvements in its attempts to tackle government corruption and to hasten development. In the latest election, in 2011, it unfolded much more smoothly, with relatively little violence and fraud. Currently, the dominant party is the People's Democratic Party (PDP), who have won every election since 1999.

3   Ethiopia is a one party ruled state, with the Ethiopian People's Revolutionary Democratic Front (EPRDF) as the dominant party. In its most recent election in 2010, the EPRDF marginalised the oppositions. Now, there is no major challenge to the EPRDF's leadership.

4   Sudan: The violent civil war and genocide in Darfur have drawn the world's 287 attention to Sudan. It is widely recognised that Sudan is an authoritarian state where all effective political power is held by President Omar al-Bashir. Sudan's legal system is based on Islamic Law, which applies to all residents of the northern state, regardless of their religion.

The four case countries represented different levels of economic development.

1   South Africa is the largest economy in Africa, accounting for 24% of its gross domestic product, when adjusted for purchasing power parity,

and is ranked as an upper-middle-income economy by the World Bank. South Africa has a comparative advantage in agriculture, mining, and manufacturing products related to these sectors. South Africa has shifted from a primary and secondary sector economy in the mid-twentieth century, to an economy driven primarily by the tertiary sector in the present day, which accounts for an estimated 65% of gross domestic product (GDP) or $230 billion in nominal GDP terms.

2   Nigeria is a middle income, mixed economy and emerging market, with expanding financial, service, communications, technology, and entertainment sectors. It is ranked 30th in the world in terms of GDP (Public-Private Partnerships – PPP) as of 2013 (40th in 2005, 52nd in 2000), and the second largest economy in Africa (behind South Africa). It is on track to become the richest country in Africa in 2014, when their new GDP rebasing result is published, and when it becomes one of the 20 largest economies in the world by 2020. Its reemergence, though currently underperforming, the manufacturing sector is the third largest on the continent, and produces a large proportion of goods and services for the West African region.

3   The economy of Ethiopia is largely based on agriculture, which accounts for 46.6% of its gross domestic product (GDP), and 85% of total employment in the country. Despite recent improvements, with an exploding population, Ethiopia remains one of the poorest nations in the world.

4   Sudan's economy is based on oil production, agriculture and foreign direct investment. The Darfur conflict and the civil war between north and south left the country with a lack of basic infrastructure and a large amount of its population living below the poverty line. The independent South Sudan is one of the World's weakest and most underdeveloped countries, with little existing infrastructure and the highest maternal mortality and female illiteracy rates in the world.

The four case countries present different characteristics. By comparing whether China has preferred to support pariah regimes or resource regimes, it can be ascertained whether China's involvement in Africa has been a scramble for oil or intentional violation of the democratic development of the continent. The results of this comparison could also be a response to the common criticism of China as a new coloniser in Africa, and China being immoral in its pursuit of oil.

According to the data in Table III.3, the amount of China's official finance to Sudan is not larger than to Nigeria or Ethiopia, which have better performing democracies. Additionally, among all the financial development projects, all the projects in Sudan have no grant element, while in Nigeria one project has 0–24% grant element, and three have 51%–99%. Ethiopia received five projects with 25%–50% grant element and nine projects with 51%–99% grant element. It showed that China has no preference for supporting the unsavory regime. Its financial support tends to focus on the host country's economic situation. Furthermore, in comparison to nonofficial finance, South Africa ranked as the top destination among the four countries, followed by Nigeria, then Ethiopia, and finally Sudan. All the funds had no grant elements. It showed that there was no particular relationship between investment and oil-rich countries. Chinese companies' investment was mainly driven by the market and stability. These comparisons echoed the discussion earlier that China's involvement in Africa is a calculation of three influential factors, rather than oil or democracy. There is no evidence that Beijing has intentionally violated the host country's democratic development.

In Table III.4, the comparison of Chinese official finance in the four case countries, one can see that Beijing has undertaken the largest number of projects in Ethiopia (91), followed by Sudan (71), then Nigeria (46), and finally South Africa (35). Of all the four countries, the largest number of officially supported projects were in the education sector, such as training and scholarship, the construction of schools and assistant teams of experts. The second largest sector was infrastructure, on power and water supply (South Africa is an exception). For example, loans for power and water infrastructure. Transportation, as an important sector within the infrastructure, also accounted for a large percentage of China's official development funds. In contrast, industry and mining construction was not a major sector for Chinese official finance. At the governmental level, aid tends to support the underdeveloped country. Among the four countries, the number of projects was in accordance with their levels of development, rather than related to their energy reserves or economic importance. The official funds were mostly invested in noncommercial sectors, notably education, which implies that the central government's funds in Africa were provided with much more consideration for expanding China's influence and reputation than economic profits.

Table III.5 compares Chinese nonofficial finance to the four host countries. It shows that Chinese companies have invested in the largest number of projects in Sudan (62), followed by South Africa (31), Nigeria (25), and then Ethiopia (18). The unofficial finance particularly focused on industry and mining construction sectors: for example, the purchase of oil stock, the construction of oil pipelines and refinery factories, and also the training of petroleum specialists. It revealed that Chinese companies have a particular concentration on the energy industry. The unofficial finance presented a different preference in countries and sectors. It tends to be invested in the energy-rich countries, with less competition from the traditional multinational corporations.

In summary, China's engagement with these four African countries has been driven by different motivations – politically, economically and diplomatically. Generally, the Chinese government has conducted a similar approach to its involvement in Africa, which comprises unconditional foreign assistance and "energy for infrastructure". At the governmental level, there

Table III.3 The comparison of Chinese development finance in the four countries

Country		Sudan	Nigeria	South Africa	Ethiopia
Official finance	Year	2002–2012	2002–2012	2001–2011	2002–2012
	Number of projects	71	46	35	90
	Amount	More than US$6.3 billion	More than US$12.5 billion	More than US$3 billion	More than US$7.5 billion
Nonofficial finance	Year	2006–2012	2006–2012	2006–2012	2006–2012
	Number of projects	43	17	23	17
	Amount	More than US$ 1.4 billion	More than US$ 27.4 billion	More than US$ 33 billion	More than US$ 7.6 billion
Military	Number		1		2

Source: Author (raw data: AidData).

Note: Some amounts cannot be identified because they are multinational and unable to category.

Table III.4 The comparison of Chinese official finance in the four countries in terms of sector

Country sector	Sudan	Nigeria	South Africa	Ethiopia
Action relating to debt				
Agriculture, forestry and fishing	3	1		
Banking and financial services			5	
Communications		4		1
Education	8	2		2
Emergency Response	4			4
Energy Generation and Supply	1	2	5	
Government and Civil Society				1
Health	13	1		
Industry, mining construction	16	14	17	6
Other multisector	1	1		
Other social infrastructure and services	3		2	1
Trade and tourism				
Unallocated	3			
Water supply and Sanitation	1			
Transport and Storage	8			

Data source: AidData.

Note: Some amounts cannot be identified because they are multinational, 291.

Table III.5 The comparison of Chinese nonofficial finance in the four countries in terms of sector

Country	Sudan	Nigeria	South Africa	Ethiopia
Action relating to debt	4	1		2
Agriculture, forestry and fishing	3	3		5
Banking and financial services		1	1	2
Communication	1	8	1	
Education	4	2	6	12
Emergency Response	9	1		4
Energy Generation and Supply	10	6		8
Government and Civil Society	7		5	9
Health	4	5	1	1
Industry, mining construction	2	3	6	8
Other multisector	1	4	4	6
Other social infrastructure and	1	1	2	
Trade and tourism	2	1	5	2
Transport and storage	9	3	1	10
Unallocated	9	5	1	20
Water supply and Sanitation	5	1	2	1

Source: Author (raw data: AidData).

Note: Some amounts cannot be identified because they are multinational, 292.

is no obvious evidence that Beijing has preferred to support pariah regimes, intentionally working with undemocratic states, or instinctively against democratic governments. It has been more concerned with diplomatic strategy and its international reputation, rather than economic benefits. This result also responds to hypobook II – that both China's and African countries' needs can be mutually beneficial, rather than incompatible. While, at the enterprise level, the investment has been more concentrated on energy supply and economic profits. There is a gap between Chinese officials and Chinese enterprises, which is mentioned in hypothesis III.

Summary

To summarise Part 2 of the book and the discussions above, there are supplementary notes for considering China's responsibility in Africa.

Hypothesis II and Hypothesis III are authenticated. These results indicate two main supplementary notes as follows:

1   Beijing could find more common ground in China-Africa engagement with African governments than with Economic Cooperation and Development (OECD) countries, no matter its political system, economic development status and energy reserves. This is partly because African leaders turn a blind eye to China's negative impact, in return for generous financial support. It is also partly reflected in the fact that China and Africa have similar grievances regarding colonisation and poverty, would be cautious towards international intervention, and would prioritise economic development over political and governmental development.

2   The western media tends to portray African countries as victims in international society. However, most African governments are capable enough to leverage between traditional OECD donors and new emerging donors and gain benefit for themselves. They have a strong willingness to develop an African agenda, rather than that of either the West or China. It is the responsibility of the traditional players and China to facilitate this willingness, rather than undermining each other. In addition, due to their experience of the colonial period, most African people have a higher awareness of law, regulations and rules than their Chinese counterparts. Moreover, it is unrealistic to devalue the African people's awareness of their right to self-protection because of their economic underdevelopment.

These results indicate that, when considering whether or not a country is responsible to/in African countries, there are more points that should be considered.

1   The receipt country's demands. The receipt country's needs and conditions are very important factors in the assessment of international

responsibility. When evaluating China's impact on Africa, it is necessary to explore what African governments need, and of what their government and people are capable. Overload conditions may bring harm rather than benefit to a fragile country.

2   The donors' capability. Traditional north–south aid patterns place the receipt country in a vulnerable position in which it is dominated by the donor. However, this unbalanced relationship in favourr of the donor could not fully explain the relations between the emerging economy and the recipient country. Hence, the evaluation of China in Africa could consider the limitations for the donor and the constraints within the host country.

From the summary of this section, I can confirm the hypotheses to be accurate and true. The concept of international reasonability is still developing, and as some developing countries become strong enough to support other countries, we cannot only use original standards to evaluate these developing supporters. There are more points that need to be considered, as has been argued in this summary.

In the concluding chapter, this book will review the topic of the book, the summary of the book, and use a supplementary standard from Chapter 3, which was also authenticated in discussions of Parts 1 and 2, to evaluate whether China is a responsible power or not. Also, the significance of the book will be discussed.

10 Conclusion and evaluation

10.1 Restatement of the topic

The evaluation of China in Africa is a broad topic and touches all elements of Africa's interests: economic, diplomatic, political, technological and military. It also reveals a dynamic interaction among the interests of China, Africa and traditional players. This book does not explore (as most of the current literature has explored) the question: 'are current Chinese actions in Africa converging with accepted international norms?'. Instead, based on the findings from the literature, it acknowledges the divergence between China and these norms, goes further to look at China-Africa by complementing the norm of 'international responsibility' with the developing countries' perspective and sets new criteria for the assessment.

The newly established criteria for China-Africa responsibility acknowledge the close connection between the state's national interests (and motivations) and 'being responsible'. It argues that China's interests in the continent are compatible with the African countries' demands, and there is space to cooperate with the traditional players.

Meanwhile, the new standards have a full understanding of emerging countries' new role as a donor. Traditional north-south patterns could not fully explain the donor-recipient relationship between China and Africa. It challenges the traditional assumption that considers Africa countries as a victim. In the China-Africa political context, even if the national strength is in favour of China, it cannot be denied that China is a weak country in shouldering responsibility on the continent; this is partly caused by Beijing's incapability of mobilising its overseas agency to adopt the central strategies effectively and smoothly within the fragmented authoritarianism framework, and partly caused by the political and economic environment within the host recipient country.

Based on the findings of the framework part, and the case studies, the book has tested three hypotheses. This chapter will first restate the answers to each hypothesis, and then evaluate China's responsibility accordingly. Finally, it will discuss the significance of the newly established criteria.

10.2 Summary of the book and verification of hypotheses

As discussed in Chapter 3, the theory of international responsibility argues that a state's responsibility policy is shaped by three influential factors: national interests, international expectations, and the recipient countries' demands. The second section of each case study confirmed the role of these three influential factors through discussing China's policy towards the host country and its motivations. The case of Sudan demonstrated the role of international expectation in pressuring China to change its policy, and the case of Ethiopia illustrated how a host country's demands could influence the of shaping China's policy. These two cases and their findings refute the criticism that China's behaviour in Africa is not responsible since China places its own economic and political interests ahead of the African societies' interest in development. Furthermore, as in the case of Nigeria, where China has oil interests, and in the case of South Africa, where China has economic and strategic interests, these two countries have little international attention, even if China's policy in the host country is mainly a matter of China's own interests, the policy is nevertheless designed to offer reciprocal benefits to the host country.

Chapter 4 tested hypothesis II, in particular, and addressed the research problem of "the compatibility of China's policy (and motivation behind it) and external requirements". This chapter highlighted that, although China's approach and philosophy are different to that of the Economic Cooperation and Development (OECD) countries, it doesn't instinctively work against the existing efforts made by both traditional players and African governments. Even the most controversial "non-intervention" principle has evolved along with China's expanding diplomatic interests. And Beijing has shown flexibility in interpreting this principle according to the changing situation. Apart from that, the ways in which China's approach differs from the Western countries' mainly lies with the following three aspects: oil for infrastructure, aid with no-strings attached, and China as a model for Africa. "Oil for infrastructure" was introduced to satisfy China's growing oil thirst while providing African countries' infrastructure which is necessary for their economic development. "Aid with no-strings attached" was not intended to undermine Western efforts to promote good governance, because the Chinese aid focuses on infrastructure building, which means there is not much cash transfer to the African governments and therefore less chance for poor aid distribution and corruption. Lastly, China has advocated that all the countries should be free to choose the best development path for their own situation. China's development path only provides African countries with one choice, which is not an absolute or the only alternative to the Western way, nor is it compulsory for these countries to follow in China's footsteps. It is the African governments' right to choose the way that best suits their situation.

Generally, the policy level decisions are compatible with African's demands and do not always contradict international expectations. The following chapters mainly explored from where China's irresponsible behaviour comes. Chapter 5 investigated the issues from China's perspective. After reviewing China's financial assistance to and business on the continent, it argued that, even if we assume China has a policy to support Africa's development, one has to consider policy implementation through all levels of Chinese agencies and actors. In terms of China's aid to Africa, the three major ministries, Ministry of Foreign Affairs (MOFA), Ministry of Commerce (MOFCOM) and Exim Bank, each with separate agendas and priorities, have affected the aid projects. The foreign aid implementer (in most of the cases, this refers to a Chinese company), with its profit-driven agenda, often deviates from the central policy. Regarding Chinese business, the State-owned enterprises (SOEs) are not as tightly controlled by the government as one may expect. They tend to operate in the host country according to local situations, with economic considerations, rather than pursuing central political goals. The private companies, in most cases, referring to medium and small companies, only seek economic gains in Africa, sometimes sacrificing environmental protection, labour safety and welfare, and returns to the local community. Some small traders even affected local industry by exporting low-quality Chinese products. In summary, the irresponsible behaviour of all these actors in Africa has had an impact on China's international responsibility as a whole.

In the case studies, the reason to China not fully responsible from African side was discussed. These chapters refuted the notion that China has an asymmetric strength in its relationships with African countries. Its responsibility in the host country is largely constrained by the political and economic context therein. As for Sudan, the deteriorated crisis and international criticism failed to recognise China's efforts in mediation. The distrust from international society, South Sudan, and rebels from Sudan have placed Beijing in an uncomfortable position, which has limited its capability to facilitate a solution to the crisis. In the case of Nigeria, the changing political agenda, mismanagement and corruption have constrained the tangible effects of China's "oil for infrastructure" approach. The suspended and cancelled bilateral contracts have negative impacts for both Chinese companies and Nigerian infrastructure construction. Regarding South Africa, the country is much more like a competitor to China in the economic field. Although China-South Africa relations enjoy close political cooperation in advancing and amplifying developing countries' voice, since the state has a limited role in representing the continent, and serves as a gateway to access other African countries, China's contribution to the country is not as much as to other underdeveloped African countries. In contrast, in Ethiopia, where there is less international attention and not much in the way of resource reserves and economic opportunity, Beijing has provided considerable financial assistance and gained positive feedback from the host country.

The discussion of the previous chapters has revealed that the evaluation of China's responsibility should employ broader criteria, relating to China's capability and Africa's situation. It echoes the theoretical chapter's argument that "the term 'international responsibility is flawed because it does not take account of the developing countries' perspectives, such as state's capability in shouldering responsibility, and the varied character of states' interaction on economic development". As a result, the assessment should be conducted on the basis of the criteria that reflect Chinese and African views, as well as the perception, do those in the West. It supplements the traditional, Western understanding of international responsibility, and provides for a more balanced understanding of the China-Africa context.

10.3 Evaluating China's responsibility in Africa

From the preceding discussion and verification of the hypotheses and research questions, the book has suggested that China and its subjects' capacity, African countries' various contexts and demands are indispensable factors for consideration when evaluating the question of whether or not China is a responsible player in Africa, or to what extent China has been responsible for Africa, and to what extend it has not. Combing through the discussion in the framework part and case studies, the evaluation of this question will be conducted according to the five criteria analysed in Chapter 3: (1) good governance (2) expression; (3) capability and behaviour; (4) consequences and impact; (5) feedback. These five standards have been discussed in the preceding chapters in order to present their importance and the dynamics among each item. The following section will analyse the five criteria and place them in the political and economic context of China-Africa relations.

10.3.1 Good governance

The first criterion was the basic requirement of a ruling government. As a ruling party, the CCP's legitimacy was believed to be built upon "an unwritten social contract between the party and the people, whereby the people do not compete with the party for political power as long as the party looks after their economic fortunes" (Breslin, 2005, p. 749). Chinese political discourse considers the successful poverty reduction, enhancement of Chinese people's welfare, maintaining economic growth, and safeguarding sovereignty and territory as the basis of being responsible. However, in reality, the Chinese government has serious corruption and transparency problems, and a wealth gap between rich and poor, rural and urban areas, along with its economic growth. This unbalanced political and economic structure has brought China a dual identity in front of Africa: strong economic development and weak governance. As a result, even if we cannot deny the fact that China has already become an important player on this continent, there are always doubts about how China could benefit Africa without solving its own problems.

On the other side, even if we assume the Chinese government's economic performance shows that it has made commitments to Africa, it depends on the host country to fully take advantage of these efforts. However, the host African governments are not always responsible, as most of the governments have issues with legitimacy. Even as the most developed state on the continent, South Africa has suffered from serious corruption, violence, and an imbalanced national income distribution system.

This criterion is not directly relevant to the evaluation of China's responsibility in Africa, but it does provide a baseline to figure out China-Africa problems and reveals that, since both the donor and the recipient country government are not always responsible, China's capability to be responsible or not in Africa is largely affected or it could say this borne deficient.

10.3.2 Expression

Due to differences in their respective political systems and interests, China has held a different approach to that of the traditional players, when it comes to engaging with Africa. Even though it does not conform to some of the accepted criteria of international responsibility deployed by OECD states, it shares the similar goals of African development with international expectation, and also serving African countries' demands. To some extent, it can be an effective actor in promoting Africa's development and a cooperator with international efforts.

The crisis in Africa could be sorted into three categories: namely security, governance, and economy. In response to the security crisis in Africa, the traditional OECD countries employed sanctions, embargoes, and joint military intervention. In the case of Sudan, the Western countries have imposed a comprehensive trade embargo and blocked the Sudanese government's assets. They called for international intervention in Sudan due to Khartoum's violations of human rights, and international humanitarian law in Sudan's Darfur region, and the war with South Sudan. In contrast, China preferred to pursue a diplomatic and economical approach to protect its overseas assets. They hold that the ultimate reasons for Sudan's crises are conflicts of interest. China preferred the provision of positive assistance over the imposition of sanctions. Beijing doubted the effectiveness of sanctions in solving the crisis in underdeveloped countries. On the one hand, China believed that the solution to the crisis lay with providing economic welfare to the local people, as Witness 23 and 24 emphasised. Considering the extent of poverty in Africa, the right to development is uppermost on Africa's agenda. Government sanctions would harm the lives of its citizens. On the other hand, it thought that neither military intervention nor sanctions were the final solution. In order to maintain peace and stability, the people needed tangible progress. Witness 3 argued that China's cautious approach towards international intervention and sanctions does not necessarily mean it placed its own national interests ahead of international responsibility because peace and stability in Africa benefits China and all other countries. There is no strong evidence to suggest that intervention and sanctions could work in solving Africa's crises. Instead, improper intervention has the danger of potentially leaving the poor country in a state of chaos.

In terms of expression (policy) in Africa, China has a different foreign strategy to that of Western countries. It places economic development in front of political and governance improvement. Prioritising the economy is not necessarily being irresponsible towards African countries: it can bring effective and tangible achievements to the country, but it may also support corruption, dictatorship, and mismanagement, since the African countries themselves are not fully responsible states. To further explore China's responsibility in Africa, one should recognise that the key to assessing China's responsibility in Africa is not whether it is consistent with the traditional donors, but instead one also needs to look at its impact on the host country.

10.3.3 Capability and behaviour

When talking about China in Africa, we are actually talking about a fragmented China confronted by a diversified Africa. China has more national strength than the four case countries. However, economic strength cannot be fully transferred to shoulder responsibility. As Witness 21 said,

> China's activities in the host countries are strictly constrained by local regulation and environment. What if the host country itself is not fully responsible?

Therefore, it requires analysis on a case-by-case basis, comparing capability and behaviour in response to common criticisms. Generally, the criticisms of China's engagement with Africa include:

1 China's "non-interference" principle provides a shield for the dictators. It provides them with an alternative source of financial support and undermines Western countries' efforts to promote democracy and human rights in Africa.
2 China has aggressively scrambled for energy and other resources in Africa.
3 The overwhelming flood of Chinese products and Chinese businesses into certain countries has destroyed local industry, increased unemployment, and violated local environmental protections, labour force protections and also working conditions.
4 China is not a good model for Africa's development.

The four case countries have evaluated the four main criticisms.

1   "Non-interference" Principle

Sudan: China's African policy is flexible and pragmatic in accordance with China's national strategy and agenda as a whole. The Chinese interpretation of "non-interference" is evolving on the basis of the changing situation in other countries. In the case of Sudan, China developed its "non-interference" principle in response to the deteriorating situation in Sudan, and in the face of increasing international pressures. But, unfortunately, China's capability in persuading Bashir regime is limited, and the oppositions in Sudan and the international community have failed to recognise China's evolving stance.

China's attitude towards "non-interference" principle reveals that the principle is no longer an obstacle to China shouldering international responsibility. The motivation behind the principle plays a more important role in determining China's stance. In the case of Sudan, China's primary concern is to protect its economic interests. On the one hand, this inevitably requires a stable and peaceful environment. This aim is consistent with international expectations. On the other hand, it is cautious to use sanctions on the host country, as the effectiveness of sanction is doubt. The second concern in Sudan is that of China's international reputation: the international community expects China to be more active in pressuring the regime. As has been mentioned, China's national interest of overseas economic safety requires peace and stability in the host country. But, it has a particular emphasis on the attitudes of the host country and regional organisations. It is worth noting that, when comparing the four case countries, China has not been particularly supportive of the undemocratic countries, nor the nations with bad human rights record. Its attitude towards African conflicts is based on a calculation of economic interests, international reputation, and the national strategy.

With China's growing connections with pariah governments, it is impossible for Beijing to escape from involvement in the resolution of local conflicts and crises. Such involvement is in the interests of both China and international society. Currently, China has shown progress in the evolution of the 'non-interference' principle, by pressuring dictators and sending a peacekeeping force. But it still has a long way to go towards being responsible in Africa. Even if we assume that China places Africa's economic development in front of other aspects of its development, Beijing still needs to make a comprehensive evaluation of their financial flow and avoid the negative impact for local people.

2   "Oil for infrastructure"

Nigeria: China has conducted the "oil for infrastructure" approach in most energy-rich countries. The approach was designed to secure China's energy safety and to pay back African countries through infrastructure construction. Witness 3 has explained that not paying money to African governments could prevent the abuse of oil income and improve conditions in African countries. The effectiveness of "oil for infrastructure" in African countries is determined by three criteria: the first is the host country's capacity – that is, to what extend the host country needs infrastructure. Considering the development status in Africa, most of a country's economic development is constrained by insufficient infrastructure. Generally, the infrastructure agreements fulfill the demands of African countries. The second criterion relates to the distribution of oil income. In the case of Nigeria, the government has a changing agenda for using its oil income, Beijing is required to adjust its approach to meet the shifting demands of Nigeria's oil distribution. The third criterion is who will enjoy the achievements.

China's foreign assistance concentrates on infrastructure construction, a sector in which traditional players are less interested, and that is complementary to the foreign aid from OECD countries. Moreover, the projects, such as highways, railways, power supplies and public buildings, provide an African country with visible contributions and, to some extent, avoid the corruption that goes with a cash transfer. However, the turnkey projects make little effort to train Africans and build local capacity. There have been complaints that Chinese companies import an unskilled Chinese labour force from home to build their projects, rather than finding a local partner or hiring local people. Although the Chinese side has argued that these problems are due to the poor competitiveness of the African labour force, Beijing cannot escape from the responsibility of training African employees and providing them with good and safe working conditions.

At the same time, providing infrastructure does not necessarily mean that it is possible to compensate for the negative effects of Chinese oil companies on the local community. As was discussed in Chapter 5, China lacks an independent agency to evaluate its overseas projects, especially in the highly sensitive oil industry, where an improper decision may harm both the interests of the local community and the safety of Chinese assets and workers. As China has become involved in oil fields that were considered too risky for western investors, it requires Chinese companies to be very cautious towards their actions in the host community.

In short, "oil for infrastructure" itself is neither responsible nor irresponsible; it is designed to benefit both sides mutually. In reality, it requires African governments and the Chinese government to work together to evaluate infrastructure projects and ensure the programs benefit local people better, rather than act as a vanity symbol for the government.

3 "Chinese Overwhelming Presence to destroy local industry"

South Africa: When considering Chinese businesses (mainly in the manufacturing industry) and Chinese labour force's impact on the local economy and working opportunity, one should first compare the host country with China. The Chinese could only replace the industrial supply chain of a host country if they have comparable manufacturing strengths. Similarly, people who can replace African workers must have the same capability. Therefore, in order to analyse whether a Chinese business has destroyed local industry, or if it has brought investment and work opportunities, one should have a look at whether the industry is competitive with its Chinese counterparts. Take South Africa as an example: the country has the most powerful capability in the continent. The country welcomes big Chinese multinationals but remains concerned about the aggressive competition from medium and small businesses. South Africa is a typical example of an African country: they hope to receive more investment from China to fuel their economies, but are afraid of Chinese people stealing their jobs. With regards to this situation, Witness 11 said, regretfully,

> We would like to hire more local employees, no matter in technical, management or labouring, because it is the most economical way for our company. But the quality of African working force is not as good as Chinese. In order to ensure the project finishing on time, we have to hire Chinese workers.

Witness 20 has also expressed willingness to transfer the supply chains to African countries, rather than importing Chinese goods from China, due to the labour and transportation costs. But he also complained that the backward infrastructure in Africa prevented Chinese companies from transferring their full production lines to local countries.

To evaluate Chinese business's impact on the host African countries, one should divide Chinese investment and Chinese goods. The investment is generally welcomed by the host country, and both the literature and interviewees have offered an optimistic expectation that Chinese investment would bring a "flying goose" model, which Would transfer its labour-intensive industry to Africa, thereby increasing local employment opportunities and upgrade China's industry. But the overwhelming flood of Chinese goods not only destroys the uncompetitive local industry but also take away local people's work opportunities. The case in South Africa reveals that, although Beijing has launched methods to promote cooperation between Chinese companies and African partners while regulating the export of low-quality products to African markets, the fundamental reasons for these problems have not been solved. The overwhelming Chinese business and products are caused by Beijing's loose control of the illegal business practice of state-own enterprises, and small and medium-sized companies. As Beijing does not have a sound supervision system to monitor its enterprises, those enterprises have brought bad operation practices and low-quality products to

Africa. Moreover, it is Beijing's responsibility to regulate its companies and avoid the negative impact on African markets.

4   China as a model

Ethiopia: China, with its successful economic achievements, has long been discussed as a developmental model for African countries. Most of the interviewees did not agree with the idea that China's development path could be considered as a model. As Witness 22 said,

> We do not attach conditions to finance African countries; we just provide them choices. The African people can choose the way they want and the way that suits them. They are free to learn the advantages of China's development path while ignoring the disadvantages.

And Witness 23 holds that,

> What African countries need is not only democratisation but also state building, political system construction and stability to maintain the democracy.

China's economic development is attractive to African countries and the African people, but the adaptability of the Chinese way to any Africa country is questionable. China itself has suffered from negative side effects resulting from its impressive, fast-paced development. For the Chinese, they only recognize that their way of development provides a choice for Africa, but they would not force another country to follow their example. Nor would China favour another country who followed a similar developmental path over another who did not. It is African countries' responsibility to distinguish which way best suits their agenda and situation.

10.3.4 Consequences and impact

Africa's voice is always absent from the current literature on China-Africa engagement. As the working paper *Afrobarometer* suggests, 'the negative rhetoric emanating from much of the surrounding literature tells only part of the story', (Gadzala and Hanusch, January 2010) and African perceptions of China-Africa are not equivalent to those they have of western countries. Generally, Africans hold positive views of China's presence in Africa. According to a Pew Survey (Table 10.1), although the data for the four countries is incomplete, the trend is that most African countries hold relatively more positive attitudes towards China than towards the United States (US) and France. However, along with China's deep involvement, the number of people who are favourable towards China is declining slightly.

A survey of 250 African university students and faculty in nine countries (including the four case countries) also illustrated this relatively positive attitude. Table 10.2 shows the results for the four case countries and the four targeted Chinese approaches.

Table 10.1 Pew survey for African countries opinion to China

Country	Survey	Very favourable	Somewhat favourable	Somewhat unfavourable	Very unfavourable	DK/Refused	General positive	General negative
Please tell me if you have a very favourable, somewhat favourable, somewhat unfavourable, or very unfavourable opinion of … China [827]								
Ethiopia	Spring 2007	19	48	22	6	5	67	28
Nigeria	Spring 2013	38	38	7	4	13	76	11
	Spring 2010	37	39	11	4	8	76	15
S. Africa	Spring 2013	18	30	21	22	9	48	43
	Spring 2008	10	27	21	30	12	37	51
Please tell me if you have a very favourable, somewhat favourable, somewhat unfavourable, or very unfavourable opinion of … the United States [844]								
Ethiopia	Spring 2007	41	36	14	8	1	77	22
Nigeria	Spring 2013	38	31	12	8	12	69	20
	Spring 2010	49	32	9	5	5	81	14
S. Africa	Spring 2013	43	29	10	10	7	72	20
	Spring 2008	28	32	8	16	16	60	24
	Summer	2002	31	34	9	19	8	65
Please tell me if you have a very favourable, somewhat favourable, somewhat unfavourable, or very unfavourable opinion of … Japan [866]								
Ethiopia	Spring 2007	40	41	5	3	10	81	8
S. Africa	Spring 2008	10	29	15	24	22	39	39

Source: Pew Research.

Table 10.2 Africa's attitudes towards China in Africa

1   For Africa, China policy of "non-interference" is

Country	A good policy (%)	Basically good, but with some problems (%)	More harmful than good (%)	Quite harmful (%)	Don't' know (%)
Sudan	43.2	33.6	8.0	4.8	10.4
Nigeria	17.3	31.0	14.7	12.7	24.4
South Africa	12.2	31.0	19.8	13.2	23.9
Ethiopia	14.3	50.5	16.3	11.2	7.7

2   Some people say China practises Neo-Colonialism in Africa

Country	Strongly agree (%)	Agree (%)	Neutral (%)	Disagree (%)	Strongly disagree (%)	Don't know (%)
Sudan	5.2	8.7	19.4	43.7	16.7	6.3
Nigeria	5.1	10.8	28.7	24.6	5.1	25.6
South Africa	2.0	4.1	42.9	29.1	8.7	13.3
Ethiopia	6.2	14.4	25.8	32.5	13.4	7.7

3   Satisfaction with Chinese companies that work on large projects in my country

Country	Very satisfied (%)	Satisfied (%)	Neutral (%)	Dissatisfied (%)	Very dissatisfied (%)
Sudan	23.1	48.6	17.1	7.2	4.0
Nigeria	12.2	44.4	33.2	9.2	1.0
South Africa	0.6	19.3	79.5	0.6	0
Ethiopia	13.0	54.4	20.7	9.3	2.6

4   My view of Chinese Small Businesses in my country is that

Country	Help with local economic development (%)	Help but also a source of problems (%)	Are not helpful to local economic development (%)	Generally harm the interests of local people (%)	Don't' know (%)
Sudan	38.7	28.4	14.0	10.7	8.2
Nigeria	44.7	28.4	12.2	8.1	6.6
South Africa	24.4	51.3	6.1	5.1	13.2
Ethiopia	40.2	40.7	6.2	7.7	5.2

Source: Sautman and Yan (2009).

The results of the survey refuted the idea that only a few members of the African political elite are positive about China-Africa links. The majority of people hold a positive attitude towards China-Africa political and economic connections. On the controversial topics (China's non-interference principle, China as a neo-coloniser, the overwhelming Chinese business in Africa), African people hold a positive or neutral role, which differs from the criticism in the western media.

If we make a comparison among the four countries considered as case studies for this book, the findings show that the four African governments welcome a close relationship with Beijing and the Chinese investment and financial support that come with it. Their greatest concern is the impact of Chinese products on local industry. The more powerful the economic development status of the African country is, the more likely it is that China's threat to local business raises anxiety. All governments welcome China's 'non-interference' stance, but they do not have a romantic view towards China. As in the African views mentioned in the cases of Nigeria and Ethiopia, the officials have distinguished between China as an 'economic model' and China as a 'political model'. They expressed appreciation for China's economic success, while rejecting China's experience of development by sacrificing social fairness and political freedom.

The public opinion survey reveals that the countries with a better governance performance and democratic system tend to have higher dissatisfaction with China's presence which shows that a close governmental relationship could lead to a friendlier attitude among African people. As Table 10.1 indicates, the African people's satisfaction declines with China's expansion. The *Afrobarometer* has given the answer to African people's concerns, as Africans are 'wary of Chinese influence, particularly when human rights and multi-party elections are of concern' (Gadzala and Hanusch, January 2010). In terms of the economic factor, it indicates that African people are at ease with China's large projects and investment. What concerns them the most is similar to the findings of the existing literature: that is, China's imports of Chinese labour and products, which are threatening the local industry and working opportunities that provide the livelihood of the majority of African people.

10.3.5 International feedback

International society is not as optimistic as are the African people. They doubt the rhetoric of Chinese political propaganda regarding 'non-interference' and a 'win-win' situation. Kaplan argues that 'China is refusing to be a responsible stakeholder in the international political system, cultivating, as it has been, good relations with some of the world's most odious regimes', and 'acts like a free rider' (Kaplan, 2010). Keet is concerned that 'whatever good intentions the Chinese government may say it has, the objective and fundamental problem is that' China-Africa economic relations 'are based upon highly uneven levels of development and a very different capacity to benefit from such interactions and cooperation' (Keet, 2008). Similar voices add that Chinese firms in Africa hire the largest percentage of workers from China and that managerial positions are filled by Chinese people.

Some researchers hold a realistic attitude towards China in Africa. Etzioni argues: 'China is surely not a responsible stakeholder, but then few nations are' (Etzioni, 2011, p. 553). Since it is inevitable that China will have a presence in Africa, it is useful to urge China to become a better co-operator in the continent, with the recognition of its inner weakness and incapability in Africa.

Finally, based on the former five standards, China is not a fully responsible actor in Africa. The fundamental reason for this is that China itself is not a fully accepted player in international society. It holds a very different approach to African countries from that of traditional players. Moreover, the fragmented authoritarianism reflects Beijing's weakness to supervise its overseas agencies and actors. Meanwhile, African interests are not as genuinely shared as it might appear. They have different requirements and different capabilities in taking advantage of China's commitments. Based on this understanding, the following section will discuss suggestions for policy.

10.3.6 Summary and policy suggestions

From the five standard evaluations for assessing whether China is a responsible actor in Africa, we can see that China has commitments to the continent that are recognised by most African countries and their people. However, much evidence is revealed of China not being fully responsible. This section will focus on how China should improve to become a more responsible actor in Africa. The first is, as suggested in former chapters, policy implementation. We cannot deny the profit-driven nature of Chinese entrepreneurs and bureaucrats: it is Beijing's responsibility to regulate these overseas agencies. Currently, China does not have an independent agency to look after its projects and business in Africa. The projects were taken without a transparent and professional evaluation of its impact on the country and the local community. China could establish an aid agency with specialists to monitor its enterprise, and to give a comprehensive assessment of their investment and projects.

Second, as argued in the former chapters, China shares similar interests in a stable and developing Africa with international society. In this case, China should be more cooperative with international efforts. Most of the cases reveal that China is incapable of dealing with the changing and risky situation in Africa. Its commitments to the continent are largely constrained by the political and economic situation there. In this situation, international support is much more important to Chinese companies.

10.4 The significance of the book

To consider whether a country takes international responsibility in a certain area is complex. Over the past few decades, developed countries have offered aid to developing countries and undereveloped countries. As Chapter 3 indicated, their emphasis has evolved from the principle of sovereignty, national diversity, and non-intervention, towards one of mutual dependence, cooperation, and then to increasing attention on human rights and humanitarian intervention. Take the US for example: strengthening democratic institutions is the primary condition when the US offers aid to these recipient states. Nowadays, when more and more countries have the ability to offer aid to recipient countries, these standards from traditional players will be used to evaluate emerging donor countries. This book, although the main topic and cases focus on China and Africa, has also tried to indicate that if we only consider the standards from the original OECD countries, one cannot properly evaluate the actions of new up-and-coming donor countries.

In the conclusion of Part 2, this book indicated that there are several factors and actors that should be added to the equation and that these factors and actors may apply to other cases and other regions when considering whether a country is a responsible actor to other states.

1   State capacity of donor countries. As the case studies and conclusion to Part 2 demonstrated, it is hard for these new donor countries to demand that recipient states change their political systems or improve their governance in a short period of time. On the one hand, the new donor country lacks the ability to pressure the recipient country; while on the other hand, the effect of using aid as a condition to pressure another government is limited.

2   Contexts of the recipient states. For most recipient states, there could be many reasons that result in their inability to develop into donor countries. For example, interest groups in Nigeria, civil war in Sudan, or South East Asia in the late 1990s with terrible financial motoring system.These problems may exist for decades, and problem solving needs time to achieve results. Therefore, it may not be appropriate to give conditions that recipient states cannot easily fulfill. For example, democracy and democratic institutions cannot be established in a very short period of time: it needs both elites and the people to establish a democratic culture and become loyal to a democratic system. If donor countries try to push the establishment of a surface democracy, which could collapse and result in an unstable situation, the elites and the people in recipient states may not support the establishment of a more solid democracy in the future. On the other hand, elites and the people from recipient states could also have their own priorities for development and survival. Pragmatic conditions that can directly fulfill their priority goals are far more attractive to recipient states. Otherwise, inappropriate or overloaded conditions for recipient states could result in negative influence, which would damage both the recipient state and the country providing the aid.

In summary, since there are more and more developing and non-Western countries joining the group of donor countries, and because the way in which aid-offering countries fulfil their international responsibility to recipient states is a continuously developing topic, this book has used China's relationship with four African countries as cases to offer supplementary standards, and to suggest a possible analytical framework for the study and evaluation of international responsibility of donor countries.

Appendix I

Interviewees list

No	Interview time	Interview location	Background	Category
1	Tuesday, August 21, 2012, 3:00–4:00	CPIFA	Vice president of CPIFA, former Chinese ambassador to Morocco	Chinese Official
2	Thursday, September 13, 2012, 10:00–11:00	CPIFA	Former second secretary to Ghana	Chinese Official
3	Friday, August 24, 2012, 5:00–6:00	Headquarter of China.com	Former Chinese Ambassador to Nigeria and Namibia	Chinese Official
4	Monday, August 5, 2012, 10:00–11:00	Beijing Academic of Social Sciences	Vice Principle of China Foreign Affairs University	Chinese Official
5	Thursday, September 27, 2012, 10:00–11:00	CAPFA	Secretary-General of the Chinese-African People's Friendship Association	Chinese Official
6	Monday, August 5, 2012, 1:30–2:00	Guangming Daily	Director of International News, Guangming Daily	Chinese Official
7	Friday, August 24, 2012, 2:30–3:30	CASS	Research Professor of Asian and African Studies, CASS	African studies researcher
8	Tuesday, August 21, 2012, 11:00–12:00	CICIR	Research Professor and Director of the Division of African Studies, Institute of Asian and African Studies, CICIR	African studies researcher
9	Friday, August 24, 2012, 11:00–12:00	CASS	Research Professor of Asian and African Studies, CASS	African studies researcher
10	Wednesday, August 22, 2012, 9:30–10:30	Peking University	Professor in the School of International Relations at the Peking University director of the Center for African Studies	African Studies researcher

(Continued)

No	Interview time	Interview location	Background	Category
11	Tuesday, August 21, 2012, 9:30–10:30 am	CICIR	Research Professor of the Division of African Studies, Institute of Asian and African Studies	African studies researcher
12	Friday, January 25, 2013	Email	Professor and Director, Institute of African Studies, Zhejiang Normal University	African studies researcher
13	Thursday, October 11, 2012	Email	Professor of Xiangtan University Law School, African law	African studies researcher
14	Wednesday, November 7, 2012	Email	Director of Integrated Development Agricultural University Center for Agricultural at Beijing	African studies researcher
15	July 25–29, 2012	Skype	Project manager of Guinea-Mali, China Geo engineering corporate	Chinese SOEs' employee
16	January 3–5, 2013	Skype	Project manager in Gabon, China Gezhouba Corporate	Chinese SOEs' employee
17	Wednesday, July 11, 2012	Skype	Engineer Nigeria, CNPC	Chinese SOEs' employee
18	Sunday, July 15, 2012	Skype	Managing Director, Tianjin Branch of Sinopec	Chinese SOEs' employee
19	Friday, January 25, 2013	QQ	Manager assistance Huawei Telecommunication Company Gambia branch	Chinese private company employee
20	Sunday, June 17, 2012	MSN	Translator of a trade company in Nigerian China Town	Chinese private company employee
21	Thursday, November 8, 2012	Email	School of Overseas Chinese and International Studies Jinan University	Chinese researcher
22	Thursday, June 5, 2014, 10:00–10:30	School of International Studies, Peking University	School of International Studies, Peking University	Chinese researcher
23	Thursday, June 5, 2014, 3:30–4:00	School of International Studies, Renmin University	School of International Studies, Renmin University	Chinese researcher
24	Thursday, June 12, 2014, 2:00–2:30	School of International Studies, Renmin University	School of International Studies, Renmin University	Chinese researcher

Appendix II

Interview Transcript Sample (The interview is conducted in Chinese and translated by the author)

1   Chinese official Interviewee No. 1 Interview time: Tuesday, August 21, 2012, 3:00–4:00 pm Interview location: Chinese People's Institute of Foreign Affairs (CPIFA) Interviewee: Cheng Tao, vice president of CPIFA, former Chinese ambassador to Morocco, who has more than 16 years of diplomatic working experiences in Africa countries, including Gabon, Mali, Benin and Morocco.

Q: What is your opinion towards China's responsibility in Africa?
A: Recently, I've been asked similar questions in an interview with People's daily on FOCAC, "Why China pay so much attention to African poor friends, isn't is a burden to the state? We are from developing country with many people in poverty. Why do we provide so much finance assistance to Africa? It even draws a lot of domestic criticism that in the recent fifth ministerial FOCAC, the Chinese government will continue to expand its assistance to Africa and pledge to provide US$20 billion in concessional loans in terms of investment and commercial properties cooperation.

I would say these people don't understand China's foreign policy. Our economic diplomacy acts as the servant of our foreign policy and foreign strategy.

Firstly, as a responsible developing country, China's support of Africa is our international responsibility, international obligation and international common morality (gongde), and is an important component of a harmonious world. In the 1960s, China has provided selfless assistance to Africa in terms of railways, roads, ports, dams and many meetings buildings, stadiums, schools and hospitals when Chinese government and people are in very difficult circumstance, which has gained its reputation and influence. China's aid to Africa with no political conditions attached contrast with the western style. Chinese experts worked with African brothers gained good local impressions. It is still an intangible asset to us now.

At the same time, China's support of Africa from the outset has been in the fundamental interests of the country. With China's development, the form and content of China-Africa relations have changed considerably, but Africa's importance for China has not, Africa's place in the structure of China's diplomacy has not. Politically Africa is still an important strategic support in our diplomatic struggle, in the logistics of the overall foreign policy situation of realising peaceful development it is indispensable as a major support. From the economic perspective, sustainable economic development can depend on Africa for energy and natural resource supplies and commodities and as an important market for investments. Good China-Africa relations will bring benefits to the people of China and Africa.

Our assistance to Africa is mutually beneficial. In the 1960s and 1970s, African countries strongly supported China to break western countries' containment, safeguard national sovereignty and territorial integrity. From the restoration of the lawful seat in the UN to defending Beijing on anti-China human rights proposal; from the Chinese campaign in many international organizations to China's bidding for Olympics Games and the World Expo, these are all inseparable from the support of African countries.

After the 2008 earthquake, Equatorial Guinea, with a population of two-million people, donated 2-million euros. The Congo-Brazzaville government donated US$1 million after the earthquake in Wenchuan, and US$2 million after the earthquake in Yushu for a boarding primary school, despite the fact that the state is a heavy debt country.

China's responsibility in Africa is not "doing things beyond its means in order to be impressive". China is a developing country richer than before. It is reasonable to increase its aid to Africa. Compared to the western countries, the scale is limited, but the quality and effectiveness is better.

Q: Since you've mentioned the mutual benefit between China-Africa, considering the asymmetric strength between China and African countries, how to realize the real mutual benefits and win-win situation?

A: I often say, the meaning of China-Africa relations is not charity, it is aid for the poor, it is not humanitarianism, it is internationalism. We are a great power which has great power responsibilities, aiding Africa's development is part of our construction of a harmonious world.

Diplomacy in any country is not selfless. Our assistance principle is considering our interests and considering the benefits of others. China-Africa's mutual benefit is not selfish. Africa is the world's resource base and rich in mineral resources. At the time that our enterprises invested in the mining industry, our government has provided finance to support "oil for infrastructure". Most of the large and medium enterprises, such as CREC and CWIC, have strongly connected with government. They were introduced to local host government through our embassy. Once these enterprises have problems or accidents, our embassy will shoulder the responsibility. Therefore, comparing to the western countries, our enterprises are more reliable. Additionally, the SOEs' projects in Africa are often supported by China-Africa Cooperation Development Fund, China Development Bank and China Exim Bank and to provide assistance, loans or buyer's credit to help African countries implement aid projects. As a result, these Chinese companies have financial advantages.

Africa now greatly resembles the early stages of China's reform and opening, China's support projects are aimed at increasing the capacity for the independence of African countries. Through developing energy resources in Africa, we help to improve local infrastructure and to enhance the ability of these countries to sustainable development.

Q: You've mentioned the embassy's guarantee for SOEs, could you please further talk about local embassy's support of Chinese enterprise?

A: Generally, the political dept. of political is responsible to collecting the local information, such as market and environment exploration and macro-management, so as to ensure the advantages and disadvantages of the local country before SOEs' "going out". The Economic and trade office is responsible to getting information on local demands and economic situations, then to contact Chinese relevant enterprises. The Dept. of Commerce is responsible for the implementation and coordination between local governments and Chinese enterprises, such as the loans and implementation of the projects. In addition, we hold regular meetings to release policy and investment opportunity while urging Chinese enterprises to abide by local regulations and corporate social responsibility.

Q: What factors do you think affect China to be responsible in Africa?

A: Currently, there are certainly some Chinese companies or some Chinese people in Africa whose conduct has triggered discontent in local populations. There are a variety of factors in this. One reason is that although China supports Africa, culturally the communication between China and them (Africans) is very limited, Africa does not understand China very much. We are currently doing a lot of work, such as through cultural exchange about our thoughts, ideas, traditions, etc., to give Africans better understanding. Western media is demonising Africa, demonising China. China-Africa should do some real things, and not let some other people slander us. Rumor is not truth, but it confuses people. We want to strengthen our influence, voice and eliminating distorted propaganda. In the past, Chinese people do not pay attention to propaganda. In the case of Africa, it lacks communication with African people and the world, between Chinese enterprises and African employees.

In addition, there are thousands of Chinese enterprises in Africa; they are far from the same. For example, I used to work in Morocco, where there are more than 2,000 Chinese enterprises, 30–50 million Chinese people, while carrying out more than 1,000 projects; they are at various levels, with different backgrounds, but they are considered to represent "China". Some of them pursue short-term benefits in the sacrifice of labor conditions, safety and other aspects. Some companies pave their way through money and believe money can do everything. Some lack of awareness of national responsibility and bring the Chinese bad habits to Africa. This phenomenon is the minority, but has very bad influence. We need to highlight our contribution, but not hide our problem. We have to deal with these problems. If the companies didn't do well in Africa, they have to receive heavy fines and legal punishment. In this way, China-Africa cooperation could be sustainable developing.

Thirdly, some African countries and people have some misunderstanding towards China and its role in the host country. In the past, our assistance to the continent is governmental oriented, but nowadys most of the bilateral economic activities are enterprise-led. Some African countries may think that in the past China has sent experts and medical groups without any payment, but now the Chinese enterprises are investing into mining industry for money. In this case, China is not as generous and selfless as it in the past. In fact, our governmental assistance has never stopped, and the enterprises are profit-driven.

Q: What do you think the criticisms, such as neo-colonization, undermining western countries efforts and China model?

A: The Western countries are envious and hostile to China-Africa cooperation. In the past they had a monopoly, accounting for 100% of Africa's natural resource exports, and now they can't prevent our cooperation with Africa because our cooperation is mutually beneficial. We are not neo-colonialists, we are not robbers. The colonialists came to Africa to plunder resources and the African people hated them for that. Africa has been the past Africa was grateful to China politically found natural resources in Africa, and the West makes a fuss about China's attraction to African resources. It is inevitable that Africa has natural resources and China has funds to help them explore and turn the resources into development.

China and Africa are cooperating, helping them to experiment, to explore. The system is one that explores the path of development. It cannot be imposed, the national development path should be decided by their people, and at different stages of development, it should be allowed to have a different form. Now some African countries learn from China's development experience, such as South Africa and Ethiopia, but China's approach should be in accordance with national conditions, China is neither exporting the Chinese model nor does it oppose learning from others. The recent

FOCAC Beijing Declaration had the proposal "to increase the exchange of experience in national governance"; this is the biggest difference with the previous sessions to which you should pay attention. At the same time, we need to admit that our development model has its own problems, such as incorrupt government, unbalance which need to deal with and overcome with African governments.

2   Chinese employee in Africa
    Interview No.: 15 Interview time: July 25–29, 2012 (due to the power supply in Guinea, the interview has lasted 4 days). Interview method: Skype Interviewee: Hu, Haowei, Project manager of Guinea-Mali, China Geo engineering corporate.

Q: How is your company deciding the people assigned to Africa?
A: Theoretically, (1) The type of project; (2) Specialty and quality of personnel (3) The employee's willingness. The company will conduct an interview for potential candidates, and then the oversea manage will review the CV and conduct a further telephone interview to decide the final candidate. In reality, most of the people do not have strong willingness to work in Africa because of the hardship here. Some young people who are interested in often want to earn some extra allowance. But the problem is these people lack of overseas experience and need to adapt to local custom and life. After they gradually get used to Africa, their contract ends.

Q: Please describe the project you have involved, its aims and scale.
A: I am currently responsible for a water supply expansion project in Guinea. The goal is to provide clean drinkable water for the capital. The project is US$273 billion. Now we have about 7 sets of drilling rigs (each set with 5–6 trucks).

Q: What are the sources of your project? Does central government or local government provide any support?
A: The funds are Chinese governmental low-interest loans applied by Guinean government. Local government has provided policy support for the project. National Bureau of Water Resources provides technical support and project quality supervision.

Q: How do you think the project will impact local community?
A: The project brings clean water to people in the capital. What's more, generally, when we finished the local projects, large equipment and machinery will not ship back to China, because the local international organizations, such as, UNICEF and International Red Cross will come to us for help. At the same time, the Chinese government may provide further assistant project from time to time. So when the project

launched, it is a snowball project. As for water projects, or other kinds of economic assistance project, African governments are particularly strong support and welcomed. They give a lot of policy support.

Q: Compared to a domestic project, how well do you profit from your project in Africa?

A: The profit of a project is different case by case. Generally, it is higher than the profit in China. And if you compare our project in Guinea with other overseas projects, we can be certain that our profit will be ranked among top three.

Q: In your project, how many African colleagues do you have and how do Chinese people get along with them?

A: The number of African employees is much more than Chinese. But most of my colleagues in at my level or and those doing clerical work are Chinese, while manual labour workers are African colleagues. I know a lot of people may say the Africa people need to learn from the Chinese for their hard working. But, but in fact, in my project, we pay extra allowances for overtime working. The African colleagues are positive towards overtime working. I think diligent diligence is encouraged by the establishment of a praise system.

As a project manager, I have a lot of opportunities to deal with all kinds of local people. I have found that in Africa money can do anything, sometimes even handle legal issues. The local governor is very sensitive to financial flow, for example, they will repeatedly confirm before signing the contract which is more serious than the Chinese, and the African people are very friendly to Chinese.

Q: What do you think is the advantage and disadvantage of Chinese enterprises, comparing it with western companies?

A: Advantages: Chinese government has provided financial support. Chinese people have paid more attention to effectiveness and efficiency.
Disadvantage: labor protection, environment protection, I didn't mean Chinese enterprise do not pay attention to it, it just not as good as western companies. At the same time, the quality of western companies' equipment is more reliable.

Q: What difficulties Chinese enterprises have encountered in Africa?

A: Poor working environment, disease. Experienced and professional technical personnel often do not choose to come to work in Africa. In addition, corruption, government inefficiency makes China's operation very difficult. Sometimes the local governor asks for a bribe.

And as more and more people entering Africa, our profit is lower than before. Most of the market is dominated by western companies; the marginalized are left to Chinese enterprise which is hard, risky, competitive and low profit.

3 Chinese private company employee in Africa

Interview No.: 20 Interview time: June 17, 2012 Interview method: MSN Interviewee: Cao, Xiaobo, Translator of a trade company in Nigerian China Town.

Q: Why do you invest in Africa?

A: My boss's relatives have done business in Nigeria since the 1990s, at that time the profit is high. Everything that was imported from China has been sold at a much higher price than in China. So my boss starts started to sell plastic products in Nigeria's China town.

Q: What's your opinion on the going global strategy and China's responsibility to Africa; do they have any influences in your daily operation in Africa?

A: Responsibility things are viewed from government to government level, and Beijing's policy is designed for large national enterprises, as far as I know, the reason for a private company to invest in Africa is mainly out of economic consideration, and since its company is still on a very small scale, they haven't considered paying back to local society at the moment. We are struggling to survive ourselves.

Q: What kinds of constraints have you experienced during your operations in the African market?

A: The hard life and competition in China town. And the local government is not nice to us. There is always someone asking for a bribe, either African or Chinese. You have no other methods than bribing local governors.

Q: Have you considered expanding business and investing in local manufacturers rather than importing from China?

A: No, transforming the industrial line into Africa can save the cost of transportation and labor, but the electricity supply here is too poor. Like in China Town, there is limited hours to have power. And the environment is risky for transportation.

Q: There is a lot of criticism and complaining about the quality of Chinese products. What do you think?

A: The reason I don't like to receive interview is that you never been to Africa. You haven't seen the hard life here. We have no other choice, the African middleman offered low prices, which leaves little profit to the Chinese manufacturers, thus, the producers have lowered the quality. And due to the mismanagement, smuggling is rampant in Nigeria. You cannot imagine how serious corruption is in Africa. Money can do anything.

Q: Have you received any help from local government? What is your suggestion?

A: No. We do our own business here. I hope the embassy could help us to understand the local policy. We are often confused about Nigeria's changing policies.

4   Chinese researcher

Interview No.: 22 Interview time: June 5, 2014, 10:00–10:30 Interview location: School of International Studies, Peking University Interviewee: Zha, Daojiong School of International Studies, Peking University.

Q: What is your opinion of China as a model for Africa?

A: In a time of globalization, countries are free to learn what that suits them. We do not attach conditions to finance African countries, we just provide them choices. The African people can choose the way they want and the way that suits them. They are free to learn the advantages of China's development path while ignoring the disadvantages. Our aim into Africa is to "hemopoiesis" rather than "transfusion".

Q: Lot of criticism is about China prefers to woo the undemocratic government and unstable market to satisfy its oil thirst, and its presence in the continent have affected local development, what do you think?

A: Lot of people have talked about China choosing to invest in the high risky energetic area, it sounds as if we have a choice. The safe oil fields with good quality energy reserves have long been controlled by the western companies. As a latecomer, China has to start from these marginalized areas. Actually, as for the overseas companies, what they concern the most is the safety of employees. They are trying everything to ensure the safety of their employees.

In response to these criticisms, there are only two ways, the first one is to expel all Chinese business, and the second one is to improve. Whether expelling all China's presence in Africa is good to the continent? We as a late comer to the continent, it is inevitable to have problems, but we are improving and learning.

Q: What do you think is the advantages and disadvantages of Chinese enterprises in Africa?

A: The technicians and specialists are the biggest advantages of China in Africa, and they have a completed procedure. In terms of the energy industry, our technic is advanced in dealing with poor quality oil and gas.

The disadvantage is that we are the late comer to the market and Chinese companies' misbehaveior in Africa.

Q: What measures do you think the government could do take to regulate Chinese companies in Africa?

A: There is a huge gap between the government and Chinese companies. I've done fieldwork in a lot of African countries. None of them have ever thought about China's imagine. What they cared about is very practical, such as, when Chinese government could help to simplify the visa application process in African countries.

References

Abdelrahman, A. (December 30, 2009). Darfur NCP civil society groups to where? *Sudan Tribune*. Retrieved from www.sudantribune.com/spip.php?article33638.

Abramowitz, M., & Kolieb, J. (June 5, 2007). Why China won't save Darfur. *Foreign Policy*.

Adem, S. (2012). China in Ethiopia: Diplomacy and economics of Sino-optimism. *African Studies Review, 55*(1), 143–160. doi: 10.1353/arw.2012.0008.

Ahmed, G. K. (2010). *The Chinese stance on the Darfur conflict*. South African Institute of International Affairs.

Ai, P. (2005). Ambassador in Ethiopia 出使埃塞俄比亚札记. *Contemporary World Studies, 4*, pp. 36–8.

AidData. Retrieved from http://china.aiddata.org.

Akidi, R. (May 22, 2012). Africa: China in Africa - Partner or plunderer? *allAfrica*. Retrieved from http://allafrica.com/stories/201205221022.html.

Alden, C. (August 1, 2005). China's growing presence in Africa introduces a new dynamic in the continent's relations with the outside world. *Survival: Global Politics and Strategy, 47*(3), 147–164.

Alden, C. (March 1, 2005). Leveraging the dragon: Toward "an Africa that can say no" *eAfrica*.

Alden, C. (2005). China-Africa relations: The end of the beginning. In P. Draper & G. L. Pere (Eds.), *Enter the dragon: Towards a free trade agreement between China and the Southern African Customs Union*, Pretoria: Institute for Global Dialogue.

Alden, C. (2007). *China in Africa: Partner, competitor or hegemon?*, London: Zed Books.

Ali, A. (2006). *The Sudanese–Chinese relations before and after oil*. Khartoum: Sudan Currency Printing Press.

allAfrica. (July 21, 2006). Ethiopia, Italian company sign $2 billion hydro power project. *allAfrica*. Retrieved from http://allafrica.com/stories/200607210970.html.

allAfrica. (April 13, 2010). Nigeria: Obama - Country critical to Africa's survival. *allAfrica*. Retrieved from http://allafrica.com/stories/201004130344.html.

allAfrica. (October 25, 2013). Ethiopia keen to take agricultural cooperation with China to higher level. *allAfrica*. Retrieved from http://allafrica.com/stories/201310270190.html.

Amosu, A. (March 9, 2007). *China in Africa: It's (still) the governance, stupid*. Foreign policy in focus discussion paper, Washington, DC.

Asche, H., & Schüller, M. (2008). *China's engagement in Africa: Opportunities and risks for development*，GTZ, Retrieved from: http://s3.amazonaws.com/zanran_storage/www2.gtz.de/ContentPages/19176160.pdf.

Aykut, D., & Ratha, D. (2003). South-South FDI flows: How big are they? *Transnational Corporations, 13*(1), 149–176.

Bathembu, C. (July 16, 2012). Dlamini Zuma elected new AU commission chairperson. *SA News*. Retrieved from www.sanews.gov.za/africa/dlamini-zuma-elected-new-au-commission-chairperson.

BBC. (November 24, 2007). Darfur rebels spurn Chinese force. *BBC*. Retrieved from http://news.bbc.co.uk/2/hi/africa/7111206.stm.

BBC. (December 11, 2007). Sudan rebels 'attack oil field'. *BBC*. Retrieved from http://news.bbc.co.uk/2/hi/africa/7138226.stm.

BBC News. (January 27, 2012). Sudan and South Sudan leaders bid to defuse oil dispute. *BBC News*. Retrieved from http://www.bbc.co.uk/news/world-africa-16754352.

BBC. (January 5, 2014). The Mint countries: Next economic giants? *BBC*. Retrieved from www.bbc.com/news/magazine-25548060.

Bell, C., & Thatcher, M. (2008). *Remembering Hedley*. Canberra: ANU E Press.

Bellamy, A. J. (2003). Power, rules and argument: New approaches to humanitarian intervention. *Australian Journal of International Affairs, 57*(3), 499–512.

Bellamy, A. J., & Wheeler, N. J. (2006). Humanitarian intervention in world politics. Retrieved from http://cadair.aber.ac.uk/dspace/bitstream/handle/2160/1925/Wheeler?sequence=1.

Berthelemy, J. C. (2011). China's engagement and aid effectiveness in Africa. Retrieved from https://www.afdb.org/fileadmin/uploads/afdb/Documents/Publications/Working%20129.pdf.

Bevir, M., & Rhodes, R. A. W. (2010). Interpretive theory. In D. Marsh & G. Stoker (Eds.), *Theory and methods in political science*. London: Palgrave Macmillan, p. 80.

Bivins, T (2006). Responsibility and accountability. *journalism.uoregon.edu*.

Blas, J., & Hoyos, C. (September 23, 2009). Chinese begin petrol supplies to Iran. *Financial Times*.

Blas, J., & Rwanda, K. (May 22, 2014). China's central bank chief admits difficulties with Africa. *Financial Times*.

Bosshard, P. (2007). *China's role in financing African infrastructure*. International Rivers Network, May, Retrieved from https://www.internationalrivers.org/sites/default/files/attached-files/chinaeximbankafrica.pdf.

Bosshard, P. (May 22, 2012). Ethiopia: World Bank to fund destructive dam through the backdoor? *International Policy Digest*. Retrieved from www.internationalpolicydigest.org/2012/05/22/ethiopia-world-bank-to-fund-destructive-dam-through-the-backdoor/.

Brautigam, D. (March 2007). "Flying geese" or "hidden dragon"? Chinese Business and African Industrial Development. *The Politics of Contemporary China-Africa Relations*. Retrieved from http://www.cebri.com.br/midia/documentos/eventos_03_ucla_papaer4.pdf.

Brautigam, D. (2008a). *China's African aid transatlantic challenges*: The German Marshall Fund of the United States.

Brautigam, D. (2008b). China's Foreign aid in Africa: What do we know? In R. Rotberg (Ed.), *China into Africa: Trade, aid, and influence* (pp. 197–216). Washington, DC: Brookings Institution Press.

Brautigam, D. (2010). *The Dragon's gift: The real story of China in Africa*. Oxford: Oxford University Press.

Brautigam, D. (2011). Chinese development aid in Africa: What, where, why, and how much? In J. Golley & L. Song (Eds.), *Rising China: Global challenges and opportunities* (pp. 203–223). Canberra: Australia National University Press.

Bräutigam, D., & Tang, X. (2012). *An overview of Chinese agricultural and rural engagement in Ethiopia. IFPRI Discussion Paper 01185*, Development Strategy and Governance Division, Retrieved from https://deborahbrautigam.files.wordpress.com/2014/02/ifpri-ethiopia-dp.pdf.

Brenner, M. (1985). Intensive interviewing. In M. Brenner, J. Brown & D. Canter (Eds.), *The research interview: Uses and approaches.* London: Academic Press, pp. 149–61.

Breslin, S. (2005). Power and production: Rethinking China's global economic role. *Review of International Studies, 31*, 735–753.

Breslin, S. (2007). *China and the global political economy.* New York: Palgrave Macmillan.

Breslin, S. (2010). China's emerging global role: Dissatisfied responsible great power. *Politics, 30*, 52–62.

BRICS. (March 27, 2013). Fifth BRICS summit declaration and action plan [Press release]. Retrieved from www.brics5.co.za/fifth-brics-summit-declaration-and-action-plan/.

Broadman, H. G. (2007). *Africa's silk road: China and India's new economic frontier.* Washington, DC.: World Bank.

Bryman, A. (1988). *Quantity and quality in social research.* London: Unwin Hyman.

Bull, H. (2002). *The anarchical society: A study of order in world politics.* Basingstoke: Macmillan.

Burnham, P., Lutz, K. G., Grant, W., & Layton-Henry, Z. (2004). *Research methods in politics.* London: Palgrave Macmillan.

Buzan, B., & Foot, R. (2002). *Does China matter?: A reassessment: Essays in memory of Gerald Segal.* London: Routledge.

Byrnes, R. M. (1996). *South Africa a country study.* Washington: Federal Research Division.

Caijing. (November 3, 2008). CCECC's project in Nigeria has been suspended 中 国铁建尼日利亚铁路项目暂停工 *Caijing.* Retrieved from www.caijing.com.cn/2008-11-03/110025675.html.

Cane, P. (2002). *Responsibility in law and morality.* Oxford: Hart.

Cassidy, E., Reynolds, F., Naylor, S., & De Souza, L. (2011). Using interpretative phenomenological analysis to inform physiotherapy practice: An introduction with reference to the lived experience of cerebellar ataxia. *Physiother Theory Practice, 27*(4), pp. 263–77.

CCS Team. (2010). Evaluating China's FOCAC commitments to Africa and mapping the way ahead. A report by the Centre for Chinese Studies, prepared for the Rockefeller Foundation. Retrieved from www.ccs.org.za/wp-content/uploads/2010/03/ENGLISH-Evaluating-Chinas-FOCAC-commitments-to-Africa-2010.pdf.

CDB. (2009). *Special Loan for the Development of African SMEs.* China Development Bank, Retrieved from http://english.mofcom.gov.cn/article/services/supply-demandofchina/supply/201204/20120408048929.shtml.

Chen, X. (Jaunary 3, 2014). Peaceful talk in South Sudan starts while Chinese oil interests suspend 南苏丹内战双方开始谈和 中国石油利益仍悬置. *First Financial Daily.* Retrieved from http://finance.sina.com.cn/world/20140103/015917828289.shtml.

Chen, Z. (2009). International responsibility and China's foreign policy. In M. Iida (Ed.), *China's shift global strategy of the rising power* (pp. 8–28). Tokyo: The National Institute for Defense Studies.

Chen, C., Chiu, P.-C., Orr, R. J., & Goldstein, A. (2007). An empirical analysis of Chinese construction firms' entry into Africa. *International Symposium on Advancement of Construction Management and Real Estate, August.* Retrieved from https://gpc.stanford.edu/sites/default/files/cp027_0.pdf.

Chen, Z., & Jian, J. (2009). *Chinese provinces as foreign policy actors in Africa.* China in Africa Programme, South African Institute of International Affairs, Retrieved from https://www.saiia.org.za/occasional-papers/128-chinese-provinces-as-foreign-policy-actors-in-africa/file.

Cheng, T. (August 27, 2012). The reason of China's aid to Africa is not complicated 中国援助非洲的原因并不复杂. *Global Times.* Retrieved from http://news.xinhuanet.com/world/2012-08/27/c_123635783.htm.

Cheng, S., & Liang, G. (May 10, 2012). Social responsibility of Chinese investment in Africa: What does it mean for EU-China cooperation on development policy towards Africa? *Trade Negotiations Insights, 10*(3), pp. 9–11.

China Daily. (April 12, 2007). US envoy defends China role in Darfur. *China Daily.* Retrieved from www.chinadaily.com.cn/china/2007-04/12/content_849019.htm.

China Daily. (March 27, 2013). China, South Africa agree to boost ties. *China Daily.* Retrieved from http://europe.chinadaily.com.cn/china/2013-03/27/content_16347571.htm.

China Daily. (September 23, 2013). South Africa has attracted Chinese investment 南非十大领域向中资 "抛绣球". *China Daily.* Retrieved from www.chinadaily.com.cn/hqcj/gjcj/2013-09-23/content_10169406.html.

China Daily. (October 26, 2013). China spends big to support SME innovation. *China Daily.* Retrieved from www.chinadaily.com.cn/business/2013-10/26/content_17060358.htm.

China Daily. (January 15, 2014). The cooperation between FAOUN and China 联 合 国粮农组织与中国合作四十年. *China Daily.* Retrieved from www.chinadaily.com.cn/hqzx/2014-01/15/content_17237977_2. htm.Chinanews.com. (July 30, 2010). Rethinking China's responsibility 中国责任论的 再 认 识. Retrieved from www.chinanews.com/cj/2010/07-30/2437173.shtml.

Chinanews.com. (January 6, 2012). Chinese foreign minister Jiang Jiechi's visit to three African countries. *Chinanew.com.* Retrieved from www.chinanews.com/gn/2012/01-06/3585854.shtml.

China News and Report. (2013). Chinese financial service providers gain foothold in Africa. *China.org.* Retrieved from www.china.org.cn/report/2013-02/07/content_27914622.htm.

Clark, I. (2005). *Legitimacy in international society.* Oxford: Oxford University Press.

CNN. (October 4, 2011). Dalai Lama scraps trip to South Africa; Tutu lashes out. *CNN.* Retrieved from www.cnn.com/2011/10/04/world/africa/south-africa-dalai-lama/.

CNOOC. (2006). CNOOC Limited acquires 45% stake in offshore Nigerian oil mining license 130 for US $2.268 billion cash. *CNOOC.*

CNPC. (2010). CNPC in Sudan. cnpc.com.cn.

Cohen, M. (December 29, 2011). China exim lends more to Africa than World Bank. *Fitch Says.*

Cohen, R., & Deng, F. M. (1996). Normative framework of sovereignty. In F. M. Deng, S. Kimaro, T. Lyons, D. Rothchild & I. William (Eds.), *Sovereignty as responsibility: Conflict management in Africa*. Washington, DC: The Brookings Institution.

Collier, P. (2007). *The bottom billion: Why the poorest countries are failing and what can be done about it*. New York: Oxford University Press.

Condon, M. (2012). China in Africa: What the policy of nonintervention adds to the western development dilemma. *PRAXIS The Fletcher Journal of Human Security, XXVII*, pp. 5–19.

Corkin, L. (December 2007). *China's contribution to the development of African infrastructure through investment in the extractive industries*. AFRODAD Occasional Paper (8).

Corkin, L. (2011). Redefining foreign policy impulses toward Africa: The roles of the MFA, the MOFCOM and China Exim Bank. *Journal of Current Chinese Affairs, 40*(4), 61–90.

Davies, P. (2007). *China and the end of poverty in Africa towards mutual benefit*, Diakonia, Retrieved from http://www.sarpn.org/documents/d0002825/China_Africa_poverty_Davies_Aug2007.pdf.

Davies, M., Edinger, H., Tay, N., & Naidu, S. (2008). *How China delivers development assistance to Africa?*: Centre for Chinese studies, University of Stellenbosch, pp. 250–5. Retrieved from http://www.ccs.org.za/downloads/DFID_FA_Final.pdf.

Davies, K., Swanson, B., Amudavi, D., Mekonnen, D. A., Flohrs, A., Riese, J., … Zerfu, E. (2010). *In-depth assessment of the public agricultural extension system of Ethiopia and recommendations for improvement*. IFPRI Discussion Paper 01041: Eastern and Southern Africa Regional Office. Retrieved from https://core.ac.uk/download/pdf/6237665.pdf.

Deng, Y. (July 2, 2011). The difficulties of Sinosteel in South Africa 中钢南非困局. *21st. Century Business Herald*. Retrieved from http://news.hexun.com/2011-07-02/131089562.html.

Devine, F. (2002). Qualitative methods. In D. Marsh & G. Stoker (Eds.), *Theory and methods in political science*. New York: Palgrave Macmillan.

dfa.gov.za. (August 01, 2014). Speech by the Minister of International Relations and Cooperation, Ms Maite Nkoana-Mashabane, on the occasion of a Public Lecture *South Africa's Chairpersonship of BRICS – from Durban to Fortaleza*. Retrieved from www.dfa.gov.za/docs/speeches/2014/mash0801a.html.

Diao, X. (2010). *Economic importance of agriculture for sustainable development and poverty reduction: The case study of Ethiopia*. Paper presented at the Global Forum on Agriculture, OECD Headquarters, Paris.

Diao, X., Hazell, P., Resnick, D., & Thurlow, J. (2007). *The role of agriculture in development implications for sub-Saharan Africa*. International Food Policy Research Institute. Retrieved from http://www.fanrpan.org/documents/d00369/Agric_dev_IFPRI_2007.pdf.

Donelly, J. (1998). Human rights: A new standard of civilization. *International Affairs, 74*, pp. 1–23.

Dong, Y. (April 16, 2012). Fitch challenged that the bad loans of three national policy bank have been undereveluated. 惠誉质疑三大政策性银行不良贷 款被低估. *First Financial Daily*. Retrieved from www.yicai.com/news/2012/04/1629278.html.

Dralle, T. (2008). Sudan, Angola and China: Oil, power and the future of geopolitics A brief case study. Retrieved from http://tilman-dralle.de.

Draper, P. (March 9, 2006). Jekyll and Hyde: China and Southern Africa. *Business Report.*

Dziadosz, A. (November 14, 2012). Special report: South Sudan's Chinese oil puzzle. *Reuters News.* Retrieved from http://uk.reuters.com/article/2012/11/14/us-southsudan-chinese-oil-id USBRE8AD0B520121114.

Edwards, L., & Jenkins, R. (2013). *The impact of Chinese import penetration on the south African manufacturing sector.* A Southern Africa Labour and Development Research Unit Working Paper Number 102. Cape Town: SALDRU.

Egbula, M., & Zheng, Q. (November 2011). *China and Nigeria: A powerful South-South alliance.* Sahel and West Africa Club Secretariat (SWAC/OECD). Retrieved from https://www.oecd.org/china/49814032.pdf.

Elizabeth, K. (1997). Environmental NGOs in China: An overview. *China Environment Series,* 9–15.

Embassy of PRC in South Africa. China-South African relations on fast track [Press release]. Retrieved from www.chinese-embassy.org.za/eng/zngx/gk/t942572.htm.

ERA. (October 2009). China in Africa: A strategic overview: Executive Research 324 associates (Pty) Ltd. Retrieved from http://202.244.105.132/English/Data/Africa_file/Manualreport/pdf/china_all.pdf.

Etzioni, A. (2011). Is China a responsible stakeholder? *International Affairs, 87*(3), 539–553.

EU Commission. (2006). EU-China: Closer partners, growing responsibilities. European Union Committee. (June 14, 2011). The EU and Sudan: on the Brink of Change: European Union Committee.

Exim Bank. (2010). About the Export-Import Bank of China. Retrieved from www.eximbank.gov.cn/tm/second/index_11.html.

Eyoh, D. (1998). African perspectives on democracy and the dilemmas of postcolonial intellectuals. *Africa Today, 45,* pp. 281–306.

Fan, J. P. H., Morck, R., & Yeung, B. (2012). Translating market socialism with Chinese characteristics into sustained prosperity. In J. P. H. Fan & R. Morck (Eds.), *Capitalizing China* (pp. 1–32). Chicago: University of Chicago Press.

FAO. (2012). *South-south cooperation.* FAO Representation China 2012. Retrieved from http://coin.fao.org/cms/world/china/SSC.html.

Feng, Z. (2005). Methods to the realization of harmonious world, a re-analysis of keeping a low profile and doing something 争取实现和谐世界之策, 也谈韬光养晦有所作为. *World Affairs, 20,* pp. 52–3.

Fin24.com. (March 14, 2010). Malema linked to R250m mining deal. *Fin24.com.* Retrieved from www.fin24.com/Business/Malema-linked-to-R250m-mining-deal-20100314.

Finch, J. (1984). It's great to have someone to talk to: The ethics and politics of interviewing women. In C. Bell & H. Roberts (Eds.), *Social researching: Politics, problems, practice.* London: Routledge and Kegan Paul.

FOCAC. (April 17, 2012). Zhong Jianhua: Chinese enterprises in Africa. *FOCAC.* Retrieved from www.focac.org/eng/zxxx/t923570.htm.

FOCAC. (July 23, 2012). The Fifth Ministerial Conference of the Forum on w Beijing Action Plan (2013–2015). FOCAC.

FOCAC. (April 9, 2013). FOCAC ABC. Retrieved from www.fmprc.gov.cn/zflt/eng/ltda/ltjj/t933522.htm.FOCAC. (October 9, 2013). Seminar on "China-Africa experiences of governance and development" "中非治国理政与发展经验国际研讨

会"在中央党校举行". *FOCAC.* Retrieved from www.focac.org/chn/xsjl/zflhyjjljh/t1086342.htm.

Foster, V., Butterfield, W., Chen, C., & Pushak, N. (2009). *Building Bridges: China's growing role as infrastructure financier for sub-Saharan Africa.*

Francis, C., Madasamy, P., Sokkary, S., & You, S. (2012). *China and the 325 Sudan-South Sudan oil fee impasse implications of Chinese foreign aid, diplomacy, and military relations.* PubPol 716: Introduction to Chinese Policy, April 24.

Frankfort-Nachmias, C., & Nachmias, D. (1996). *Research methods in the social sciences.* London: St Martin's Press.

Friends of the Earth. (2010). *Chinese banking industry environmental record 2010.* Friends of the Earth. Retrieved from https://www.banktrack.org/download/chinese_banking_industry_environmental_record_ngo_analysis_executive_summary.

Gadzala, A. & Hanusch, M. (January 2010). *African persepctive on China-Africa: Gauging popular perception and their economic and political determinants.* Afro Batometer Working Paper No. 117. Retrieved from https://www.files.ethz.ch/isn/112383/AfropaperNo117.pdf.

Garwood-Gowers, A. (2012). China and the "responsibility to protect": The implications of the Libyan intervention. *Asian Journal of International Law, 2*(02), 375–393. doi: 10.1017/s204425131200015x.

Gebre-Egziabher, T. (2009). The developmental impact of Asian drivers on Ethiopia with emphasis on small-scale footwear producers. *The World Economy, 32*(11), 1613–1637.

Geda, A., & Meskel, A. G. (2010). *Impact of China-Africa investment relations: Case study of Ethiopia.* African Economic Research Consortium (AERC). Retrieved from https://www.africaportal.org/documents/6675/Ethiopia-China_Eth_Invest_Fina.pdf.

Gelb, S. (2010). *Foreign direct investment links between South Africa & China.* China-Africa Economic Relations.

Gill, B., & Huang, C.-H. (February 2009). *China's expanding peacekeeping Role: Its significance and the policy implications.* SIPRI Policy Brief.

Giry, S. (November 5, 2004). China's Africa strategy- Out of Beijing. *The New Republic.*

Global Times. (September 20, 2010). Sudan Rebellion: Never anti-China 苏丹反政府武装:绝不反华尽快释放中国工. *Global Times.*

Gold, R. (1958). Roles in sociological field observation. *Social Forces, 36*, pp. 217–223.

Gordimer, N. (May 24, 2012). South Africa: The new threat to freedom. Retrieved from http://www.nybooks.com/articles/2012/05/24/south-africa-new-threat-freedom/.

Gramizzi, C., & Tubiana, J. (2012). *Forgotten Darfur: Old tactics and new players* (Vol. Norwegian Ministry of Foreign Affairs), Switzerland.

Grimm, S. (June 2011). *China as Africa's ambiguous ally why china has a responsibility for Africa's development.* Center for Chinese Studies, Stellenbosch University.

Gu, J. (2009). China's private enterprises in Africa and the implications for African development. *European Journal of Development Research Special Issue, 24*(1), pp. 570–87.

Guo, J. (July 27, 2010). How the irresponsible concept "China's economic responsibility" has been concocted? 不负责任的 "中国经济责任论" 如何 炮制出来. *People's Daily.*

Harding, H. (2009). China rediscovers ethics in foreign policy. *Policy Innovations.* Retrieved from https://www.carnegiecouncil.org/publications/archive/policy_innovations/commentary/000101/:pf_printable?.

Harrison, R. (June 19, 2009). Moeletsi Mbeki: Black empowerment has failed. *Mail and Guardian*. Retrieved from http://mg.co.za/article/2009-06-19-moeletsi-mbeki-black-empowerment-has-failed.

Hathaway, T. (September 17, 2010). Chinese loan underwrites lake Turkana Destruction. *International Rivers*. Retrieved from www.internationalrivers.org/resources/chinese-loan-underwrites-lake-turkana-destruction-3746.

Hawke, G., & NZIER. (November 19, 2011). The TPP: What are Asia's alternatives? *East Asia Forum*.

He, W. (2008). China-Africa cooperation: Partnership and global influence 中非 合作: 伙伴关系及全球影响. *International Affairs Forum, Summer*.

He, W. (February 27, 2012). More soft power needed in Africa. *China Daily*. Retrieved from http://usa.chinadaily.com.cn/opinion/2012-02/27/content_14697700.htm.

Heilmann, S., & Perry, E. J. (2011). *Mao's invisible hand the political foundations of adaptive governance in China* Cambridge: Harvard University Asia Center.

Hellström, J. (May 2009). *China's emerging role in Africa: A strategic overview*. FOI Studies in African Security.

Hertz, R., & Imber, J. B. (1995). *Studying elites using qualitative methods. Studying elites using qualitative methods*. Thousand Oaks, CA: SAGE Publications, Inc.

Higgins, K., & Prowse, S. (2010). *Trade, growth and poverty: Making aid for trade work for inclusive growth and poverty reduction*. Overseas Development Institute. Retrieved from https://www.odi.org/resources/docs/5778.pdf.

Holslag, J. (August 15, 2007). China's diplomatic victory in Dafur. *BICCS Asia Paper, 2*(4), pp. 1–12.

Hopkin, J. (2002). Comparative methods. In D. Marsh & G. Stoker (Eds.), *Theory and methods in political science* (pp. 249–270). London: Palgrave Macmillan.

Hou, W. (December 4, 2012). China's investment promotes African development 中国投资促进非洲发展. *ChjnaAfrica*.

Hu, J. (2007). China's responsibility and peaceful development "中国责任论" 与和平发展道路. *Contemporary International Relations, 12*, pp. 43–7.

Hurrell, A. (2007). *On global order: Power, values, and the constitution of international society*. Oxford: Oxford University Press.

IBtimes. (March 17, 2011). UN vote approves Libya no-fly zone; China, Russia Abstain. *IBtimes*. Retrieved from www.ibtimes.com/un-vote-approves-libya-no-fly-zone-china-russia-abstain-276107.

ICBC. (April 18, 2011). ICBC pursues with vigor to be world-class green financial institution. *ICBC*. Retrieved from www.icbc.com.cn/ICBC/ICBC%20NEWS/ICBC%20Pursues%20wi th%20Vigor%20to%20be%20World-Class%20Green%20Financial%20Institution.htm.

ICG. (April 17, 2009). *China's growing role in un peacekeeping*. International Crisis Group. Retrieved from https://www.crisisgroup.org/asia/north-east-asia/china/china-s-growing-role-un-peacekeeping.

ICG. (April 4, 2012). China's new courtship in South Sudan. *International Crisis Group*. Retrieved from www.crisisgroup.org/~/media/Files/africa/horn-of-africa/sudan/186-chinas-new-courtship-in-south-sudan.pdf.

ifeng. (June 30, 2010). ICBC's project has been accused of destroying African ecology 工行贷款项目被指破坏生态非洲水利贷款引争议. *Ifeng*. Retrieved from http://finance.ifeng.com/bank/zzyh/20100630/2357704.shtml.

ifeng. (May 16, 2012). CNPC's dilemma in Sudan. *ifeng.*ifeng. (July 10 2012). The first China-African civil forum. *ifeng.* Retrieved from http://news.ifeng.com/opinion/gundong/detail_2012_07/05/15802402_0.shtml.

Information Office of the State Council. (April 2011). *China's foreign aid.* Beijing: China's Information Office of the State Council. Information Office of the State Council. (2013a).

Information Office of the State Council. (2013b). The diversified employment of China's armed forces. *White paper on China's armed forces.* Beijing information Office of the State Council.

Jackson, R. H. (1990). *Quasi-states: Sovereignty, international relations and the Third World.* Cambridge: Cambridge University Press.

Jackson, R. H. (November 1998). *Surrogate sovereignty? Great power responsibility and "failed states".* Working Paper, No. 25, pp. 1–20.

Jackson, R. H. (2000). *The global covenant: Human conduct in a world of states.* Oxford: Oxford University Press.

Küng, H. (2004). *Global responsibility: In search of a new world ethic.* Eugene: Wipf & Stock Pub.

Kang, X. (2012). Regional indentity, power structure and international conflicts 地位认知、权力结构与国际冲突. *World Economics and Politics, 2*, pp. 99–118.

Kaplan, R. (Janurary 28, 2010). Don't panic about China. *The Atlantic.*

Kaplinsky, R. (July 2007). *Asian drivers and sub sahara Africa - The challenge to development strategy.* Report for the Rockerfeller Foundation.

Kaplinsky, R., & Morris, M. (2009). Chinese FDI in sub-Saharan Africa: Engaging with large dragons. *European Journal of Development Research, 21*(4), 551–569. doi: 10.1057/ejdr.2009.24.

Kassa, z. (May 21, 2013). Hailemariam Desalegn sits with BBC's George Alagae. *ERTA gov.* Retrieved from www.ertagov.com/news/index.php/component/k2/item/692-hailemariam-desalegn-sits-with-bbcs-george-alagae/692-hailemariam-desalegn-sits-with-bbcs-george-alagae?latestlimitstart=108.

Keet, D. (2008). The role and impact of Chinese economic operations in Africa. In *China's new role in Africa and the South: A search for new perspectives.* D.-G. Guerreo and F. Manji (Eds.), (pp. 78–86). Oxford: Fahamu.

Keller, E. J., & Rothchild, D. (July/August 1997). *Africa in the new international order: Rethinking state sovereignty and regional security* Colorado: Lynne Rienner.

Kenneth, T. (April 26, 2012). South Sudan: 'CNPC infrastructure can be compensated through oil industry in RSS', President Kiir. *allAfrica.* Retrieved from http://allafrica.com/stories/201204270608.html.

Kent, A. (2007). *Beyond compliance China, international organizations, and global security.* North Yorkshire: Stanford University Press.

Kim, Y. (2013). Chinese investment and African peace and security: The case of Ethiopia. In M. G. Berhe & H. Liu (Eds.), *China-Africa relations governance, peace and security*: Institute for Peace and Security Studies (Addis Ababa University) and Institute of African Studies (Zhejiang Normal University). Retrieved from http://www.ipss-addis.org/index.php?option=com_docman&task=doc_download&gid=48&Itemid=132.

Kleine-Ahlbrandt, S., & Small, A. (2008). China's new dictatorship diplomacy: Is Beijing parting with pariahs? *Foreign Affairs* (January/February).

Kong, F. (2011). *Research on big power's responsibility in the process of China's rising* 中国崛起过程中的大国责任研究 (Master's Degree). Suzhou Univerisity.

Kotecki, S. (2008). The human rights costs of China's arms sales to Sudan–A violation of international law on two fronts. *Pacific Rim Law & Policy Journal, 17*(1), pp. 209–35.

KPMG. (October 19, 2011). Focusing on Africa-China trade and investment. *KPMG report.*

Kragelund, P. (2008). The return of non-DAC donors to Africa: New prospects for African development? *Development Policy Review, 26*(5), 555–584.

Kramer, M. H. (2004). Review: Responsibility in law and morality. *Philosophical Review, 113,* pp. 133–5.

Krause-Jackson, F. (June 12, 2011). Clinton chastises China on internet, African "new colonialism". *Bloomberg,* Retrieved from www.bloomberg.com/news/2011-06-11/clinton-chastises-china-on-internet-african-new-colonialism-.html.

Lancaster, C. (2007). The Chinese aid system. *Center for Global Development,* June.

Large, D. (2008). Sudan's foreign relations with Asia China and the politics of "looking east". *Institute for Security Studies, 158,* pp. 1–20.

Large, D. (2009). China's Sudan engagement: Changing northern and southern political trajectories in peace and war. *The China Quarterly, 199,* 610. doi: 10.1017/s0305741009990129.

Large, D., & Patey, L. A. (2011). *Sudan looks east: China, India and the politics of Asian alternatives.* NY: James Currey.

Lavers, T. (2011). The role of foreign investment in Ethiopia's smallholder-focused agricultural development strategy. *Global Land Grabbing,* April 6-8, paper presented at the Institute of Development Studies, University of Sussex.

LEBELO, M. (March 27, 2004). Charting way forward for BEE. *Fin24.com.*

Leech, B. L. (2002). Interview methods in political science. *Political Science & Politics, 35*(04), 663–664.

Lesch, A. M. (1998). *The Sudan: Contested national identities.* Oxford: James Currey.

Li, A. (2006a). The adjustment and evolution of China's African policy 论中国对非洲政策的调适与转变. *West Asia and Africa, 8,* 11–20.

Li, A. (2006b). China-African relations in the discourse on China's rise 论"中国崛起"语境中的中非关系. *World Economics and Politics, 11,* 7–14.

Li, Z. (2007). China, Africa and world factory. *CASS Forum.*

Li, H. (2008). An analysis of Deng xiaoping's keep a low profit 论邓小平的韬光养晦外交战略思想. *Journal of University of International Relations, 3,* pp. 1–6.

Li, A. (November 12 2008). South-South cooperation in the process of globalization, China's aid to Africa 全球化过程中的南南合作: 中国对非援助的理念与行动. *People Daily.*

Li, H. (2009, March 23). Reflect on China's responsibility. *People's Daily.*

Li, D. (2011). The analysis of China's international responsibility through the features of international responsibility 从国际责任的认定与特征看中国的国际责任. *Contemporary International Relations, 8,* pp. 52–7.

Li, Y. (2013). China-Africa development fund in South Africa. *China in Africa: The Real Story.*

Li, H., Meng, L., Wang, Q., & Zhou, L.-A. (2008). Political connections, financing and firm performance: Evidence from Chinese private firms. *Journal of Development Economics, 87*(2), 283–299.

Li, H. (2009, March 23). Reflect on China's responsibility. *People's Daily.*

Lichtman, A., & French, V. (1978). *Historians and the Living Past.* New Jersey: John Wiley & Sons.

Lin, l. (June 2007). An rational analysis of "China's responsibility" 理性辨析 "中国责任论". *People's Forum.*

Liu, J. (March 6, 2008). China should interpret international responsibility from self identity 中国应从自身角色来认定国际责任. *Economic Information Daily.*

Liu, Y. (March 11, 2011). Chinese expert on China-Africa relations over past 55 years 非洲专家解读中非关系55年 In China.org.cn (Ed.). Retrieved from http://fangtan.china.com.cn/2011-02/21/content_21965753.htm

Liu, L. (July 5, 2011). The risk in overseas projects in the case of Sinosteel's loss 海外项目遇险凸显中钢扩张之痛. *Shanghai Business*. Retrieved from www.shbiz.com.cn/Item/160522.aspx.

Liu, H., & Huang, M. (2013). *Strategic research on China's foreign aid and international responsibility* 中国对外援助与国际责任的战略研究. Beijing: Social Sciences Academic Press.

Lofland, J., & Lofland, L. H. (1984). *Analyzing social settings*. Belmont, CA: Wadsworth Publishing Company, Inc.

Lü, H. (2000). *Cadres and corruption: The organizational involution of the Chinese communist party*. North Yorkshire: Stanford University Press.

Lucas, J. R. (1993). *Responsibility*. Oxford: Clarendon Press.

Lum, T., Fischer, H., Gomez-Granger, J., & Leland, A. (2009). *China's foreign aid activities in Africa, Latin America and Southeast Asia*. CRS Report for Congress, Congressional Research Service. Retrieved from https://fas.org/sgp/crs/row/R40361.pdf.

Luo, J. (August 11, 2014). How to understand the annual foreign aid volume of 30 billion RMB? 如何认识年均 300 亿元的对外援助. *CPCnews*. Retrieved from http://theory.people.com.cn/n/2014/0811/c40531-25440978.html.

LUSAKA. (June 11, 2011). Clinton warns against "new colonialism" in Africa. *Reuters*. Retrieved from www.reuters.com/article/2011/06/11/us-clinton-africa-idUSTRE75A0RI20110611.

Macharia, J. (March 10, 2013). China keen to invest in SAfrica mines. *Reuters*. Retrieved from www.reuters.com/article/2010/03/10/us-kh-mining-summit-safrica-idUSTRE6293VA20100310.

Maglad, N. E. A. (2008). *Scoping study on Chinese relations with Sudan*. AERC Scoping Studies on China-Africa Economic Relations.

Mail and Guardian. (March 27, 2009). Manuel: Dalai Lama spat 'a matter between states'. *Mail and Guardian*. Retrieved from http://mg.co.za/article/2009-03-27-manuel-dalai-lama-spat-a-matter-between-states.

Marthoz, J.-P. (2012). *The challenges and ambiguities of South Africa's foreign policy*. NOREF Report, September.

Matisoff, A. (July 26, 2010). China's green credit policy. *China Dialogue.*

McDoom, O. (February 2, 2007). China's Hu tells Sudan it must solve Darfur issue. *Reuters*. Retrieved from www.washingtonpost.com/wp-dyn/content/article/2007/02/02/AR2007020200462.html.

McGreal, C. (March 23, 2009). Dalai Lama's South Africa conference ban causes uproar. *The Guardian*. Retrieved from www.theguardian.com/world/2009/mar/23/dalai-lama-south-africa-world-cup-ban.

Mertha, A. (2009). "Fragmented authoritarianism 2.0": Political pluralization in the Chinese policy process. *The China Quarterly, 200*, 995. doi: 10.1017/s0305741009990592.

Mills, G., & Shelton, G. (2004). From butterflies to take-off? Asia-Africa trade and investment ties. In G. Mills & G. Shelton (Eds.), *Asia-Pacific and Africa: Realizing economic potential* (pp. 17–46). Johannesburg: South African Institute of International Affairs.

MOFA. (March 29, 2005). Liu Jianchao's press release on AU in UN reform 外交部 发言人刘建超就非盟在联合国改革问题上的共同立场答记者问 [Press release]. Retrieved from www.fmprc.gov.cn/mfa_chn/gjhdq_603914/gjhdqzz_609676/lhg_610662/fyrth_610670/t189320.shtml.

MOFA. (July 7, 2009). Foreign ministry spokesperson Qin Gang's press conference on UN security council Resolution 1874 -DPRK nuclear test.

MOFA. (2010). Jiang Zemin's visit to six African countries *MOFA*. Retrieved from www.mfa.gov.cn/chn//gxh/xsb/wjzs/t8969.htm.

MOFA. (February 17, 2013). Xi Jinping's meeting with Chairperson of the African Union Commission Zuma 习近平会见非盟委员会主席祖玛. Retrieved from www.fmprc.gov.cn/mfa_chn/zyxw_602251/t1014206.shtml.

MOFA. (June 14, 2013). President Xi Jinping meets with Prime Minister Hailemariam Desalegn of Ethiopia. *fmprc.gov.cn*. Retrieved from www.fmprc.gov.cn/ce/ceke/eng/zgyw/t1051197.htm.

MOFA. (July 2, 2013). Ambassador TIAN Xuejun writes for Chinadaily Africa Weekly. *fmprc.gov.cn*. Retrieved from http://wcm.fmprc.gov.cn/pub/eng/wjb/zwjg/zwbd/t1055484.shtml.MOFCOM. (2011). *2011 Statistical Bulletin of China's Outward Foreign Direct Investment 2011* 年度中国对外直接投资统计公报. China Statistics Press.

MOFCOM. (February 17, 2011). Eight Commerce Associations crack down on the potential export to Africa of counterfeit and shoddy products and commodities 八大商协会联合发布对非出口打假保知. *MOFCOM*. Retrieved from www.mofcom.gov.cn/aarticle/ae/ai/201102/20110207405266.html.

MOFCOM. (2013a). Foreign Investment Blueprint Ethiopia 2013. *MOFCOM*.

MOFCOM. (2013b). Foreign Investment Regional Blueprint South Africa 2013.

MOFCOM. (March 8, 2009). Major Function 主 要 职 能. Retrieved from http://jjhzj.mofcom.gov.cn/article/guanywm/200401/20040100167568.shtml.

MOFCOM, & China's Embassy to Nigeria. (2013). Foreign Investment Blueprint (Nigeria) *MOFCOM*.

MOFED. (2010). National development plan. Retrieved from www.mofed.gov.et/English/Information/Pages/NationalDevelopmentPlan.aspx.

Moser, G. G., Rogers, S., Van Til, R. H., Kibuka, R. D., & Lukonga, I. (April 4, 1997). *Nigeria: Experience with structural adjustment*. International Monetary Fund.

Moyo, D. (2010). *Dead aid: Why aid is not working and how there is another way for Africa*. NY: Farrar, Straus and Giroux.

Mthembu-Salter, G. (2009). *Elephants, ants and superpowers: Nigeria's relations swith China*. South African Institute of International Affairs. Retrieved from http://www.voltairenet.org/IMG/pdf/Nigeria_s_Relations_with_China.pdf.

Muekalia, D. J. (2004). Africa and China's strategic partnership. *Africa Security Review*, *13*(1), 5–11.

Naidoo, S., Molele, C., & Letsoalo, M. (February 3, 2012). State of the nation: Zuma adopts Chinese model. *Mail and Guardian*. Retrieved from http://mg.co.za/article/2012-02-03-zuma-adopts-chinese-model.

NEPAD. (2010). Africa launches an ambitious programme for infrastructure development. *nepad.org*. Retrieved from www.nepad.org/regionalintegratio-nandinfrastructure/news/162   8/africa-launches-ambitious-programme-infrastructure-de.

NetEase. (May 28, 2007). Sarkozy: Darfur Issue could not be solved without China's active involvment 萨科齐: 中国不积极介入达尔富尔问题无法解决. *NetEase*. Retrieved from http://news.163.com/07/0528/05/3FIB7U3B0001121M.html.

Neumann, I. B., & Waever, O. (1997). *The future of international relations: Masters in the making?*: London: Routledge.

New Century. (December 13, 2010a). Chinese enterprise in Africa: Opportunities and traps. *sina.com*. Retrieved from http://news.sina.com.cn/c/sd/2010-12-13/164421632897.shtml.

New Century. (December 13, 2010b). Gold rush in Africa 非洲淘金启示录. *New Century Weekly*. Retrieved from http://magazine.caixin.com/2010-12-11/100206503.html.

News One. (April 17, 2011). Ethiopia's biggest dam to help neighbours solve power problem. *News One*. Retrieved from www.inewsone.com/2011/04/17/ethiopias-biggest-dam-to-help-neighbours-solve-power-problem/43904.

Nigeria2Day. (April 28, 2006). *Daily email bulletin*.

Nina Hachigian, W. C., & Beddor, C. (November 2009). *China's new engagement in the international system-In the ring, but punching below its weight*. Center for American Progress. Retrieve from https://cdn.americanprogress.org/wpcontent/uploads/issues/2009/11/pdf/chinas_new_engagement.pdf.

Niu, H. (2007). The analysis of China's international responsibility "中国责任论析论". *Contemporary International Relations, 3*, pp. 46–50.

Niu, J., & Wu, K. (2011). China's international responsibility under the harmonious world concept 和谐世界理念下的中国大国责任. *Tribune of Study, 27*(7), pp. 44–7.

Nolan, P. (2005). *Transforming China: globalization, transition and development*. London: Anthem Press.

Nour, S. S. O. M. (2010). *An assessment of effectiveness of Chinese aid in financing development in Sudan*.

Odeh, L. E. (2013). Sino-Nigeria investments: prospects and challenges 1971–2010. *African East-Asian affairs the China monitor, 4*. OECD, The 0.7% ODA/GNI target - a history. Retrieved from www.oecd.org/dac/stats/the07odagnitarget-ahistory.htm.

Ogunseye, T., Okpi, A., & Baiyewu, L. (November 25, 2012). N5tn stolen under Jonathan–Investigation. *Punch*. Retrieved from www.punchng.com/news/n5tn-stolen-under-jonathan-investigation/.

Osayande, A. (June 10, 2014). Minister urges ban on fake Chinese goods. *News24*. Retrieved from http://m.news24.com/nigeria/Business/News/Minister-urges-ban-on-fake-Chinese-goods-20140610.

Payandeh, M. (2010). With great power comes great responsibility? The concept of the responsibility to protect with the process of international lawmaking. *The Yale Journal of International Law, 35*, pp. 470–516.

Pei, M. (January 20, 2012). Viewpoint: China's Iran dilemma. *BBC News*.

People's Daily. (June 5, 2005). Li Zhaoxing: Group 4's proposal to UN has undermined the interests of developing countries 李肇星称四国集团入常 草案有损发展中国家利益. *People's Daily*. Retrieved from http://news.sina.com.cn/c/2005-0605/01316081728s.shtml.

People's Daily. (October 17, 2006). Ethiopian PM: China not looting Africa. *People's Daily*. Retrieved from http://english.people.com.cn/200610/17/eng20061017_312372.html.

People's Daily. (October 29, 2006). Premier Zhou's Visit to Africa has launched the first wave of diplomatic relations establishment 周总理访非掀起第一 次建交高潮. *People Daily*.

People's Daily. (February 22, 2008). Sinosteel's "Xuri Project" launched in South Africa 中钢 "旭日工程" 在南非上马. *People's Daily*. Retrieved from www.people.com.cn/GB/other3983/4024/4061/6910656.html.

People's Daily. (December 22, 2008). Interview: Ethiopian PM lauds China's reform policy. *People's Daily*. Retrieved from http://english.people.com.cn/90001/90776/90883/6558450.html.

People's Daily. (February 16, 2011). What kinds of international responsibility should China takes? 中国应承担的国际责任是什么?. *People Daily*. Retrieved from http://news.xinhuanet.com/politics/2011-02/16/c_121083795.htm.

People's Daily. (April 8, 2011). Changes in three major oil companies 三大石油公司高层大调整. *People's Daily*. Retrieved from http://energy.people.com.cn/GB/115016/140072/218777/.

People's Daily. (October 15, 2013). State council has issued plan for eliminating outdated and excess capacity in key industries. 国务院关于化解产能严 重过剩矛盾的指导意见(全文) *People Daily*.

Pere, G. L. (2007). China and Africa: Dynamics of an enduring relationship. *Global Dialogue, 9*(Winter/Spring).

Peters, B. G. (1998). *Comparative politics: Theory and method* NY: NYU Press.

Prinsloo, L., & Marais, J. (February 10, 2013). SA's status as a mining national slips. *Business Day Live*. Retrieved from www.bdlive.co.za/business/mining/2013/02/10/sa-s-status-as-a-mining-nation-slips.

Qin, J., & Li, X. (February 27, 2008). Rice expects more solid Sino-US relations. *China Daily*. Retrieved from www.chinadaily.com.cn/cndy/2008-02/27/content_6487100.htm.

Qu, X. (February 18, 2011). China's real responsibilities *China Daily*. Retrieved from http://usa.chinadaily.com.cn/opinion/2011-02/18/content_12037299.htm.sh.

Qu, X. (March/April 2012). *The UN charter, the responsibility to protect, and the Syria issue*. China International Studies. Retrieved from http://www.ciis.org.cn/english/2012-04/16/content_4943041.htm

Ragin, C. C. (1987). *The comparative method: Moving beyond qualitative and quantitative strategies*. Oakland: University of California Press.

Raine, S. (2009). *China's African challenges*. London: Routledge.

Reisen, H. (2007). *Is China actually helping improve debt sustainability in Africa?*. G-24 Policy Brief No. 9.

Reuters. (February 23, 2012). China urges dialogue in South Sudan dispute with oil firms. *Reuters*. Retrieved from www.reuters.com/article/2012/02/23/ozatp-china-southsudan-idAFJOE81M04O20120223.

Reuters. (March 25, 2013). China's Xi tells Africa he seeks relationship of equals. *Reuters*.

Rone, J. (2003). Rebels, regional and oil-Sudan. *World Today, 59*(12).

Rotberg, R. I. (2008). *China into Africa: Trade, aid, and influence*. Brookings Institution Press and World Peace Foundation.

SA News. (August 19, 2013). BRICS Business council set for first meeting. *SA News.gov.za*. Retrieved from www.sanews.gov.za/south-africa/brics-business-council-set-first-meeting.

SAnews.gov.za. (September 12, 2013). SA seeks "balanced trade" with China. *SAnews.gov.za*. Retrieved from www.southafrica.info/news/international/china-120913.htm#.U_wMjYPmgup.

Sarkin, J., & Paterson, M. (2010). Special issue for GR2P: Africa's responsibility to protect. *Global Responsibility to Protect, 2*(4), 339–352.

Sautman, B., & Yan, H. (2009). African perspective on China-Africa links. *The China Quarterly.*

Schiere, R., Ndikumana, L., & Walkenhorst, P. (2011). China and Africa: An Emerging Partnership for Development?. *African Development Bank Group.*

Servant, J. C., China's trade safari in Africa. Le monde diplomatique. Retrieved from http://mondediplo.com/2005/05/11chinafrica.

Shi, Y. (2008). The interview of Professor Shi Yinhong, School of International Relations, Renmin University. In C. Daily (Ed.): China Daily.

Shih, T. H. (June 2, 2011). ICBC Quiet over controversial dam project. *International Rivers.* Retrieved from www.internationalrivers.org/resources/icbc-quiet-over-controversial-dam-project-2721.

Sidiropoulos, E. (2007). South Africa's regional engagement for peace and security. *FRIDE's Comments.*

Sina. (June 11, 2014). Chinese enterprises explore Africa 中国企业探路非洲:劳 动力成本上升倒逼产业转移. *Sina.com.cn.* Retrieved from http://finance.sina.com.cn/world/20140611/001919371122.shtml.

Slim, H. (2010). Values versus power: Responsible sovereignty as struggle in Zimbabwe. *Global Responsibility to Protect, 2.*

Sofaer, A. D., & Heller, T. C. (2001). Sovereignty: The practitioners' perspective. In S. D. Krasner (Ed.), *Problematic sovereignty contested rules and political possibilities* (pp. 28–52). New York: Columbia University Press.

Solla, M. F. P. (2004). The notion of international responsibility: A 'classic' in times of change?, Retrieved from www.esil-sedi.eu/fichiers/en/PerezSolla_812.pdf.

Stanford Encyclopedia of Philosophy. (2011). *Stanford Encyclopedia of Philosophy.*

Stearns, S. (May 10, 2012). China plays bigger Diplomatic role in Sudan conflict. *VOA.* Retrieved from www.voanews.com/content/china_plays_bigger_role_in_sudan_co nflict/566047.html.

Stedman, S. J., Jone, B., & Pascual, C. (2009). *Power and responsibility: Building international order in an era of transnational threats* Washington: Brookings Institution Press.

Stering-Folker, J. (2004). Realist-constructivism and morality. *International Studies Review, 6*, pp. 337–52.

Sudan Tribune. (April 1, 2007). DARFUR - China faces mounting calls to boycott Olympics game. *Sudan Tribune.* Retrieved from www.sudantribune.com/spip.php?article21092.

Sudan Tribune. (March 18, 2008). EU turns up heat on China over Darfur crisis and divest from PetroChina. *Sudan Tribune.* Retrieved from www.sudantribune.com/spip.php?article26401.

Sudan Tribune. (February 22, 2012a). Head of Petrodar oil company expelled from South Sudan. *Sudan Tribune.* Retrieved from www.sudantribune.com/spip.php?article41676.

Sudan Tribune. (February 22, 2012b). South Sudan to reviews oil contracts after expelling PETRODAR chief. *Sudan Tribune.* Retrieved from www.sudantribune.com/spip.php?article41682.

Sudan Tribune. (February 23, 2012c). South Sudan gives PetroDar President 72 hours to leave Juba. *Sudan Tribune.* Retrieved from www.sudantribune.com/spip.php?iframe&page=imprimable&id_article=41686.

Sudan Tribune. (February 24, 2012). China downplays expulsion of Petrodar boss from South Sudan. *Sudan Tribune.* Retrieved from www.sudantribune.com/spip.php?article41704.

Sudan Tribune. (June 10, 2013). South accuses Khartoum of "making up" rebel claims. *Sudan Tribune.*

Sun, Z. (2008). Review of China international position report-explaining China's responsibility to the world 说明明中国的责任-读 2008 中国国际地位报 告有感. *World Economics Studies, 10*, pp. 83–4.

Swan, J. (May 3, 2007). Civil war and genocide in Darfur: Chinese and Saharan dimensions. Retrieved from http://2001-2009.state.gov/p/af/rls/rm/84401.htm.

Taylor, I. (2002). Taiwan's foreign policy and Africa: The limitations of dollar diplomacy. *Journal of Contemporary China, 11*(30), 125–140. doi: 10.1080/10670560120091174.

Taylor, I. (2004). The "all-weather friend"? Sino-African interaction in the twenty-first century. In I. Taylor & P. Williams (Eds.), *Africa in international politics external involvement on the continent.* London: Routledge, pp. 84–7.

Taylor, I. (2005). Beijing's arms and oil interests in Africa. *China Brief, 5*(21), Retrieved from: https://jamestown.org/program/beijings-arms-and-oil-interests-in-africa/.

Taylor, I. (2006a). China's oil diplomacy in Africa. *International Affairs, 82*(5), 937–959.

Taylor, I. (2006b). *China and Africa: Engagement and compromise* London: Routledge.

Taylor, I. (2007). China's relations with Nigeria. *The Round Table, 96*(392), 631–645.

Taylor, I. (2009). *China's new role in Africa.* Boulder, CO: Lynne Rienner.

Taylor, I. (2012). *The forum on China- Africa cooperation (FOCAC).* London: Routledge.

Teitt, S. (2008). China and the responsibility to protect: Asia-Pacific center for the responsibility to protect.

Thakur, M. (2009). *Building on progress? Chinese engagement in Ethiopia.* South African Institute of International Affairs, July.

The Daily Times. (2013). South Africa signs deals with Russia, China. *The Daily Times.* Retrieved from www.thedailytimes.com/business/south-africa-signs-deals-with-russia-china/article_7fbe53c5-7ce7-5620-8558-befaa1d5d9d3.html?TNNoMobile.

The Embassy of Ethiiopia in China. (2013) Press Brief: Diplomacy and politics. The Embassy of Ethiiopia in China.

The Guardian. (March 7, 2011). Ethiopia's controversial dam project. *The Guardian.* Retrieved from www.theguardian.com/global-development/poverty-matters/2011/mar/07/ethiopia-controversial-dam-criticism-communities.

The Guardian. (March 24, 2013). South Africa: More of a briquette than a Bric? *The Guardian.* Retrieved from www.theguardian.com/world/2013/mar/24/south-africa-bric-developing-economy.

The news. gov.za. (2010). The new growth path.

Thisdaylive. (March 1, 2013). Jonathan meets Cote d'Ivoire's parliament today. *Thisdaylive.* Retrieved from www.thisdaylive.com/articles/jonathan-meets-cote-d-ivoire-s-parliament-today/140930/.

Thisdaylive. (July 2, 2013). UNIDO Prods Nigeria to Transform into Value-adding Economy. *Thisdaylive.* Retrieved from www.thisdaylive.com/articles/unido-prods-nigeria-to-transform-into-value-adding-economy/152199/.

Tian, X. (June 28, 2013). A 15-year relationship worth celebrating. *China Daily.* Retrieved from http://africa.chinadaily.com.cn/weekly/2013-06/28/content_16678063.htm.

Tong, X. (September 6, 2012). To get clear information on oil investment overseas-interview of academician Tong Xiaoguang. In C. News (Ed.).

Tronvoll, K. (2010). The Ethiopian 2010 federal and regional elections: Re-establishing the one-party state. *African Affairs, 110*(438), 121–136.

UHRC. (2012). Genocide in Rwanda. Retrieved from www.unitedhumanrights.org/genocide/genocide_in_rwanda.htm.

UIA. (2009). *Yearbook of International Organizations 2009–2010* (Vol. 2). Munich: KG Saur Verlag.

UNCTAD. (2012). World investment report 2012-Towards a new generation of investment policies. New York and Geneva: United Nations Conference on Trade and Development.

UNSC. (March 17, 2011). Security council approves "No-Fly Zone" over Libya, authorizing "all necessary measures" to protect civilians, by Vote of 10 in Favour with 5 Abstentions [Press release].

USAID. (2012). U.S. small businesses: Creating Opportunities with USAID: USAID.

Van der Wath, K. (2004). Enter the dragon: China's strategic importance and potential for African business. *Convergence, 5*(4), 72–75.

Vanguard. (October 26, 2013). UN security council: Nigeria should be among 10 world's powers – Ambassador Dahiru. *Vanguard*. Retrieved from www.vanguardngr.com/2013/10/un-security-council-nigeria-among-10-worlds-powers-ambassador-dahiru/.

Vanguard. (September 23, 2011). Nigeria's investment environment more transparent, says Jonathan. *Vanguard*. Retrieved from www.vanguardngr.com/2011/09/nigerias-investment-environment-more-transparent-says-jonathan/.

Vincent, J. (1974). *Non-intervention and international order.* New Jersey: Princeton University Press.

Vincent, J. (1986). *Human rights and international relations.* Cambridge: Cambridge University Press.

Waal, A. D. (February 7, 2013). Sizzling South Sudan why oil is not the whole story. *Foreign Policy.*

Wade, A. (January 23, 2008). Time for the west to practise what it preaches. *Financial Times.* Retrieved from www.ft.com/cms/s/0/5d347f88-c897-11dc-94a6-0000779fd2ac.html#axzz39ijTa5XE.

Wallace, R. J. (1994). *Responsibility and the moral sentiments.* Cambridge, MA: Harvard University Press.

Wang, Y. (1995). *International politics* 当代国际政治析论: Shanghai People's Publishing.

Wang, Q. (1999). The great development of China-Africa relations in the past 20 years 中非关系巨大发展的 20 年. *Journal of Foreign Affairs, 1.*

Wang, Y. (2007). China's state security in a time of peaceful development: A new issue on research agenda. *China & World Economy, 15*(1), pp. 77–86.

Wang, G. (2008). National interests and national responsibility–An analysis of China's Responsibility 国家利益与国际责任观–兼论中国国家责任观. *World Economics and Politics, 9*, pp. 21–8.

Wang, Y. (2012). *South Africa's role in the BRICS and the G-20: China's view.* South African Institute of International Affairs, pp. 5–15.

Wang, X., & Ozanne, A. (September 2010). *Two approaches to aid in Africa: China and the west.* Paper presented at the Ten Years Of War Against Poverty: What Have We Learned Since 2000 And What Should We Do 2010–2020?. Retrieved from http://www.sfu.ca/global-nutrition/@GH/ghO/ghoChineseVs-WesternAidInAfrica.pdf.

Watson, A. (1997). The limits of independence: Relations between states in the modern world. London & NY: Routledge.

Wax, R. H. (1968). Participant observation. In *International Encyclopedia of the Social Sciences*, NY: Macmillan and Free Press, Vol. 11, 238–241.

Welle-Strand, A. (2010). Foreign aid strategies: China taking over?. *Asian Social Science, 6*(10), pp. 3–13.

Wen, Z. (July 31, 2010). What is the real means of China's economic responsibility? 西方国家爆炒中国责任论醉翁之意是什么. *People's Daily*.

Weston, J., Campbell, C., & Koleski, K. (September 2011). *China's foreign assistance in review: Implications for the United States*: US-China Economic and Security Review Commission.

Wheeler, N. J., & Dunne, T. (2002). Hedley Bull and the idea of a universal moral community: fictional, primordial or imagined?. In B. A. Roberson (Ed.) International society and the development of international relations theory. London: A&C Black.

Wilson III, E. J. (July 28, 2005). China's influence in Africa-implication for U.S. policy *Testimony before the Sub-Committee on Africa*. US House of Representatives, Washington DC: Human Rights and International Operations.

Wolfgang, B. (1989). *The economic aid of the PR China to developing and socialist countries*. Berlin: De Gruyter.

Wu, F. (2010). China's oil diplomacy and international responsibility, in the case of Durfur issues 中国能源外交与国际责任-以达尔富尔问题为例. *Arab World Studies, 3*, pp. 59–66.

Xiaojuan, W. (January 2, 2012). Thorns in the African dream. *Chinadialogue*. Retrieved from www.chinadialogue.net/article/4748-Thorns-in-the-African-dream-1.

Xinhua News. (November 4, 2006). Hu Jintao: China will launch eight measures to promote China-Africa cooperation. *Xinhua News*. Retrieved from http://news.xinhuanet.com/world/2006-11/04/content_5288773.htm.

Xinhua News. (April 7, 2014). Nigeria has become the largest economy in Africa 尼日利亚跃升非洲第一大经济体 *Xinhua News*.

Xinhua News. (December 19, 2004). China, Nigeria sign oil development agreement. *Xinhua News*. Retrieved from www.chinadaily.com.cn/english/doc/2004-12/19/content_401418.htm.

Xinhua News. (February 2, 2007). Hu Jintao meets Bashir 胡锦涛同苏丹总统巴希尔会谈 *Xinhua News*. Retrieved from http://news.xinhuanet.com/world/2007-02/02/content_5688877.htm.

Xinhua News. (February 28, 2008). China-Nigeria joint press communique. *Xinhua News*. Retrieved from http://news.xinhuanet.com/english/2008-02/28/content_7687564.htm.

Xinhua News. (October 24, 2007). Hu Jintao's Report at 17th Party Congress. *Xinhua*.

Xinhua News. (November 17, 2008). Africa wishes to participate into the reform of international financial system. *Xinhua News*. Retrieved from http://finance.people.com.cn/GB/42773/8353245.html.

Xinhua News. (November 24, 2009). Hu Jintao's Viewpoints about the Times 《瞭望》载文阐述胡锦涛时代观的五大中国主张.

Xinhua News. (December 24, 2010). South Africa joins BRIC as full member. *Xinhua News*, Retrieved from http://news.xinhuanet.com/english2010/china/2010-12/24/c_13662138.htm.

Xinhua News. (November 28, 2011). The CSR risk of "going out" 企业 "走出去" 的 社会 责 任 风 险 *Xinhua* Retrieved from http://news.xinhuanet.com/fortune/2011-11/28/c_122343987.htm.

Xinhua News. (May 3, 2012). China calls for balanced position on Sudan-South Sudan issue. *Xinhua News*. Retrieved from http://english.peopledaily.com.cn/90883/7805908.html.

Xinhua News. (July 21, 2013). China Focus: Banks boost green credit for green growth. *Xinhua News*. Retrieved from http://english.peopledaily.com.cn/90778/8334766.html.

Xinhua News. (September 13, 2013). Li Keqiang's speech at Summer Davos opening ceremony 李克强在第七届夏季达沃斯论坛上的致辞. *Xinhua News*. Retrieved from www.china.org.cn/chinese/2013-09/13/content_30015908.htm.

Xinhua News. (October 31, 2013). Ethiopia, China have to work hard for common aspirations: Ethiopian president. *Xinhua News*. Retrieved from http://english.peopledaily.com.cn/90883/8442075.html.

Xinhua News. (October 30, 2013). SA deputy president invites Chinese infrastructure investment. *Xinhua News*. Retrieved from http://english.people.com.cn/90883/8441914.html.

Xinhua News. (September 25, 2013). Liu guijin: China wishes to help Africa realizing industrialization 刘贵今:中国愿助非洲大陆早日实现工业化. *Xinhua News*. Retrieved from www.chinadaily.com.cn/hqcj/xfly/2013-09-25/content_1018930 4.html.

Yan, X. (1997). *The analysis of China's national interests* 中国国际利益分析 Tianjin: Tianjin People's Publishing.

Yan, X. (2011). International leadership and norm evolution. *The Chinese Journal of International Politics, 4*(3), 233–264.

Yan, X. (March 31, 2011). How assertive should a great power be? *The New York Times*. Retrieved from www.nytimes.com/2011/04/01/opinion/01iht-edyan01.html?_r=0.

Yang, J. (March 29, 2013). China, Africa have shared destiny: Xi *Global Times*.

Yang, C. (August 2008). *Corporate social responsibility and China's overseas extractive industry operations: Achieving sustainable natural resource extraction.* FESS Issue Brief. Foundation for Environmental Security and Sustainability: USAID.

York, G. (December 20, 2012). South Africa's ANC vetoes plan to nationalize mining. *The Global and Mail*. Retrieved from www.theglobeandmail.com/report-on-business/international-business/african-and-mideast-business/south-africas-anc-vetoes-plan-to-nationalize-mining/article6611394/.

You, Z. (2007). *Research on China's oil policy to Africa* (Master's degree), National Chengchi University.

Zadek, S., Chen, X., Li, Z., Jia, T., Zhou, Y., Yu, K., ... Morgan, G. (November 2009). Responsible business in Africa: Chinese business leaders' perspectives on performance and enhancement opportunities. *Corporate Social Responsibility Initiative*. Account Ability and the Enterprise Research Institute, Development Research Centre of the State Council of P.R. China.

Zafar, A. (2007). The growing relationship between China and sub-Saharan Africa: Macroeconomic, trade, investment, and aid links. *The World Bank Research Observer, 22*(1), 103–130. doi: 10.1093/wbro/lkm001.

Zeng, Y. (2012). The strategic analysis of China in Darfur 中国处理达尔富尔危机的 战略分析. *Arab World Studies, Issue 6*.

Zhang, X. (2010). A rising china and the normative changes in international society. *East Asia, 28*(3), 235–246. doi: 10.1007/s12140-010-9131-y.

Zhao, X. (2010). China's foreign policy from "doing something" to "doing something in light of general trend" 中国外交:从" 有所作为" 到" 顺势而为". *Contemporary International Relations, 11*, 8–10.

Zhao, Z. (November 24, 2011). New interest groups have impacted national policy 新部门利益正在影响国家决策. In F. F. Daily (Ed.). Retrieved from http://finance.ifeng.com/opinion/zjgc/20111122/5110268.shtml.

Zheng, Y. (August 8, 2007). International responsibility has impacted China's rising 国际责任关系着中国崛起. *Sin-Chew Lianhe Zaobao*. Retrieved from www.zaobao.com/special/forum/pages5/forum_zp070731.html.

Zhong, S. (February 6, 2012). What is the real "to be responsible" to Syrian people? 怎样做才是真正对叙利亚人民负责. *People's Daily*. Retrieved from http://paper.people.com.cn/rmrb/html/2012-02/06/nw.D110000renmrb_20120206_1-03.htm.

Zheng, Y. (June 8, 2013). Chinese people's real story in Africa, why poor country should aid to poor country? 中国人在非洲的真实故事:穷国为何要援助 穷 国. *BJNews*. Retrieved from http://history.sohu.com/20130608/n378343389_1.shtml.

Zheng, Y., & Chen, M. (2006). *China moves to enhance corporate social responsibility in multinational companies*. Briefing Series-Issue 11: China Policy Institute, University of Nottingham.

Zhou, S. (2008). Adhere to the principle of never becoming a leader and to promote new international order 坚守不当头方针 推动建设国际新秩序. *Contemporary International Relations, 9*, pp. 32–3.

Zhou, G. (2009). China's rising and the international responsibility coming with it 中国崛起过程中的国际责任. *Jianghai Academic Journal, 5*, pp. 170–5.

Zhu, L. (September 2010). China's foreign policy debates: Institute for Security Studies (EUISS).